It's All About the Dress

ST. MARTIN'S PRESS ⋈ NEW YORK

It's All About the Dress

WHAT I LEARNED IN FORTY YEARS ABOUT MEN, WOMEN, SEX, AND FASHION

Vicky Tiel

IT'S ALL ABOUT THE DRESS. Copyright © 2011 by Vicky Tiel. All rights reserved.
Printed in the United States of America. For information, address St. Martin's
Press, 175 Fifth Avenue, New York, N.Y. 10010.

www.stmartins.com

Book design and composition by Gretchen Achilles

Library of Congress Cataloging-in-Publication Data

Tiel, Vicky.
   It's all about the dress : what I learned in forty years about men, women, sex
and fashion / Vicky Tiel. —1st ed.
      p. cm
   ISBN 978-0-312-65909-7
   1. Tiel, Vicky. 2. Women fashion designers—United States—Biography.
3. Fashion design—United States—History. 4. Taylor, Elizabeth, 1932–2011.
I. Title.
   TT505.T54A3 2011
   746.9'2092—dc22
   [B]

                                                            2011004442

First Edition: August 2011

10   9   8   7   6   5   4   3   2   1

This book is dedicated to Mike, who handed me a broom.

ACKNOWLEDGMENTS

To four special women: Carmelita de Jesus and Jan Kearney, who loved my stories and encouraged me to keep writing them down; Bonnie Nadell, my agent; and Elizabeth Beier, my editor, who made the book happen.

Thanks, as well, to the wonderful women I met along the way: Elizabeth Taylor, Liza Todd Burton, Mia Fonssagrives, Vivien Best Demonge, Sue Bloomberg, Diane Johnson, Maria Floyd, Claudette Candib, Amy Baron, Martha Fox, Jacqui Goldman, Arlene Goldfarb, Kate Green, Suzanne White, Yanou Collart, Andrea Holtz, Sivia Loria, Christine Lambert, Suzie Lambrechts, Beth Levine, Marie O'Neill, Mary Alice Orito, Lynne Rodgers Rabineau, Susanna Moore, Gayle Martz, Carolyn Williams, Carolyn Farb, Amy Zerner, Michelle Richter, Suzanne Pleshette, Joan Snitzer, Shirlee Fonda, Goldie Hawn, Barbara Warner, Geraldine Stutz, Dawn Mello, Dorian Leigh, Lisa Fonssagrives, Edith Head, Coco Chanel, Romy Schneider, Nathalie Delon, and Joy Philbin.

Here's to Aunt Dora, who taught me there's always sex.

Here's to the men who counted: Ron, Rex, and Richard Berkeley, Steve DeNaut, Mike Arquette, Woody Allen, Dick Sylbert, Charles Feldman, John Heyman, Peter Katz, Frank Nicoletti, Andrew Charles, Peter Cheney, George Wong, Burt Tansky, Ira Neimark, Joe Boitano, Ron Frasch, Morris Goldfarb, Michael Wilbourn, Ken Noland, Serge De Vatedski, and Richard Burton.

Undercover at Bergdorf's

Vicky Tiel? Isn't she dead yet?" The beautiful, slim young woman pointed to the sign in Bergdorf Goodman's couture salon. She and her friend stopped briefly to inspect a Vicky Tiel gown on display. They didn't seem to notice me, the designer, sitting nearby. In my white lace peasant dress and gold platform sandals, I probably looked like another customer. Some designers might have been embarrassed or angry, but not me. I knew that being "undercover" could be instructive.

"I wore her pleated lavender lamé dress to my junior high prom," said the woman in the pale pink suit.

Her friend chimed in, "I wanted to wear her strapless lace empire gown for my wedding but my mom vetoed it. She reminded me that Grandma was buried in a Vicky Tiel 'Pretty Woman' Goddess dress."

I had to smile. The old lady probably wanted to go out looking her best, I thought, but kept quiet. It wasn't the first time someone was ready to write me off. After forty years in this business, I've developed a fairly thick skin.

I thought back to the early sixties, when I was a student at Parsons and the head of the school told me that I had no future in the commercial fashion world of Seventh Avenue.

In my time, I've been thrown off movie sets by Mike Nichols and John Frankenheimer, snubbed (and then approved) by Coco Chanel, and arrested in the Middle East and then again in

Pigalle. I've been kicked off an airplane for being "inappropriately" dressed, sucked out a helicopter door and pulled back in by Elizabeth Taylor, had my nude body printed on matchbook covers, then been banned by the French government. I've had some wild ups and some spectacular downs, and I've managed to survive through it all.

Surviving is what I do best. More than thirty years ago, my own survival—my very life—was literally at risk.

It was back in 1974, off the coast of Palermo, Sicily. I was lying on the floor of Elizabeth Taylor and Richard Burton's bedroom on the *Kalizma*, their 165-foot yacht. I was trying to grab on to the long strands of the fuzzy beige carpet while the boat rocked back and forth, almost upside down. Gale-force winds were churning the sea and tossing the boat around like a child's toy. Each time we lurched to one side, Elizabeth's Louis Vuitton trunk with the gold *LV* flew past her king-size bed. Fortunately the trunk was empty, since Elizabeth had flown the coop, leaving Richard once again.

As the boat threatened to tip all the way over, I desperately looked for anything to grab—the bathroom door frames, the bedposts, the deep-pile carpet. I stretched out my arms and legs like a rock climber on the side of a steep mountain, holding on for dear life. The fierce typhoon had already sunk almost every boat in the Palermo harbor. We had begun the day with two crew members on board, along with my husband, Ron Berkeley (Burton's makeup man), and my eighteen-year-old stepson, Craig. The boat was about to capsize, and I didn't know where they were or even if they were still alive.

Then I heard Ron's voice coming from the hallway, where he also was lying on the carpet. "Good-bye," he yelled. "I love you. We're all going to die."

I yelled back, "*No!*" I was *not* going to die in the *Kalizma,* not sleeping on Pratesi sheets. What about the dinner we had started? What about the $600 bottle of Château Palmer waiting in the galley? We were going to make it to Naples and I would visit Pompeii.

I will not die today.

You might ask why I was even on Liz Taylor's yacht in the middle of a crazy storm. Ron had been working on *The Voyage* in Italy, and the Sicilian location shooting was finally over. During the shoot, Richard had fallen in lust with Sophia Loren, and now it was time for them to part. At the wrap party the night before, Richard was not willing to leave Sophia. He asked us to take the boat, with all his books and clothes, to Naples while he stayed behind to woo Sophia. Like so many men before him, he thought (wrongly) he could persuade her to leave Carlo Ponti, her older husband.

During a previous filming in Italy, Elizabeth and Richard had been Sophia's houseguests in Rome. Elizabeth had immediately sensed the animal attraction between her husband and the Italian temptress and had been extremely upset. Now it was happening all over again, but this time Elizabeth was not going to stand for it. She bolted. And for the last time, it turned out.

At the wrap party, Sophia had cut Richard off abruptly and retired to her room before the festivities were over. Having drunk one (or more) too many and forgetting that at almost fifty he was too old to play Romeo, Richard had impulsively decided to climb the wall of the Villa Igiea. The antique castle, converted to a grand hotel, hung over cliffs jutting above Palermo harbor. Richard scaled the thick vines on the hotel's front wall, and in spite of his age, managed to make it to the third-floor balcony adjoining Sophia's room. He was about to go inside but peeked through the window and stopped himself.

Without making a sound, he spun around, climbed back over the balcony, and gingerly made his way down to ground level, with just a few minor scrapes and cuts. Later he tearfully told me that Sophia had been sharing her bed with another person . . . and *not* Carlo Ponti. Not elaborating, he said he had decided not to join Ron and me on the boat. He urged us to leave at once. A storm was coming and we had to cross before the typhoon got to Sicily.

Richard's plan was to join us in Naples with Sophia at his side. But he sounded more desperate than hopeful. I tried to console him by explaining that Sophia had an inglorious reputation as the "Goddess of Love." He was not the first man to fall under her spell. Every actor she worked with (most notably Cary Grant) was seduced and then discarded. She never left her husband.

The storm eventually stopped and we all survived. The *Kalizma* had been caught at sea in the same region as the spot referred to in *The Odyssey*: the Strait of Messina, Europe's most dangerous sea passage. Ulysses had almost come to grief there, tempted by the Sirens, sea demons. Unlike the mythical wanderer, Richard Burton did not return to the welcoming arms of his wife. He arrived in Naples dejected and alone, with no Sophia at his side.

And now, thirty-five years later, here I was at Bergdorf's, waiting on customers, lightly amused by their comments. All these years later, my dresses, lingerie, and perfumes were still selling. In fact, I named my men's perfume Ulysses and my women's perfume Sirene, in honor of that night aboard the *Kalizma*.

This book is the story of how I survived—and yes, even *thrived*—as a fashion and fragrance designer, and an occasional costume designer for Hollywood. It's about how I managed to keep my business going, no matter what and how many highs and lows occurred on my journey.

Back then, tossing on the Tyrrhenian Sea, I was weary but not ready to call it quits. Today I am the longest-surviving female designer in Paris. For more than forty years, I have experienced great glory moments being a "fashion favorite," then being dismissed as a "has-been," and finally being rediscovered as the designer everyone copied. I have had wild times followed by reflective times, which led to growth as an artist and as a human being.

Along the way, I learned much from the beautiful and alluring women (and a few men) I had the privilege to dress. Many are stars you will recognize by their first names only. Many were kind enough to share their secrets of seduction and power with me. I wrote this book to share their amazing stories, along with some fairly outrageous adventures of my own.

Growing Up With Shaky Status

My parents divorced when I was a baby, and my mother dropped me off with her parents in her hometown of Hudson, New York, while she went to Hollywood. She worked as a secretary at MGM during the war, hoping to get "noticed," but the best she did was to walk past Clark Gable, who winked at her.

Mother remarried to a top gun at the IRS when I was eleven. We moved to posh Chevy Chase, Maryland, the leafy suburb of Washington, D.C.

Our entire neighborhood ran the country—or tried to. The

father of my next-door neighbor and best friend, Amy Perlmeter, was assistant press secretary to President Harry Truman. The mother of my other neighbor, Jean Huang, was the voice of Radio Free China. My stepgrandfather was an engineer and head of roads and bridges in Siam (later Thailand), but the family knew he worked for the OSS (forerunner of the CIA). Our neighbors never knew exactly what Dad did for a living.

They were all spies, lobbyists, and obscure lawyers for government committees. Everything was about information and disinformation, and every four years many families picked up and moved away somewhere. Senators, congressmen, and judges all maintained homes in Montgomery County while also keeping a place in their "home states." Chevy Chase was the preferred suburb, as it had eight of the best country clubs where presidents often played golf and tennis and members could dress up in formal wear Friday and Saturday nights, dine and dance and network while drinking very dry martinis.

In spite of our parents' government jobs, we grew up (my class of '61) typical American kids, very *Ozzie and Harriet*. Our parents repeatedly stressed that "nice girls get the guys, the bad girls end up with a shaky status in life."

Amy's mother was the couture manager of the new Chevy Chase Saks Fifth Avenue. She brought home *Vogue* and *Harper's Bazaar*, and by the age of twelve Amy and I had both decided to become dress designers. I bought a sewing machine and learned to cut and sew my own designs. I was already a cheerleader at Kensington Junior High School and walked around school two days a week in my cheerleader uniform: a white sweater with a giant red *K* and a white pleated skirt. I quickly realized that my female classmates wanted to copy anything I wore. That was my first lesson of personal power in fashion. After a few tries, I created two items, a wrap skirt in burlap with flower appliqués that I fringed five inches so my knees showed and a muumuu in cotton floral prints with white cotton fringe trim that we could wear at pajama parties and feel like perky pop princesses next to girls in boring pajamas.

I sewed my own label—Vickie Tiel—inside my designs and charged $25 for each item (today's value, $500). In our high school yearbook, my fellow cheerleader Merilly Siepert wrote, "I'll see you in Paris where I'll buy your dresses."

In my last year, now at Bethesda—Chevy Chase High School, and a cheerleader for the previous five years, I learned the power of clothing—and of *no* clothing—as I developed a strategy to help our football team go undefeated:

1. You must know the exact moment a game is on the line and the next play is a game breaker.

2. The center of our team must spread the rumor that "one of our cheerleaders in the middle is not wearing underpants."

3. Our front line must pass the rumor down the line until the opponents are distracted and turning to check out the cheerleaders on the sidelines.

At this point I started my cartwheels in my short white pleated skirt.

Years later I dressed Goldie Hawn during a movie promotion in Paris. We realized she had cheered for Blair High School against me during a game where we defeated Blair by a stupefying score of sixty-three to zero. Goldie asked me, "Vicky, are you that infamous cheerleader with no underpants? That's something so low only a fashion designer could conjure it up."

Love Lessons

My first love, at age eleven, was the most beautiful boy on the planet, Tom Bacas. We were all in love with Tom, boys and girls alike. He was Greek, a Greek god. Our sixth-grade class was shy with puberty setting in, and only I had the nerve to pursue him. He hated girls and loved only sports. He was the star of the football team and the brainy class president.

Tom *had* to be mine. How could I win his love? I decided to learn everything about all sports and become a cheerleader. Tom would love me forever.

My plan worked. I was his date for the prom at Anacostia High, and later, when he went to Harvard to become a Washington civil rights lawyer, I was his date for the Harvard-Yale football game weekend. We finally had sex in a Cambridge hotel and completed our seven-year romance with tender, first-time lovemaking.

I was Tom's first, but he wasn't mine. I couldn't wait and fell in love in high school with Michael Wilbourn, the dreamy Monty Clift–type star of our high school plays, not a jock. I fell in love with Michael watching him perform in Tennessee Williams's *The Glass Menagerie*.

We dated throughout high school. When I was a junior and

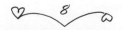

he a senior, we lost our virginity together one night on the golf course of nearby Columbia Country Club. Our love affair ended when I went to college in New York and he slept with my best friend, Amy, who had stayed home. I broke up with him and moved on. I stayed friends with Amy, as it wasn't her fault—he was beautiful, sensitive, and available.

Lesson 1   Learn what men like and be good at it.

Lesson 2   Never keep a man who seduces your friends.

Lesson 3   Move on. A new man comes along every ten minutes, just like a bus.

No Sex for Shoes

New York, 1961

I was seventeen and about to start college. My father, a successful Washington builder, took me to lunch in Greenwich Village, and later we sat together on a bench in Washington Square Park. I had just finished an interview at Cooper Union, considered by some to be the best art school in the country. (I didn't get accepted, being unable to draw a decent egg for their entrance exam; my line drawing didn't impress.) But on this day, Daddy wanted to tell me some serious stuff about men and women.

I was his only child and he wanted to steer me toward a happy adult life. Had I been his only son, I'm not sure he would have imparted such insider male wisdom. He said, "Vicky, if you marry for security and don't have your own money, you're going to have to have sex with your husband if you want a pair of shoes." (He was smart to use shoes as an example; at that point in my young life, I had nearly fifty pairs.)

"Better to earn your own money and pay for all your own shoes. Better yet, buy the car you want, the home you want. Don't ever ask or beg. Men hate women who beg for shoes. They can confuse a wife with a prostitute."

Hmmm . . . Women with their own money? No need for men? Except maybe to procreate? His advice, revolutionary at that time, inspired me more than he could ever have imagined. It was a lot to take in while eating my strawberry shortcake with Daddy.

After lunch, while we were sitting on that park bench, he gave me the news that would change my life forever.

"Vicky, I've been taking care of you and paying for things for you your whole life. This life has been costing me close to twenty-five thousand dollars a year. And I'm happy to pay it because when you graduate, you'll be able to get a good job and be self-reliant. I'm telling you now so you can be prepared: When you graduate, I'm cutting you off financially. You'll have to stand on your own, make something of yourself, by yourself. I love you and always will, but if you make your own money, you never have to eat shit from a man. You can show him the door and you can be the one who's screwing the pool man."

I was stunned, paralyzed with shock and fear. I thought Daddy would always pay for everything. Now what? But really, it was the best thing my father could have done for me.

Back home in Chevy Chase, my mom offered the opposite advice. A frustrated artist herself, her youthful dream had been to live in Paris with Amedeo Modigliani, the handsome Italian painter, to be his muse and clean his brushes. I always listened to her when she told me I was beautiful and talented, but, being a rebellious daughter, I turned a deaf ear to her other opinions. She thought the only way a female artist could make it was to sleep with a successful male artist, an art dealer, or a critic. Failing that, she needed to marry a rich Jewish man.

Years later, I shocked her when I announced, "Mom, I *am* that rich Jewish man!" I decided to listen to my dad and not depend on any man for my success or security.

Postscript, 2011: While reading my manuscript, my mother told me her divorce from my father was over a pair of very expensive shoes she bought with money he was stashing away to start his construction business.

A Really Fabulous Woman

Greenwich Village, 1961

When I wasn't accepted by Cooper Union, I decided to attend Pratt Institute in Brooklyn since I loved fashion. One autumn Saturday night I left my all-girl dorm at Pratt for my first Greenwich Village party with John Barrick, an actor I'd met in D.C. during the summer. We were sitting on the piano bench of a baby grand in a glorious living room at 1 Sheridan Square. A fashionable lady who lived at this address threw a party every weekend, and the "in" crowd of the Village entertainment world was always invited. A large silk-damask-draped window overlooked the square. The furniture and art were European, tufted, gilded, and elegant. The smoky room was filled with crazily dressed artists of all colors and shapes. My modest black shift dress stood out (I would never make this mistake again).

The party would get wild after the clubs closed. The Village Gate, Café Wha?, and Gerde's Folk City were just a few blocks away. The male entertainers would come and go with the latest pretty young things.

A guy on the piano bench passed me a joint. I'd never seen one before. I took a puff, trying to be cool, and he told me his story.

"I'm so messed up," he confided. "This woman I'm in love with has gone to L.A. I want to be an actor on the stage here in New York. Should I follow her there, or stay here?"

I was only seventeen, pretending to be twenty-one. "What's so special about her?" I asked, trying not to cough. "If she's worth it, go to L.A. Forget your career—only love matters!"

"It's not so easy," he said. "She has not quite realized that she's in love with me."

"Oh," I said, hoping I sounded worldly wise.

Then he told me something else I will never forget. "You see, she's something special. She's a really fabulous woman. It's not that she's so pretty, but she has such unusual style. You can take her to a White Tower at midnight in a Dior couture gown and she's perfectly at home. Or you can take her to a society party where everyone's all dressed up and she arrives in jeans with a big jeweled necklace and she's at ease. She has 'it'"

The woman was Brooke Hayward, the daughter of Leland Hayward, the theatrical agent of Broadway stars in the 1940s. Brooke never married the guy on the piano bench. She married Dennis Hopper and later Peter Duchin. I met Brooke in Paris in 1984 and we went to lunch at Brasserie Lipp. She had written her memoir, *Haywire*, and was on tour promoting the book in France. She described her terrible childhood. Her mother had committed suicide, as had Jane Fonda's. Both women had been married to Leland Hayward. *Hmmm.*

I told her about the guy on the piano bench, how impressed I had been by his description of her, and about my trying as a young girl to emulate her incredible style. She didn't even remember the guy's name.

The Birth of the Mini Skirt

Parsons School of Design, New York, 1962

After my first semester at Pratt, I switched to Parsons School of Design. The world's most exclusive fashion school was situated on East Fifty-fourth Street over a six-story parking garage. The inside looked like a dump, but it worked. The school's fame was based on the fact that the teachers were famous designers. It was hard to imagine the most exquisitely dressed male designers having to take the dirty freight elevator to the top two floors that housed the school, but they all did.

My teachers (and critics) were Norman Norell, James Galanos, and Rudi Gernreich. At the year-end fashion show, these famous designers would often select the most promising students as their assistants in the fashion world.

I was thrilled that the school was closer to Greenwich Village and I could have my own apartment instead of living in a dorm in Brooklyn. My apartment on Jones Street was the first floor of a pink brownstone with a little garden in the back, complete with a brick barbeque and a flagstone patio. The walls inside were exposed brick with two wood-burning fireplaces. My father rented it for me for $175 a month, an amazing amount then.

My Parsons classmate Ingeborg introduced me to her friend Antonio, later to become a famous fashion illustrator. Antonio taught me how to shop in thrift stores for antiques, a passion that is still with me. In Chevy Chase, antiques are inherited. My parents bought everything new. Antonio had a passion for Tiffany lamps, and we bought every one we could find, some real, some Tiffany style, all from the 1920s and '30s. My mattress was on the floor, and running alongside it was a long, skinny mirror. Above was a patchwork of mirrors and framed fashion sketches. Quite pleased with myself, I thought the whole look screamed "art" and "sex." The place was perfect for parties, or "happenings," as they were called then, since friends and fellow students "happened" to drop by on Friday nights to congregate, smoke pot, and hook up with friends or lovers.

The Café Figaro at the corner of Bleecker and Macdougal was the spiritual center of the Village. It stayed open practically twenty-four hours a day. With sawdust floors, smoke-filled wood-paneled rooms, and old French Thonet chairs and benches, the Figaro looked as if it had been there for a hundred years. There were poetry readings at midnight by William Burroughs, Allen Ginsberg, and Lawrence Ferlinghetti.

My next-door neighbor on Jones Street was a serious-looking twenty-five-year-old schoolteacher, Judy Kaplan. Her boyfriend, Tom Ziegler, who owned the Figaro, was married and visited Judy at odd hours. On weekends when her parents came to visit from Philadelphia, she would hide his clothes in my closets. Judy wore conservative dresses and pearls for her parents and my handmade leather outfits when going to clubs with Tom. (Tom and Judy eventually married.)

The Village Gate was where the singers and jazz musicians played. We heard Thelonious Monk, the Modern Jazz Quartet, and Stan Kenton. We had Peter, Paul and Mary; Bob Seeger; Joan Baez; and Buffy Sainte-Marie to listen to any night of the week. When invited, the musicians would follow you home and play together free-form until dawn.

There was one singer I had a mad crush on. While still at Pratt, I had developed an infatuation with a charismatic folksinger named Steve DeNaut, even though I had never met him in person. Almost every girl in the Pratt dorm had a full-size poster of him. "The Golden Boy." He was the first man to wear skintight big-bulge see-everything black leather pants with a white shirt and a leather vest, holding a huge guitar in front of him like a giant erection. He wore black sunglasses, long sideburns, blond curls, and a lost-but-love-me look on his face. Every night the Playhouse Café would hang up his life-size poster on MacDougal Street, and by morning it would appear over some girl's bed.

Steve fit my idea of the perfect rebel. No wonder. I had fallen in love with my first rebel at age eleven when I saw *On the Waterfront*. I didn't understand a thing about the mob or labor disputes, but when Marlon Brando kissed Eva Marie Saint in a white silk slip and they slid down that wall, I felt a new kind of quiver in my whole body. I was eleven and experiencing actual lust, even though I hardly knew what it was! From then on, my teenage heartthrobs were in that same rebellious mold, especially Elvis and James Dean—bad boys. But I dreamed of a bad boy who would only be really bad with me.

I was inspired by Steve's black leather pants and vests. I started to sew leather clothes and sell them to my friends, turning my little apartment into a boutique. I hung my creations on the brick wall and they sold quickly. The leather skirts and matching fringed, beaded vests went for $175, one month's rent on my apartment.

One day I decided to make a bag to go with the skirts and vests. Cutting the pattern from a piece of black leather, I wove beads into the fringe and wove straps out of leather cords. After I made the vest, with matching beaded fringe, I realized that there wasn't enough leather left to make a decent skirt. With a lot of effort, I managed to cut out an extremely indecent skirt that landed four inches above my knees (the current fashionable skirt covered the knees). I decided to wear the miniskirt myself, thinking no one would want to buy it. For a top, I wore a lace undershirt not meant to be worn without a blouse—allowing my full breasts and nipples to be clearly visible. I made lace panty hose by sewing stretch lace around my legs. A new look was born, the miniskirt! When I walked down the street, men's heads turned! What a feeling! I would make the next skirt shorter, then shorter.

Parsons School of Design was not impressed by me or my new look. I was not an A student by a long shot, and I alienated the teachers when I showed up at school draped on the back of my current boyfriend's motorcycle, sometimes hungover and still wearing a cocktail dress from the night before. They also were not amused when I brought my Yorkie puppy Wuffles to class, snuggled inside a red-and-green-striped original Gucci tote bag that I had proudly brought back from a summer fooling around in Italy. I had seen Audrey Hepburn with a tiny Yorkie in a bag and a French scarf tied under her chin, and the photo of her was etched permanently in my mind.

I didn't like the kind of fashion being taught then at Parsons, boxy constructions that looked like they could stand up on their own, even without the models inside. This basic H shape was late fifties French couture, Dior, Balmain, and Cardin. Oleg Cassini brought the box shape to America when he dressed Jacqueline Kennedy in her famous sleeveless sheath in 1960, a style that Michelle Obama favors today.

The teachers, all well-known male designers, were shy and nervous. They seemed to fret and worry about where to place each button, and every decision prompted a major discussion. I found all this fussiness extremely tedious. I wanted to design clothes that were easy and simple, and didn't hide the beautiful female body under a box. I instinctively knew that "nice girl" clothes like those from the '50s and Jackie Kennedy—Oleg Cassini boxy sheaths for mothers and grandmothers were soon to be a thing of the past. I loved my body; years of ballet had given me confidence. The clothes I designed were part of me, not wearing me. With a drape here and a dart there, my body had never looked better. I could help other women be their most beautiful selves, not hide in a box of cloth.

My favorite professor was the painter Paul Brach, who taught art history. He said, "Art is struggle, with the struggle erased." I understood and learned not to worry about being an A student. Artists are not A students. Artists are rebels and creators, definitely not the teacher's pet. I would learn to politely listen then blow off my critics, a lesson Parsons gave me to use for the rest of my life.

The first day I dared to wear one of my sexy leather miniskirts to class, the head of the school, Ann Keagy—dressed in a boxy brown short-sleeve dress, a Maggie Thatcher look-alike—called me into her office. She looked me over from head to toe, with her eyes almost popping out of her head. She told me that if I wore my "cocktail party" mini-outfits to school again, I would be thrown out.

I told her that my creations could be worn anytime, not just in the evenings, and I intended to sell the same designs to my class-mates. "Covering the knees is over," I announced. "I thought this was a fashion school!"

She informed me, in the coldest tone, that I had no future in the commercial fashion world of Seventh Avenue. "You should consider Hollywood or Las Vegas."

"No thanks," I said. "I've got another plan. I'm going to be a couturier in Paris."

Peaches in the Village

Greenwich Village, 1962

When I wasn't in class or selling my leather creations, I hung out at the Café Wha? on MacDougal Street, hoping to get hired as a "pass the hat" girl. Since coffee shops did not pay musicians directly, pretty buxom girls in sexy beatnik outfits—high-neck T-shirts, ethnic skirts, and heavy beaded necklaces—passed the hat (or basket) on their be-half. Collection girls were often the musicians' girlfriends, like

Mary Travers of Peter, Paul and Mary. They often became musicians themselves or they inspired the folk music, which was either politically controversial or just plain sad.

One night at the Playhouse Café, a talented black bongo player named Cyril Jackson invited me to a party. Tall, elegant, and incredibly charming, he had been in a show on Broadway, *House of Flowers*, written by Truman Capote. He also was Marlon Brando's bongo instructor.

The party was in a huge apartment overlooking Washington Square. There were musicians, painters, poets, actors, and a few bums. People were having impassioned conversations, smoking pot, and passing around a plate of hash brownies. Wow. The parties back in Chevy Chase were never like this! Someone was playing the piano and singing Broadway songs, and a very pretty small woman was dancing with Harry Belafonte.

I ordered a Singapore Sling from the white-gloved waiter, grabbed Cyril's arm, and strolled the party with him, comfortable in a black leather jacket and skirt.

Late into the night, I spotted *him*. Steve DeNaut was dancing close to a beautiful redheaded woman in a tight Chinese dress and red heels. They began to fight and pull apart and he was suddenly alone. He started to walk toward us to speak to Cyril and seemed upset about the redhead, who had by then left the party. I gathered that the woman was his ex-wife, and Steve looked distraught.

Our eyes connected and the thunderbolt one hears about but rarely happens happened to me. I fell madly in love and lust and knew I had to be with this man. I learned that Steve and his wife, Brenda, had just separated, and he had moved into Cyril's apartment. Steve left the party; I assumed he went to look for Brenda.

Later, I wound up at Cyril's place on West Twenty-third

Street, a third-floor walk-up brownstone next to the Chelsea Hotel. When we got to his apartment, a man was passed out in the hallway, sprawled across an overstuffed chair. He had curly blond hair and skintight pants. It was *him*! I was flushed with excitement.

"Vicky, help me get Steve inside," Cyril said. "I'll get him some coffee." Cyril took too long to make the coffee.

When he returned, Steve and I were in his bedroom. *Instant lust:* We fell into each other's arms as if we'd known each other through a zillion lives. Our sex was perfect. Steve was endowed like no man should be. I couldn't get enough.

Because of my unique look, I was hired at the club to pass the hat for Steve. When he first saw me collect money, Steve spontaneously said, "Now Peaches LaTour will pass the hat." That is how I became known in the Village as Peaches LaTour. Some of the other performers I got to see during that era were Woody Allen and Lenny Bruce.

I passed the hat for an unattractive singer with a gravelly voice, Bobby Zimmerman (who later renamed himself Bob Dylan), and an ordinary-looking man with the deepest, sweetest voice of all, Fred Neil, the star singer of the Playhouse Café. Fred later wrote the music for 1969's *Midnight Cowboy*—"Everybody's Talkin'" became a worldwide hit. Of course, Bob Zimmerman had serious drive and became the superstar folksinger of our '60s generation.

For my new persona, Peaches, I created outfit after outfit to keep Steve interested, each one more outrageous than the last. At the beginning of our relationship, he had said, "Surprise me!" and I worked hard at it. My apartment in the pink brownstone became the scene of many Saturday night drop-by costume parties.

At one, I wore only a G-string along with autumn leaves glued to my breasts. When the leaves dried out and fell off, I was all out there! Some men photographed me for a new magazine called *Show*, which was published by the A & P supermarket heir Huntington Hartford. My bare butt was in the opening edition. Thereafter, strangers passing by on the street would greet me with a friendly wink and "Hi, Peaches!"

I truly think that my motivation as a designer sprung from that primal desire to be outrageously sexy for Steve and make sure his attention stayed on me. To this day, my designs have much more to do with pleasing men than with any passing fashion trends.

After that first night together, Steve took me to the Margaret Sanger birth control clinic and registered me as Mrs. Steve De-Naut. I became part of the trial of the first two hundred women for something called the "pill." The brochure at the clinic promised that as long as you didn't miss a day for thirty-six days, you would not get pregnant. It was given away for free. Now Steve and I could have sex whenever we wanted and not worry.

The full import of how revolutionary this little pill would turn out to be didn't occur to us back in 1962. But I knew I felt suddenly liberated and powerful, and could enjoy my pleasure consequence-free, like a man.

For my twentieth birthday, Steve bought me an album he promised would be the next big thing. We made love to "I Want to Hold Your Hand," by The Beatles. Lying on my mattress on the floor, opposite the wood-burning fireplace, watching ourselves on a wall of patchwork mirrors strategically placed, candles and incense burning, surrounded by satin pillows and delicious, penetrating tongue kisses, we looked at each other and trembled over this new sound. It was electric.

A new sound was born. I saw on Steve's face a look that told me that he knew that his moment had passed—he was no longer the "next new thing."

Steve moved from the apartment he shared with Cyril to the Lower East Side, near Avenue B. It was a sad, poor neighborhood, but Steve felt this would be the exciting new area, as artists could no longer afford the Village rents.

East Eighth Street was already becoming a hippie boutique destination with the first vintage clothing stores selling retro furs from the forties called chubbies. I wore them over leather minis in the winter with fishnet stockings and tight knee-high boots. A new look was born when I added long straight hair with bangs cut to my eyes.

Steve's new railroad brownstone apartment was decorated with a floor-to-ceiling collage of photos of movie stills, art, posters, and pages of songs he had written. On the wall directly over Steve's bed were two things: a beautiful black-and-white nude photo of Brenda and a large three-by-three-foot chart.

Steve's Chart

Steve's chart had names on the left of all the girls he'd slept with and on the right his categories in order of importance in the art of lovemaking.

The first category was oral sex (he felt it was essential for women to learn to "give good head"); followed by enthusiasm, which he felt was superimportant; then classic sex; kissing; and beauty—the last item until he added fashion after I became his latest conquest.

Steve also gave out stars: green, silver, gold, and red, which was tops. One could earn up to five stars. He used the same stars we got in school as kids.

I was determined to have five red stars in every category and asked Steve for lessons, which he promptly provided, thrilled to have a willing pupil.

"Baby," he said, "you're the only one who's not angry over my chart. Sometimes I even hide it."

"No," I told him. "I want to know what men want."

How the Arquette Family Came to Be

1963

Fashion school and life on Jones Street went smoothly for a few months. Steve would take my father's $175 rent money and buy pot from a certain dealer who later turned out to be a megamogul on Wall Street. Within a day Steve would return my $175 and we would have free pot. Sometimes I got an extra hundred to buy leather for my clothes.

After six months of bliss, after the party with the "falling leaves," Steve was not happy with men taking photographs of me, bare-assed, for a magazine. I didn't understand, because Brenda was a nude model. He got angry and we had a huge fight in Sheridan Square Park. We were hitting each other, knocking each other to the ground, and he ran off. I chased him but lost him on MacDougal Street. I later heard he went to L.A.

While he was gone, I started dating his best friend, Mike Arquette, the son of TV comic Cliff Arquette. Mike and Steve had both attended Hollywood High and had been best friends since childhood. Mike was a change from leather cowboy Steve. He was well mannered, well-off, and well dressed, and loved taking me to clubs, restaurants, and concerts. Mike and I became the latest "couple" in the Village. He was an aspiring actor, and I could picture a rosy future for the two of us in Hollywood. I didn't let him know that Steve was my Pygmalion. I also didn't let him know that my heart would always belong to Steve.

In 1963, Mike and I were having dinner at the Café Rienzi on MacDougal Street when Steve walked in. He had been gone for more than six months. I was wearing my first wrap dress with high boots. Steve grabbed my arm and pulled me outside, leaving Mike sitting at the table. Steve slowly unwrapped my dress and kissed me passionately. There on the street, with Mike looking on through the big picture window, Steve and I made up for lost time.

Mike and I never spoke again or said good-bye. He left town and returned a few months later, married to Brenda, Steve's ex-wife. They moved to Chicago, taking Steve's baby, Lisa. In Chicago, they all became actors, taking on new names. Mike became Lewis, Brenda became Olivia and later Mardi, and baby Lisa became Rosanna Arquette.

Steve moved back to his apartment on Avenue B and kept his independence. Rejecting a record career, he became the editor of 16 Magazine and flew around the country interviewing teenage heartthrobs and rock stars. Whenever I mentioned Paris, he rolled his eyes. We knew we were lovers for now, nothing more. We were too young, too wild, and too sexy to commit only to each other and break each other's hearts. We had our lives to live, but the impact of our love had transformed both of us. Each had left indelible marks on the other. We could always close our eyes and remember.

Mike and Brenda stayed married until her death in 1998. Mike died shortly after, leaving the Hollywood dynasty of Rosanna, Patricia, David, and Alexis Arquette alone to mourn their beloved parents.

Mia Fonssagrives, My Best Friend

1963

I wasn't the only student at Parsons who created her own clothes. Mia Fonssagrives did, too, but Mia was really the "it" girl. She was the girl the other students feared would get all the awards at the year-end fashion show. Everyone noticed Mia when she entered a room; with her long legs she moved like a colt. Tall and brunette, with the body of a *Playboy* Playmate, she was the daughter of the model Lisa Fonssagrives and the stepdaughter of the photographer Irving Penn.

Mia's look was offbeat. She sewed simple outfits in vibrant colors, and she'd do striking things like mix a hot pink T-shirt and a bright orange skirt. Her designs were easy to sew but the shapes were new. The T-shirt dress had originated in Italy with Emilio Pucci, but Mia added colorful cutouts in Matisse colors to the clingy shirt shape. She was a class act. A Dalton graduate, she wore private school uniforms until she began creating her own clothes.

Mia did not cultivate my sexy see-through shocking fashion, but she approved of what I was doing. She understood my message. Her clothing was edgy and new. My clothing expressed my sexual freedom, my power: Look but don't touch. I am not a hooker; I am a modern woman. I am hot. Mia was both cool *and* hot.

With a famous stepdad like Irving Penn, Mia had to watch her step. Her classmates were intimidated by her family and status. I was quite the opposite, open and friendly, qualities I acquired as the perennial cheerleader. One day I walked into our classroom at Parsons wearing a turquoise burlap wrap skirt with a black lace see-through T-shirt. Mia was wearing a purple rectangle wrap skirt with two strings that crossed around her narrow hips. Wrap skirt meets wrap skirt. I decided to approach her. I moved my chair next to Mia's and attempted to break through her cool demeanor. "Our skirts have to meet," I told her with a smile. She looked up. To my surprise, and in spite of her colorful outfits, I discovered a shy person.

I could feel Mia's intense interest in my "wild girl" image, and after a few weeks of school, we were drawn to each other. Her famous parents had her on a tight schedule. School and home afterward, and none of her friends were allowed into their apartment. She had a little brother, Tom, the only child of Irving Penn, many years younger than she. There was little room for friendships. She confessed to me that her parents were so famous they were obsessed with privacy. I told her how mine never asked me where I went or what I did. At that instant, I knew we could trade places. We had lessons to learn from each other.

After school we sat in Greenwich Village cafés and she introduced me to frothy cappuccino. Sometimes she would sneak me into her apartment. She lived across the street from Bloomingdale's on the fashionable Upper East Side. The décor was creamy beige and starkly modern. Nothing was out of place, no pillows or knickknacks. Instead of colorful paintings, there were black-and-white photos taken by her stepfather on the walls.

Mia confided her anxieties about being the daughter of one of the world's most beautiful women, the same anxiety to compete I would later recognize in the children of celebrities I dressed. Lisa Fonssagrives was unusual, a Swedish ice goddess like Greta Garbo. She was aloof. She did not giggle. A laugh was "hah;" *yes* or *oui* was a breathy swallowing sound of "owee." Like me, Mia was a child of divorce, and she wasn't sure which parent's path to follow—the romantic, passionate French father, Fernand Fonssagrives, or icy cool Lisa. I suggested that she follow a path of her own.

Mia wasn't convinced. Her stepfather and mother were so famous they were known to the press and the fashion industry by the single names Penn and Lisa. She was worried about any bad publicity that would result if she happened to be spotted at the wrong place doing the wrong thing. When she was sixteen she had been photographed for *Vogue* on the lawn of their French country home on Long Island, wearing her own black sweater dress and playing a guitar. Would Penn object to her striking out on her own, with her own sexy look, so un-*Vogue*? Could she compete with her mother as a great beauty or as an artist?

Competition played an important role in the life of Mia and her family. Her mother had married Fernand Fonssagrives, a beautiful ballet dancer she had met in dance class, who then became a photographer in Europe. She left him to marry superstar Irving Penn in New York. Unable to compete with Penn, Mia's father became a sculptor. He found personal happiness but never huge commercial success.

Fernand was given a little cottage on James and Carolyn Tyson's estate on East Hampton Beach as a second home. The Tysons' son David was not a boyfriend but was Mia's great companion. His mother's home on Further Lane was a center for the local fine arts community. Carolyn Tyson was one of the financial backers who was just starting to put East Hampton on the map. With her family's fortune gained from the postwar sales of mass-produced linoleum called Kentile (she was born Kennedy), she sponsored young artists and backed their shows in her bookstore-cum-gallery on rue de Seine in Paris. She also renovated downtown East Hampton. She bought Home Sweet Home, a graceful old house built in the 1720s, and moved it to a place of honor, establishing it as a wonderful museum on the town square.

Mia, David, and I would drive to the Hamptons for square dances with the "townies" and meet the local artists who were Carolyn's "discoveries." Carolyn owned a painting studio in the Carnegie Hall Studios; a pied-à-terre in the Gainsborough Studios that Mia and I used later on in our lives; a sumptuous apartment in the Hampshire House; a home in Carmel, California; and a home in Paris. Despite the homes and her fabulous wealth, Carolyn was simple, direct, and funny. She hated snobs and bigots, and delighted in bringing Jewish artists to the restricted Maidstone Club for dinner. No one would dare say anything to the doyenne of the Hamptons. In 1962, East Hampton was a sandy, run-down beach town with small wooden cottages and old-timey country shops. There were miles of empty dunes and emptier beaches.

Since Carolyn also lived in France and had a European attitude, guests in East Hampton were allowed to sunbathe and swim topless. Her home was filled with Early American antiques, large art books, French houseguests, and cooks preparing cocktails galore and serving trays of delicious whatnots all summer long. We ate off blue-and-white Meissen china on long refectory tables in weather-beaten wooden shacks.

By our last year at Parsons, Mia and I were inseparable. We decided on the beach one afternoon to become business partners and called ourselves Fonssagrives-Tiel even before we had a label to sew in a dress. As our school days were drawing to a close, Mia and I lay on the deserted beach with Carolyn and Fernand and pondered our future. Carolyn's advice to us was to take a chance and go to Paris. She never said be careful; instead, she just told us not to miss rue de Seine, where her apartment, gallery, and bookstore, Fischbacher, were located.

With Mia and me, there was no *I*—all our sentences began with *we*. We told each other our dreams and fears, and it felt so calming and complete to have a "sister" at last, who was more than a friend. As long as there was a phone, we were connected. We spoke two or three times a day. We even cut each other's hair. In spite of our differences, we learned to trust each other. We gave each other courage. Eventually, Mia broke free from her family.

I learned a lot from my occasional glimpses into Mia's family. Lisa and Penn exuded sophistication, and I witnessed a way of life I had never known before. They did not belong to country clubs or do the New York social circuit. They owned a French-style country home where they could escape from the city to relax and work as artists. Penn had a darkroom and Lisa had an atelier for sculpture. They had a flower and a vegetable garden and a huge kitchen with lots of large copper pots hanging on hooks. They made their own simple meals, and even with their large incomes had no staffs tending to their needs.

It also intrigued me that Lisa was six years older than her husband. From her I learned the power of mystique in attraction, no matter the age. Lisa's beauty and grace defied her age. In her career as a model, she was careful never to overexpose herself to anybody either publicly or privately. Lisa was a mystery.

Thanks to her, I also got the world's best recipe for apple pie, fantastic tips on wrinkle prevention (always hold your head high), and most of all I learned you can choose to be thrifty even if you're rich.

DARTOIS

Dartois means "wrapped in pastry." This is Lisa Fonssagrives's French apple pie, and I taught it to every houseguest.

    1 cup flour, sifted
    1 cup sugar (all white or ½ white and ½ brown)
    1 large egg
    1 stick unsalted butter, softened
    3 large apples (any kind), peeled, cored, and diced into
        1-inch chunks

½ teaspoon cinnamon
crème fraîche, whipped cream, or vanilla ice cream
(optional)

1. Preheat the oven to 350°.

2. In a large bowl, mix the flour, sugar, egg, and butter with a fork. The mixture will be sticky. Mash it into a ball (neatness doesn't count).

3. Sprinkle a handful of extra flour on a wooden board. Scoop out spoonfuls of the dough and flatten with your hands, then turn it over so both sides are lightly coated with the flour.

4. Put half the dough in a pie pan to cover the bottom and sides of the pan. Add the apple chunks and lightly sprinkle on the cinnamon.

5. Put the remaining dough pieces on top. There's always enough. Sprinkle more cinnamon on top. Bake until the top is lightly brown and melts down, 45–50 minutes.

I like to serve this warm, with crème fraîche, whipped cream, or ice cream.

Lisa's dartois became my trademark dessert. I taught it to each houseguest in Normandy and in Florida, where I live today. I have peach and pear trees and often replace the apples with pears or peaches. As the recipe has been handed down from person to person for more than forty years, hundreds of people may now make Lisa's pie. It lives on after her.

At least once a year some stranger will come up and tell me she made my pie. I tell her it's called dartois and that its creator was the world's most beautiful woman.

Falling In Love With Paris

We decided to move to Paris and take the French fashion world by storm. Mia was half French; I was not. Could we pull it off?

Parsons had an eight-week summer program in Europe. I convinced my parents I should attend. Unfortunately, Mia was unable to join me on the trip. One glorious June morning, Parson's summer school bus dropped us off on boulevard Saint-Germain. Our class of thirty students scattered, carrying their bags off to taxis.

My fellow fashion student John Warden and I just stood transfixed, drinking it all in: the beautifully dressed people, the glorious architecture, the light a sort of mysterious blue-gray that highlighted every detail of outfit and building. We eased ourselves down upon the infamous green-and-red straw chairs, symbols of the Café de Flore, and ordered our first frothy café crème and crusty feather-light hot croissants. We eavesdropped on the animated conversations of the French at the neighboring tables.

I fell madly in love with Paris that exact moment. Paris was the place of my dreams.

I turned to John and said, "I'm never leaving here for the rest of my life." (Only a slight exaggeration, as it turned out. My shop today is one street away on rue Bonaparte and I bought a studio, my first apartment, across the street, on rue du Dragon.)

John and I dragged our suitcases through Saint-Germain-des-Prés to boulevard Saint-Michel to the street I'd read about in Elliot Paul's *The Last Time I Saw Paris*, which was also a favorite movie starring Elizabeth Taylor. There stood the Hôtel de la Huchette, right out of the book, and John and I moved in without hesitation and sans reservation.

"Where are you taking me?" he moaned. At this time John was a boy just off the farm in Niagara Falls, but he later became a dress designer in Canada in the style of Yves St. Laurent.

The hotel turned out to be an "*hôtel de passe*," where Parisians took lovers or call girls, renting their rooms by the hour. Never mind, I had to be there! Across from the hotel was the tiniest street in Paris, rue du Chat qui Pêche, "street of the cat that fishes." This street once butted up to the quai where the Seine often flooded. Also across from the hotel was the celebrated jazz club with the same name as the street, where music vibrated up into our creaky bedroom at night.

On the ship on the way over, John and I had briefly experimented with becoming lovers, but we agreed that we did much better as buddies. As nonromantic roommates, we shared various hotel rooms and cut our expenses for summer school. Our extra cash allowed us to blow everything we had left on cafés and clubs at night. We stayed out until dawn in Montparnasse at La Coupole, searching for Jean-Paul Belmondo, on whom we both had a crush.

Parsons Paris was actually a trip throughout Europe led by Stanley Barrows, an extremely elegant, elderly gay gentleman who dressed in three-piece suits with a red carnation in his lapel, a boulevardier from another time. He was the respected dean of interior design and a connoisseur of architecture, furniture, tapestries, moldings, and such.

I kept asking him why the five fashion students along with the twenty-five interior design students were being dragged to all these Austrian palaces in Vienna and Palladian villas in Vicenza. We wanted to see boutiques and shops. "Where are the dresses?" I asked.

He told me to "study big before small. Learn about architecture for line, decorating for color and space. Art is art. Good line is everything. Train your eye, Vicky."

I could manage it for only three weeks. There were so many gorgeous men with small swimsuits and big accents. Somehow I made it through Austria and Italy, but as the class was crossing Lake Lucerne on a ferry, we intersected with a tall, well-built, blond, tan German boy with a beautiful chiseled face and large hands, riding a Vespa. I jumped on his bike and left the class behind. His name was Rainer Hoppe and he called me "Schatzie."

We lived in a tent on the beach on the road to Saint-Tropez. I saw my first topless woman and checked out the fashions and jazz in Nice and Monte Carlo. He drove me to Barcelona and we dined on the Ramblas and swooned over Gaudi architecture. We drove to Cadaqués and saw Salvador Dalí's home and ate at the local bistro where signed Dalí and Picasso drawings on the menus are framed. (Little did I know I would meet Dalí later and he would draw for me in my Dalí book the same signature.)

Rainer and I began to learn each other's languages. He was an engineering student, loved art and sex, especially kissing me on his bike! I agreed to marry him when I came back to Europe after school.

When I returned to Le Havre and the class to get the boat back to America, Mr. Barrows gave me an F (for Fashion).

Parsons had its annual end-of-year fashion show with our designer-teachers giving out awards. I was up for the Norell award, for a slinky black jersey gown with a triple-layer white organza collar and a black rose in the décolleté. I lost to a pink chiffon number, but the next morning the fashion journalist Eugenia Sheppard praised me and my gown in *The International Herald Tribune*: "Although she didn't win a Golden Thimble, Vicky Tiel designed something new." I realized they would read about me in Paris! I decided this was the sign that I was waiting for: Paris called.

In May, Mia and I solidified our plans. I had $2,000 saved from selling my leather dresses. Mia had little money saved, but she had something even better, a wonderful "gift" from her mother. Lisa Fonssagrives told her, "I want to give you only one name, the name of a friend of mine in Paris, Dorian Leigh. She will help you." Our dream was starting to take shape, just like our designs. We would take our bright colors, novelty fabrics, and minidresses to Paris.

Both sets of parents (especially Penn) wished us well and expected us to fail. Celebrity children are often underachievers (often turned off by their parents' absences). Our classmates knew we would not fail in Paris. When school ended in May 1964, they gave us a Going to Paris party on the cruise ship *Île de France*. We left with eighteen bags, two sewing machines, and my Yorkie, Wuffles. Our classmates, destined for Seventh Avenue, waved good-bye as the ship pulled away from the pier. They knew we weren't coming back.

Dorian Go Lightly

Paris, 1964

Mia and I arrived in Paris with only one address, for Dorian Leigh; Lisa Fonssagrives had explained that Dorian's name was enough. "She knows everybody who counts," she said, "and she's married most of them. Besides that, she runs the number one model agency in town." Along with Ava Gardner, Dorian was considered to be the most beautiful, alluring woman in the world, a Southern belle and—much like Ava—a free spirit, collecting and discarding lovers on a whim.

Dorian had already been famous for decades. I remembered first seeing her on the Edward R. Murrow show *Person to Person* with her sister, Suzy Parker. They were being interviewed in Dorian's sixteenth-century Paris apartment. The antiques were museum quality, and the sisters sat on pearl gray gilded Louis XV settees under giant crystal chandeliers hanging from twenty-foot ceilings. The walls were boiserie, the mantel gray marble. Both sisters wore black-and-white Chanel suits and ropes of pearls. Dorian was drinking pink Krug champagne (her favorite) in a tall Baccarat flute. When I saw all that glamour and style, I promised myself that one day I would have a beautiful apartment in Paris with antique molding and old marble fireplaces and, of course, a twenty-foot ceiling.

I learned later from Dorian herself what a long way she had

traveled to be in that luxurious setting. Back in the early '50s, she had left her two kids and husband back home in San Antonio, Texas, and moved to New York, in the hopes of making it as a model. She lived upstairs from Truman Capote and he wrote a novella based on the hillbilly girl who comes to New York to make it big. It was called *Breakfast at Tiffany's*.

Dorian became a top model in the '50s in spite of being only five foot six. I remember her photo in a beauty ad campaign. She was the Fire and Ice girl in the Revlon ads and she had many American men falling instantly in love, as she lay draped across a black-and-white zebra-skin rug wearing a white Grecian draped gown, with her dark brown hair, white skin, and red-orange lips taunting men as her red-orange nails clawed the zebra's head. In another Revlon campaign, this time standing, Dorian (in a red taffeta cape and slinky silver gown) again struck a don't-mess-with-me pose, her hand forming a claw, red-orange nails in front of her face. She provoked women to empowerment.

Mia and I moved into a simple hotel room and took a taxi to see Dorian on our very first morning in Paris. We both wore cut-velvet see-through lavender and peach minidresses with ostrich-feather boas.

The first thing Dorian said, looking us over, was, "You're both very pretty. You've got a great look. You may not become famous fashion designers but you'll have a lot of fun." Then she said, "Go get dressed in your latest creations. You're coming to my wedding tomorrow."

The next afternoon, Dorian, then in her late forties, was getting married for the fifth time—this time to Iddo Ben-Gurion, who was twenty-three. Their wedding took place in an open courtyard in the Marais. A few of Dorian's five children were there. Most of French society was not, due to the age and religion of the groom.

The fashion industry, however, was in full attendance. Mia and I met Loris Azzaro, Jean-Louis Scherrer, and Marc Bohan, who were all accompanied by beautiful models wearing the latest spring creations. The haute couture fall collections were in July, two months away.

Louis Féraud and his young associate Guy Rambaldi sat next to Mia and me, on golden chairs in the cobblestone courtyard. "Are you new models with Dorian?" Féraud inquired.

"No," we answered, "we're fashion designers from New York," just stretching the truth a wee bit. After all, we had designed the dresses we had on, the hemlines of which were six inches higher than any others at the wedding party.

Guy Rambaldi spoke to me in broken English, "Come to Louis Féraud's couture house on Faubourg Saint-Honoré next week and we talk. Louis loves zee short dresses you are wearing. We show couture in July, and maybe we present zee new short dresses. They're very new and *très amusant*."

Dorian Leigh's wedding was a romantic affair. Her gown was Balmain and her hair was in a chignon by Alexandre of Paris. Her jewels were rubies and diamonds, heirlooms from her previous lover, the Marquis de Portago, a race-car driver who had died tragically in the Italian Grand Prix. Their eleven-year-old son, Kim de Portago, was best man.

So there she was in person, the gorgeous model from our old copies of *Vogue*, the real Holly Golightly, now marrying her fifth husband in Paris. She had "reinvented" herself to resemble a grande dame of Parisian society, living in a gilded apartment and running the country's finest modeling agency.

Our friendship outlasted the marriage to Iddo Ben-Gurion. Dorian became my surrogate mother in Paris. She was one of the most beautiful, fascinating women in the world and, for me, the most influential. "Don't do as I do, do as I say," she warned.

DORIAN'S DOS AND DON'TS

- Don't trust your beauty; trust your brains.
- Save some money; don't spend it all on champagne and taxes.
- Buy real estate.
- Never marry a man for money, only for sex.
- Learn to cook. Your body is a temple, feed it luxuriously.
- Always buy good furniture. You can sell it if you run out of money.
- Read and always be learning a new thing.
- Follow the trends of the youth of today.
- Don't judge men by their accents. Elegant, eloquent men are often phonies. Working-class men can be more driven and interesting.
- Always try to have fun.

One afternoon while Dorian and I were sipping Krug, Dorian confessed a little secret. She had a private reason to help Lisa Fonssagrives's daughter. Lisa, she told me, had taken Irving

Penn off her hands. Apparently, Dorian had been romantically involved with Penn but not seriously. Yet she didn't want to hurt her career by ending the relationship. Luckily, along came Lisa, who became his favorite model, and Dorian could move on to another, wilder man more her style, specifically, the writer Irwin Shaw. Dorian, however, could not resist upstaging Lisa in the famous and often copied Penn photo of the dozen supermodels of the '50s staged in various poses.

Lisa had been positioned in a chair, in profile, in the center. Dorian waited until all the models were placed and then walked across the stage and lay down across the floor in her "Fire and Ice" pose, dead center, hogging the camera, and Penn let her get away with it.

Years later, Dorian's agency failed due to unpaid taxes on the models' salaries. Seventy percent of each month's salary was supposed to be paid on top of their salary to the government by the fifteenth of the month. Dorian felt that models should be exceptions to this rule, so she paid the models their full salaries and the government *rien*. The apartment was seized for taxes. Kim de Portago died tragically. He jumped off an apartment building in New York. Dorian decided, once again, to start over. She opened an *auberge*, Chez Dorian, outside Paris. She cooked, and all her friends came. We all became "partners" to keep her in business.

The meals were exquisite, but nobody ever got a bill. Unable to run a business, she closed. She returned to the States and moved to Virginia, where she baked cakes and pies and sometimes wrote for *Gourmet* magazine. Dorian passed away in 2008 at age ninety-one.

Dorian said that you can't live in France without a good vinaigrette recipe, and the best one is very simple. If kept in a jam jar it can travel with you. Tie a gray velvet ribbon around the jar and the vinaigrette becomes a great gift when you're invited to dinner.

DORIAN LEIGH'S PLAIN & SIMPLE VINAIGRETTE

2 tablespoons wine vinegar

6 tablespoons vegetable oil

½ teaspoon Dijon mustard

1 clove garlic, minced

salt and freshly ground pepper

Combine all the ingredients in a jar with a lid. Shake until frothy.

The dressing will keep for a week in the refrigerator.

"Anyone Over 25......"

Paris, 1964

After Dorian Leigh's wedding, Mia and I worked very hard in our little hotel room, furiously sewing our designs to be ready for Louis Féraud's fashion show. Two weeks wasn't much notice, but we were young and full of ambition and energy. Féraud wanted us to present two outfits, with each of us wearing her own design. We had been taught at Parsons to sketch twenty drawings around one idea, then wait a day and go back to the drawings with fresh eyes, circling the best design for each concept.

Mia and I sketched away in our own drawing books and then decided together which two designs we would wear. We never disagreed and we adored each other's work; we were each other's favorite designer. Mia's designs were wild and innovative, often with modern cutouts and shapes. She had no fear of mixing colors. My designs were all about fitting the body or showing off body parts. We knew the two designs we chose would make us or break us, as the world fashion press never missed a Louis Féraud show.

In Louis's show, Mia wore a purple suede minidress cut down past her belly button, with an orange snakeskin belt, orange fishnet stockings, and purple mules. I wore a denim minicoat lined in lime green fake fur, pale green lace stockings, and miniboots. We pranced down the runway at the end of the show, neither of us ever having set foot on a runway before. I had some ballet experience, and Mia had watched her mom all her life, so we were both fearless when our turn came. We sauntered and strutted like old pros. The show ended with "Bravo's."

We made the front pages of the European papers and *The International Herald Tribune* the next day, where once again Eugenia Sheppard wrote about us. Her headline was, "Anyone over 25 in the world of fashion might as well drop dead."

Mia and I spent the entire summer being photographed in Paris. Our photos were taken on the Champs-Élysées, in Castel's nightclub, photographers' studios, and while wearing bikinis on swings in the Luxembourg Gardens. We even made the French movie gossip magazines. We were invited to London to be photographed by the *Sunday Times* fashion editor. We boarded the plane wearing our outrageous cream lace minidresses made out of matching antique tablecloths and lace stockings.

At Heathrow, we realized we had left the paper with the address and instructions on the desk in Paris. We sat on our suitcases, lost and forlorn in the middle of the London airport, trying to figure out what to do. We couldn't remember whom we were supposed to meet from the *Times* or where to go. Eventually, two cute-looking Englishmen walked past and flirted with us. We boldly asked them to drive us into town. One of the men, Roy Cuthbert, was a photographer and was just returning from Africa. He drove us to his studio near Knightsbridge and called the *Times*. He found out that we had an appointment with Ernestine Carter and David Bailey—and we were late.

David Bailey was Jean Shrimpton's handsome boyfriend who later married Catherine Deneuve. David took one look at us in our see-through lace dresses and told us how to pose.

"Stick out your titties and wet your lips," he commanded from behind the camera. "Open your mouths and each of you look at me like we are having sex."

We did our best to obey. I thought, If only Miss Keagy at Parsons could see us now!

Our sexy photos were in the next Sunday's *Times*. Soon after, we were offered a contract with Wallis shops, a popular chain of youthful ready-to-wear clothes. Our new short dresses were to be sold on Oxford Street. A woman on Beauchamp Place offered to carry our couture dress in a popular shop next door to San Lorenzo, the number one royalty hangout restaurant. We were now part of swinging London.

Back in Paris, we rented our own beautiful apartment, a miniversion of Dorian Leigh's, on the Right Bank near Place de l'Étoile. It had antique molding (thanks, Mr. Barrows), boise-

rie paneling, a pale gray marble fireplace, and balcony windows with a view of the Eiffel Tower. On our Louis XIV dining room table were stacks of magazines featuring our photos—*Life, Look, Newsweek,* and *Elle.* A Swedish newspaper called Mia "the newest Swedish beauty to dazzle Paris."

I was twenty years old and thought I had it made. I thought that for the rest of my life this excitement would never stop. With so little life experience, I had no way of knowing that this peak experience was just that—a peak, not a permanent condition.

But at that moment, only three months after graduation from fashion college, the world was ours. As Françoise Sagan said, "Get success out of the way young."

Overnight Pussycats

1964

Louis Féraud was a man of his word. He had kept his promise to include us in his July fashion show, launching us into the world of Parisian haute couture. Far from being the typical chauvinistic Frenchman, Louis loved everything American. To him, America was fantastic, the future, and he wanted to be part of it.

Louis and Mia fell passionately in love in the weeks after they met. He saw his beautiful young American girlfriend as the perfect match: He was a common Frenchman from Arles who spoke patois, and Mia was descended from fashion royalty with an Upper East Side private school accent. For the first two years of their relationship, they barely understood a word the other was saying. Unfortunately, those turned out to be their best times together. Contrary to what therapists preach, once this couple completely understood each other, things started to fall apart.

Louis was the son of a baker from the south of France, and he remained a simple man all his life despite becoming rich. To him, fashion was a business like any other. He joked that he won his first shop in a poker game in Nice. Then he opened a shop in Cannes. On a bus in Cannes, he met a perky French girl aptly named Zizi, who became his designer and then his wife. Neither could draw or sew—that was for "the others." He was a strong man, short and a bit round. He had an infectious smile and a permanent air of not taking life too seriously. But he took it seriously enough to join the Resistance in World War II and received a little rosette medal that he wore on his suits when he had to get dressed up—something he hated to do. Louis was an adorable slob. He hated anything tight, so he always wore baggy corduroy pants (à la Picasso) and layers of T-shirts topped with a cashmere sweater worn backward and inside out.

Brigitte Bardot was filming *And God Created Woman* in Cannes and Saint-Tropez in 1956. Louis met Brigitte in his shop, dressed her in a gingham dress with a tight top and a full skirt, and the BB look was born. Gingham, called vichy in French (like the French government during the war), was a style of tablecloth in the south of France. Worn with flat ballerina slippers, the gingham-check look became a worldwide fashionable teenage girl uniform. With the success of his Cannes shop, the Férauds took the plunge and opened a couture shop in Paris, on rue du Faubourg Saint-Honoré directly opposite the Élysée Palace, the home of the formidable President Charles de Gaulle.

Louis loved women, especially his models, a little too much. Louis and Zizi had *une arrangement*. Before each fashion show, Louis would select his favorite model, whom he often cast as the bride in the finale. She would receive his full attention—often sex but more often just kisses and squeezes on the derrière. His models were exotic; he preferred Brazilians, a first in France. Their dark skin complemented the bright, electric, pure colors Louis preferred for his fashions: yellow, orange, lime green, and magnificent prints he designed himself. Once he met Mia, she inspired him to paint like the colorful designs of his prints. He created a painting studio out of a series of maids' rooms above his apartment.

Louis and his neighbor de Gaulle, however, never saw eye to eye. With Louis being a free-spirited baker's son from Arles and de Gaulle being quite conservative, this made for very nasty clashes. Louis loved to rattle de Gaulle, who Louis claimed spied on him night and day. When Louis fell in love with Mia and Zizi moved out, he often invited me to stay in the guest suite in his apartment. Each morning the three of us would descend the staircase to Café Faubourg Saint-Honoré for breakfast. On the street, exactly opposite de Gaulle's bedroom window, we would do our little routine. Louis would grab Mia's breast and kiss her on the lips. Then he would grab my butt and kiss me on both shoulders just below my ears. He wanted to drive the president crazy!

September found us overwhelmed with offers, some serious, some not. After the show with Féraud in July and our great press coverage, we were showered with contracts for swimwear and cocktail dresses. One of our contracts was with the American firm Madcaps Hosiery to introduce our lace panty hose to the

United States and another with Rose Marie Reid for swimwear. We designed two triangles that moved on a string and a string bottom with two ties in a soft cotton terry sponge that we sold to Brigitte Bardot. (These days you have to give free clothes to celebs to wear or even pay them.)

Then one night at Castel's, one of the first discotheques in Paris, two handsome American men approached us on the dance floor, claiming to be producers from Hollywood. Mia was wearing a navy-blue-and-gold minidress, with a large triangle cut out to show off her belly button. I was wearing a gold lamé bra and matching hip-hugging miniskirt. The way they studied us convinced me that they had never seen anyone wearing a bra in public. The men claimed to be doing a movie in Paris and said they were in the club scouting locations. Would we be interested in doing the costumes? Naturally we were a bit skeptical.

We demanded proof that they were bona fide producers. So Charles Feldman (agent-producer) and Richard Sylbert (art director-producer) showed us their cards and even pulled out their driver's licenses, complete with legitimate-looking Beverly Hills addresses. Right there on the disco floor, Feldman and Sylbert officially hired us to do the costumes for Woody Allen's *What's New Pussycat?* about to be shot in Paris. Not knowing much, we managed to ask for a single screen credit and a chauffeured limousine, which we got (without an agent).

Mia was twenty-three and I was twenty. We had graduated from Parsons in May, arrived in Paris in June, by July were working with Féraud, and now we had been asked to do costumes for a movie. I was so excited when I found out it was Woody Allen's first movie, the maiden voyage of my quirky comic friend from the days at Café Wha? in the Village.

When Woody saw me on the set the first day, he yelled, "Peaches! What are you doing here?" When he found out that Mia and I were designing the costumes, he offered to write a part for me in the opening scene, but I declined. I told him I couldn't act but would be happy if he put my leather outfit on a French "Peaches LaTour" look-alike. So in the opening scene, Woody is playing chess outside the Closerie des Lilas café with a carbon-copy Vicky, and my "Peaches in the Village" leather look went worldwide.

Pussycat had some extraordinary females for Mia and me to dress, each one an emotional wreck, each one a rising star. The leading lady was Romy Schneider, Europe's number one star, constantly in the press because of her recent breakup with heart-throb Alain Delon.

Romy plays the good-girl fiancée of Peter O'Toole, and the seductresses are Capucine, the fashionista; Paula Prentiss, the kook; and Ursula Andress, the sensual bombshell.

Paula and Capucine struggled with their place in the hierarchy of the film, competing for more time on-screen, by any means possible, which is generally earned by seducing the director or cameraman. It was a four-way competition, but it was evident to cast and crew that no one could compete against the formidable Ursula Andress, unique in power and determination. One of the highlights of my life was getting to know and admire her.

In the sixties, Andress was the new Brigitte Bardot. Her figure (35-22-35) was beyond perfection. The missing inches at the waist (the average model was 35-24-35) were natural; this was before liposuction. Whenever we walked down Parisian streets together, all the men became dumbstruck by her blond, tan, natural beauty. She was also extremely intelligent, multilingual, and

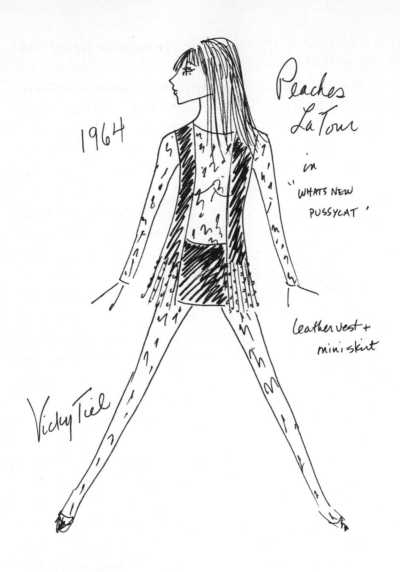

1964

Peaches
La Tour

in

"WHATS NEW
PUSSYCAT"

leather vest +
mini skirt

Vicky Tiel

reputed to be the lover of James Dean just before his death (yes, I know, but apparently he could go either way).

Ursula, like Marilyn Monroe, preferred to go commando (without underwear *ever*). It made for some intimate fittings with the costume designers of both sexes. Ursula wasn't trying to be provocative; it was her nature. She was just a "natural Swiss miss."

One morning while getting dressed, she announced, "Vicky, I want a white jersey gown for tonight. I must look like a Greek goddess and the dress must be able to come off in a hurry!"

"Where are you going?" I asked.

"I have a big party tonight and I am going to meet Jean-Paul Belmondo," she replied.

Belmondo was France's James Dean. Along with Alain Delon, he was the top leading man. Frenchwomen preferred either one or the other since they were so different: Belmondo, the sensual, athletic lover; Delon, the cool-eyed, dark-haired sophisticate.

"Ursula," I asked innocently, "isn't Belmondo married?" She gave me a look—perhaps because she, too, was married, to John Derek—that shut me up. Okay, fine. I made a goddess dress that didn't take long to sew, since it was one big piece of jersey that wrapped around the neck and could come undone with two hooks. At the neck we attached a large diamond pin.

The next morning I went to the Hôtel du Quai d'Orsay to pick up Ursula for the day's filming at the studio outside Paris. Her room was a mess. The white gown was lying on the floor. Ursula was draped nude across the bed, wrapped partially in a sheet.

"*Oh, ma petite* Vicky! *Merci beaucoup pour la robe!*" She thanked me for the dress. "I'm in love. It was zee dress. He loved it!"

This was a most important lesson in my life. Ursula Andress taught me the power of a dress. A gown I had designed had been instrumental in causing France's leading man to stray from his wife. Belmondo moved in with Ursula soon after that, and they remained together for years. Fashion could disrupt the status quo. At the very least, certain clothing could push buttons, and Ursula knew which ones to push. Forget Parsons fashion school.

Ursula would teach me all the little tricks men liked. I would use them for the rest of my career.

> ### URSULA'S FASHION SEDUCTION SECRETS
>
> - Tiny black spaghetti straps on the shoulders
> - Animal prints . . . *grrrr*
> - Fabrics that are soft and furlike
> - Sexy heels that flatter the leg, but not too crazy
> - Boots with sexy heels, some for day, some for evening
> - Tight belts
> - White jersey, white chiffon, white dresses: the Greek draped-goddess look
> - Black lace over skin, especially over arms
> - A must: hard nipples showing through a top
> - Natural-look makeup, always with shiny lips and big eyes
> - No underwear (just the thought arouses men)

My boyfriend Rainer came to Paris for a romantic visit. We had stayed in touch by letter. I visited his family in Düsseldorf. Then all hell broke loose. In the German magazine *Bunte*, a revealing photo of me appeared under the title "I Know What Men Find Sexy."

Rainer phoned me and broke up. "I can't marry someone like you."

I didn't suffer for long. As *What's New Pussycat?* went on, I began dating Woody and sometimes the director, a divine silver-haired Englishman named Clive Donner. Clive was charming, intellectual, and seventeen years older. After I spent several months dodging the sexual advances of both, permitting nothing beyond deep good-night kisses, Dick Sylbert told me emphatically, "You have to go to bed with one of them. You have to choose." I couldn't. I really didn't lust after either. I was stuck on a type: blond, built, and *hot*. . . but I agreed.

My birthday was coming up; I was about to turn twenty-one. Dick Sylbert, ever the art director, created a birthday party fit for a movie scene, with a "Vicky" contest. Both Clive and Woody would present a gift to me at my party, and the cast of the movie would vote on which was better. The winner would get to sleep with me that night, the night I became an official adult. This was not just for fun but also for a commitment to a relationship. Both Clive and Woody were serious, and I felt both wanted me for a long-term romance or more. Once I turned twenty-one, I couldn't continue to "date" both of them.

At the party, the film crew of about twenty gathered around a birthday cake, ready to vote. Clive gave me the largest tapestry box of Godiva chocolates. Woody had two guys carry a giant pinball machine up the five flights to the new red velvet garret apartment that I shared with Mia. Woody won.

Victorious Woody, ever the director, gave me very specific instructions. He did not want to sleep with me that night, but planned it for the next so he could "set the stage." I was to arrive at the Hotel George V at precisely eight o'clock. I was then directed to go into the bathroom, take a long shower with the door open, come out nude, and walk to the bed. He promised he would also be nude—and erect—under the sheets, waiting for me.

Sexuality Counts
(And Size Helps!)

As Joan Rivers says, "Can we talk?"

The genius who said "size doesn't count" was probably rationalizing. In my experience, two things count: sexuality and, well, let's face it, size.

I measure sexuality on a scale of one to ten. Ten being enthusiastic and capable of having sex daily, zero being very happy to do without sex day after day. Tens should mate with tens, or maybe a nine or an eight, but never with a seven. A two is best with a two or three but not with a five or a zero and definitely never with a ten. A zero can make it only with another zero.

Many people fake enthusiasm until they marry and then their true sexuality emerges. After only one year, 30 percent of couples *never* achieve the sexual rhythm or intensity they had in their debut. After their first sexual encounters, 14 percent of couples *never* have sex again yet remain together.

Besides all the other potential clashes in marriage, such as social and economic differences, philosophies of child rearing and careers, it is very dangerous to add in the lack of compatibility in bed. While it's true that opposites attract, it's not a good idea to go for your opposite in sexual intensity. Tens will not be happy with zeros or ones or even fives. Like should marry like as far as our sexual energies are concerned. Are you with me so far?

Let's get down to brass tacks. Women are the receptors and

men are the objects. This cannot change. As a receptor, a woman is formed at an early age by the sexual object inside her. If a woman has had a normal penis inside her for twenty years, a ten-inch-long one would present a painful ordeal. On the other hand, some women who have had a very well-endowed first lover might have a difficult time achieving an orgasm through penetration as they are stretched. Lacking size, imagination and enthusiasm are necessities.

Trying to make something work that doesn't is a big mistake. I always tell my friends who are looking for Mr. Right, if no one comes along, that is because no one was meant to!

Time alone is time we need to learn a life lesson. When you are ready, the door opens and Mr. or Ms. Right will walk in. Just make sure you watch those numbers.

"At Lunch?"

1964

On the day after my birthday—the day of my "date" with Woody Allen—I was enjoying a gossipy girls' lunch with Paula Prentiss and Ursula Andress. We were in the commissary of Billancourt Studio, a redbrick building on the west side of Paris. I was their designer trying to become their confidante. Dick Sylbert had pulled me aside after asking Mia and me to do *Pussycat* and told me he had had two reasons for choosing me specifically to work on the set. Besides wanting the actresses to have the Mia/Vicky look, he wanted me to look after Paula Prentiss personally. "She's a nut, and you're a nut too," he said, "so you can take care of her. Follow her around and look after her."

I began to see Dick's point of view that day at lunch. Paula had a peculiar habit when she ate. She would put her salad, main course, and dessert all on one plate, mix them together, and gobble everything down with a Coke. She eventually did feign a big suicide scene, when she climbed the rafters of the set to the ceiling boards and threatened to jump. I was asked to follow her up to the roof of the soundstage, which I did, and calmly asked her to come down, adding that it was my first job and I would be fired if I couldn't bring her down. She very sweetly agreed, and we became lunch buddies.

Suddenly the swinging doors to the dining room opened and in walked the most virile man I had yet to see in Paris. He didn't look French. He had blond buzz-cut hair, blue eyes, and a dimpled chin à la Kirk Douglas. He was tan and muscular, wearing a black-and-white polka dot shirt, tight black jeans, and black-and-white Top-Siders, no socks (even though it was cold outside). He must be American, I thought. I caught his eye and he walked directly toward us. He walked like a surfer. Coming through the swinging doors right behind him were Elizabeth Taylor and Richard Burton. The commissary went silent.

The handsome stranger left the Burtons, walked over to Paula, flashed a toothy grin, and gave her a big hug that brightened her up. They spoke for a few moments, until he got her phone number, then he turned to me and said, "Hi, who are you?" He stared at me up and down in my see-through lace jumpsuit, then asked me for my phone number, too. I wasn't worried enough about Paula's mental health not to give it to him. The stranger was Ron Berkeley, makeup man to Elizabeth Taylor. When he left to join the Burtons, Paula said, "He's the hot stud of MGM." She wouldn't say if she had learned that from personal experience, but I wondered whether she had, and it seemed to me that she was anticipating a repeat performance. He had also been the makeup man on her first film, *Where the Boys Are*.

I listened to Paula but was thinking about my date with Woody that night. I was an adult and promised to Mr. Woody Allen.

That night at six thirty my phone rang in my apartment on rue Lauriston. "Hi," said the voice, "it's Ron, from lunch today."

"Oh, yes!" I answered.

He seemed rushed.

"Can I see you tonight?" I was surprised at the urgency in his voice.

"No, I have a date."

"Well," he went on, "I'm downstairs from your apartment and calling from the café on the corner. I found your address. I have to see you for just a quick drink. I'll come up and get you."

A few minutes later, I opened the door wearing a long black satin bathrobe. He grabbed me and we kissed in the doorway. The kiss was beyond great, and I melted. We fell to the floor and had sex right there in the hallway (thank God there was only one neighbor and Mia was out), continued in the living room on the couch, then finally made our way to the bedroom, where hours later we finally finished. We were lying there exhausted when I realized it was nearly eleven o'clock.

I screamed, "Oh, my God, Woody!" And then I told Ron the whole plan of what was supposed to have taken place that night at the George V. He was mildly amused, and our night continued as before.

The next day at the studio I saw Woody early in the morning

before filming. I could tell he was very upset with me. I said, "I'm so sorry. I meant to come to the hotel, but I fell in love yesterday at lunch with a guy I met and am going to marry. He's already asked!"

Woody looked skeptical. "At lunch?" he asked, with that trademark woebegone look.

Years later, after I married Ron, we went to see *Manhattan*.

In the last scene of the film, Woody races across New York City to tell Mariel Hemingway that he loves her and not to leave for Europe. She answers, "Don't worry, I'll be back."

Trying to persuade her that six months is a long time, Woody says sadly, "You'll be working in the theater there, you'll be with actors and directors, and you'll, you know, you'll go to rehearsal and you'll hang out with those people, you'll have lunch a lot and before you know it, attachments form . . ."

She tells him, "You have to have a little faith in people." And that is the end of the movie.

When I saw *Manhattan*, I realized the mark that my falling in love at lunch had left on Woody's psyche. If I had slept with Woody and not Ron, how different would all three of our lives have been?

Ron Berkeley's World

1966–1985

I must get out of these wet clothes and into a dry martini.
—ALEXANDER WOOLLCOTT

The man I fell in love with at lunch was MGM's top makeup man and had film credits on more than thirty major motion pictures. After a passionate week together, one morning at breakfast on the balcony of his hotel room we got around to talking about ourselves, our families, and our pasts.

I described my middle-class life in Chevy Chase and learned that my life up until the day we met held little interest for Ron except for the fact that he had found out Elizabeth Taylor was intrigued by the outfits I wore to work. Even the article written about me in the *Times* did not impress him. I realized how boring my life was compared to his.

On this cool morning over coffee and croissants, with a view of the Paris rooftops, he described his childhood growing up in Laurel Canyon in Hollywood, the third generation of Berkeleys in the film industry. For starters he said, "Errol Flynn was my godfather and his home, the Liar's Den, is just up the street from where I grew up. My dad, Mowbray Berkeley, was nicknamed Bunny, as his father was also Mowbray Berkeley. My dad was a set decorator, Errol's closest pal and running-around mate." I could picture those suave, dazzling loverboys.

I was impressed.

Ron explained that starting in the 1950s he worked on eight movies with Elvis, including my favorite, *Jailhouse Rock*. Ron had been Sinatra's makeup man on *The Manchurian Candidate*, another of my favorite films. Then he worked with Marlon Brando, Rock Hudson, and Debbie Reynolds before the Debbie Reynolds–Eddie Fisher–Liz Taylor scandal. He left for Europe with Elizabeth when she fled the States with Burton after having been declared unfit by the American press for her erratic love life.

Our twelve-year age difference and Ron having begun his career in his early twenties with Elizabeth on *The Last Time I Saw Paris* (ironically) meant he had worked on most of the great movies of my childhood: *Giant*, *Cat on a Hot Tin Roof*, *Raintree County*, *The Misfits*, *Sayonara*, and *Mutiny on the Bounty*. He knew *everyone*. He had been *this close* to all the great movie beauties—and he fell in love with *me*.

The Berkeleys were a notorious family in the film industry. Ron's grandmother, Aimee Berkeley, was the stunt double of the silent film star Nazimova. Aimee was a reknowned horsewoman and part black South African. She was first cousin to her husband, who ended his life as a vaudeville star. The Berkeleys slept with whomever they wanted, damn the consequences. The Berkeley (the Brits pronounce it BARK-lee) family owned the oldest inhabited castle in England, built in the 1100s in the town of Dursley on the Welsh border. Ron's real first name is Dursley, but in Hollywood everyone called him Ron.

Berkeley Castle was—is—infamous in England. In his play *Edward II*, Christopher Marlowe writes that the king's murder took place in the castle dungeon. The favorite knight of Ron's ancestor Sir Thomas Berkeley, Marlowe tells us (I paraphrase!), stuck a hot poker up Edward's ass. Some say that the knight's headless ghost, with fire coming out of where his head would be, rides the castle's parapets on cool summer nights. To this day, local legend has it that the "curse" of homosexuality and financial ruin hangs over the Berkeleys in England.

Perhaps the curse is real? There were many gay Berkeleys, and the family did lose all their money and land. Humphrey Berkeley, Ron's great-uncle, sat in Parliament. He sponsored the law in England that allowed homosexuality. There is also Berkeley Square in London, named after the family, and Berkeley (Yanks say BERK-lee), California, was named after Bishop George Berkeley, a philosopher and poet in the 1700s.

Richard Burton enjoyed the fact that a poor Welsh boy from a coal mining town could have as his trusted makeup man and companion someone from the oldest noble family in England. Ron certainly did not look noble: He dressed like a California surfer. Apart from women, his passion was surfing, and he was proud to be a founding member of the San Onofre Surfing Club in San Clemente, California. Ron was part of the beach culture, with a wife and son in Malibu. She was wife number two. His first marriage had ended in divorce and their son lived with him and Lea.

Ron's mother's uncle, the writer William Desmond Taylor, was murdered in 1922 in Hollywood (the case is still unsolved). The great noir film *Sunset Boulevard* is—loosely—based on that story, with William Holden playing Taylor. In fact, the name Norma Desmond (Gloria Swanson's role) is a combination of Taylor's middle name and the last name of the actress Mabel Normand, a friend of Taylor's. Ron told me his current close beach friends were Peter Lawford, Alan Ladd Jr., Rod Taylor, and Gardner McKay, and that they played volleyball on the Santa Monica beach in front of Lawford's house (where Lawford often entertained Marilyn Monroe in her trysts with John Kennedy). I could not imagine one man connected to so many famous people.

Elvis gave Ron a motorcycle after a movie with Ann-Margret. Sophia Loren was a friend. He confided that she had a special beauty trick: She put her hair in very tiny braids and pulled the braids into a knot at the back of her head. This pulled up all the skin, especially around her neck. An instant face-lift without surgery. Over the braids, Sophia would wear a wig. If you see old pictures of Sophia, even in a swimsuit, she is wearing a wig. This trick was taught to Sophia by Marlene Dietrich, who worked with Ron's dad, Bunny Berkeley, Mike Todd's personal decorator.

Ron met Elizabeth Taylor at MGM when they were both teenagers and he did the makeup for her early movies *Giant* and *Raintree County* with Montgomery Clift. He told me Elizabeth truly loved Monty, but he went gay. They were in the middle of filming *Raintree County* when Monty totaled his car in a crash after leaving Elizabeth's house, destroying his face; it was never the same again. Elizabeth was devastated.

She had loved four husbands before she met Richard, and Ron knew them all well, but he adored Burton, who was the love of Elizabeth's life. Ron was working with the Burtons on *The Sandpiper*, which was shot in Paris even though the movie was supposed to take place in Big Sur on the beach. The exterior shots had been done before on a beach in California, but Elizabeth had insisted on Paris for the interiors so she could eat real French food. *Bien sur.*

The Burtons had been thrown out of America (Elizabeth relinquished her U.S. citizenship and their passports were taken) because Elizabeth had broken up the marriage of America's sweetheart, Debbie Reynolds, to Eddie Fisher, only to abandon Eddie five years later for Burton. She was an outcast in society and the public couldn't read enough about her.

Ron swore that his marriage was over sexually and he was getting a divorce. He assured me that he and his wife had separated and he was buying another house for her off the beach and he would be moving to Europe. After *The Sandpiper*, he would return to California for Christmas, tell his wife about us, and we would marry as soon as his divorce was final. He had promised me all this the night we met, sometime before dawn. I didn't know if it was the challenge of taming a bad boy or the desire to enter his seductive Hollywood world—perhaps a bit of both—but my heart fell in love at first sight. My body fell in love at first kiss.

Finding Husbands Married to Someone Else

Those who maintain that all is right talk nonsense,
they ought to say that all is for the best.
—VOLTAIRE

The idea of falling in love with someone else's husband had been incomprehensible to me and I don't think I would have slept with Ron at our first meeting had he been wearing a wedding ring. But after a week of nonstop candlelight dinners in all the romantic bistros in Saint-Germain-des-Prés wearing my latest bra tops and miniskirts even in crisp fall weather, I was hooked. Ron had become a habit and I wanted him to be all mine.

He introduced me to vodka tonic, the requisite drink in the Burton world. I would learn that Richard and Ron could each easily drink a bottle of vodka a day on or off the set and continue working with no effect. On our first real date outside of my bedroom, we met at the bar in his hotel, the Montalembert, and I had eight vodka tonics to his eleven. Drinking was followed by dinner at the bar where various *Sandpiper* actors and crew joined us, not one revealing that Ron was more married than he let on when he introduced me as his fiancée.

Life with Ron was exciting, a movable cocktail party, filled with fabulous conversation and unusual combinations of characters. He could befriend a boxer, a drunken poet, or a schoolteacher on vacation from Iowa with his wife. He fascinated everyone with intimate stories of life with Sinatra in Vegas with the Rat Pack, such as the day the entire crew locked Sinatra in the bedroom and brought up call girls to the living room, where they partied all night to drive Sinatra crazy. He pounded on the door. (Ron later mentioned that one of the "girls" was his first wife.) We would all be drawn in and he could peel off the layers of sophistication or innocence from his audience and find a common ground (alcohol). His barroom parties were thrilling for a girl six months out of college, and they were followed by proof of his sexual prowess after drinking endless vodkas. Of course, he was only thirty-three.

One morning we were in bed together at the Montalembert when his then-wife, Lea, called from L.A. He asked me to go to the bathroom to give him privacy. I obliged and did not eavesdrop; I trusted him. When the next phone call happened a week later, I asked why I couldn't listen and he said I made him nervous. He wanted the divorce to go well and not to let her know he was remarrying.

After a month of being together every night, we were celebrating Thanksgiving with the Burtons at Leroy Haynes's restaurant in Pigalle. I was invited to join them as a dress designer rather than as Ron's girlfriend. The charade was too much. Fueled by vodka and great wine, I pretended to be unattached and flirted with one of the film's costars, the bad man in all the '50s films, Robert Webber. Later that night Ron and I had our first fight. Ron admitted that he was a liar, really married, not separated at all. But he insisted he was not lying about loving me. He promised me we would get married. I fell for him all over again.

Mia, meanwhile, had her own problems with Louis Féraud, which we discussed endlessly each morning at the local café. Their fledgling romance had begun as one of the flings Louis constantly had with his fashion models—he employed only the sexiest, most exotic models in Paris. He had his pick of the litter. What model could turn down the only male couturier capable of having sex with a woman?

Louis's wife, Zizi, tolerated his extramarital affairs, as most Frenchwomen do. This gave her permission to have love affairs of her own with attractive men she met at the chic dinner parties Louis refused to attend. Zizi was a pixie painted in shades of taupe and brown, with a shag haircut and big eyes. She was the first woman I ever saw wear a tight white blouse unbuttoned below her bra so the tips of lace and her puffed-up breasts popped out of her décolleté. Zizi flirted with young Frenchmen selling fabrics in the atelier. Louis didn't seem to mind. Indeed, he appeared to take pride in the fact that other men desired her. He even seemed aroused.

Mia was another story: Not ready for French games, she taunted Louis with her aloof air. He had to possess her. She was a challenge. He had never been in love with a woman who was born into a family of wealth and celebrity. Louis had had a fling with a celebrity, Kim Novak, but Kim was from a Midwestern American family, not fashion royalty. Mia's feelings for Louis grew, and as they became a couple, something changed. The ice melted and she would sit on Louis's lap and kiss him endlessly in public, in front of everyone but Zizi. The aloof Mia had disappeared. She looked deliciously happy.

One morning on the phone, Mia confessed that she loved Louis. Until this moment I had never heard these words from her about anyone. She had never been allowed a serious romance living with the Penns. Mia had dated the handsome model-actor Michael Nouri in college, but she never showered him with attention in public.

She told me she hoped Louis would get a divorce so they could marry. She envisioned herself in all the workrooms on Faubourg Saint-Honoré. I told her I preferred the Left Bank because it was more youthful; let Zizi keep the Faubourg, which eventually happened.

Zizi agreed to a divorce and half ownership of the brand Louis Féraud, which included clothes, perfume, and all licensing. Zizi bought a magnificent apartment with a view of the Seine where she entertained in great style with a maid and a cook. She moved a handsome new conquest into her bedroom. She then diplomatically allowed Louis to move Mia into his bedroom and me into the guest room of their former apartment. Zizi also gave Mia and me a wonderful Christmas present: a French encyclopedia on the history of costume fashion design with a loving inscription welcoming us to French couture. Everything they say about Frenchwomen is true. They are unlike the rest of the planet.

One big difference in relationships with our sexy, older lovers began to emerge: Mia's desire to work suffered as a result of her need to keep an eye on Louis. I never felt a man should impose on my job. I never felt insecure or worried enough to leave work, and I loved working long, late hours. I told Mia, "If my man left me for another woman, I would find someone else even if I was in love with him. The world is filled with men." I recited to her my mantra: "A new man comes along every ten minutes, just like a bus."

She said, "I know," and yet she kept running home early to check on Louis. My romance with Steve in the Village had helped me to let go of the obsession of possessing a man. I could compete until I was number one in his heart, but once we were a committed couple I wanted to be free and not clingy, and most of all, I didn't want ever to check up on someone and I didn't want anyone who would ever do that to me.

THREE WAYS TO TELL IF A MAN IS IN LOVE

1. He wants to spend his *time* with you.

2. He wants to spend his *money* on you.

3. He wants to have *sex* with you.

   If you get all three, it's the jackpot.

   If you get only two, beware. If you choose to compromise, you are settling for less than you deserve.

   If you get only one, move on.

Johnny Carson Calls

The week of Christmas 1965, Johnny Carson's office called Mia and me in Paris. Would we fly to New York the next day and bring our minidresses and have a fashion show on TV? We screamed, "Yes!" They even let us bring Wuffles on TV.

I wore a green miniculotte jumpsuit and Mia wore a minicoat in purple cut velvet. Two models showed our latest creations, the bra dress and the jumpsuit. Would the school that gave me an F in fashion notice?

After the show, Steve found me, as he always managed to do, sleeping at the Tysons' apartment at the Hampshire House. He ran over and we made love in Carolyn's giant bedroom overlooking Central Park.

I didn't tell Steve about Ron. Steve was irresistible to the majority of women, myself included. Would I ever lose this magnetic attraction?

At dawn we looked over the beautiful winter haze as the sun rose over the park. This was the real good-bye. Steve said to me, "I'm moving to L.A. to try acting. I'm so proud of you, Peaches, now come back to this bed. Man, these sheets are something else, nothing ever felt so good." They were French, signed by Porthault. I had to buy some when I got back to Paris.

Lessons From Elizabeth Taylor

Little did I know at sixteen, when I cut my hair for my junior prom into the Elizabeth Taylor "artichoke," the hairstyle she made famous at the 1961 Oscars, that at the age of twenty-one I would be hanging out with Elizabeth as a girlfriend in Paris. Or even better yet, that she would want to dress young like me and wear my clothes.

How to describe Elizabeth Taylor? She was not a movie star; she was the entire galaxy of stars in one package. That was the energy she emitted when she walked into a room. People froze. When they spoke to her, they stuttered. The only other person I've met who ever came close was Elvis. Ron, who did Marilyn Monroe's makeup in her later years, said Marilyn was just the opposite: Toward the end of her life when Marilyn came around, people ran. She was so desperately unhappy that her gloom was contagious.

Elizabeth's eyes were not the clear blue of Paul Newman's or Cameron Diaz's but dark navy blue, like the deep sea, with an indigo light that most people call violet. They were very large, and she could use them as the actress she was: just open them up and *glare*. Since her blackened eyebrows were a good two inches above her eyes, the glare was so intense it went right through you and the gaze could shock you silly. I saw many a nervous producer go faint when he told Elizabeth she had taken too long for lunch, and she snapped open her eyes and said, "I *what*?!"

Yes, life with Elizabeth was an amazing time. Ron and I lived with her and Richard for the good part of ten years and rented apartments nearby for another ten. Elizabeth invented the entourage. At times there were twelve of us all flying around together. Richard Hanley, Elizabeth's secretary, had been secretary to Louis B. Mayer, the head of MGM, and traveled with his partner, John Lee. Jim Benton, Burton's secretary, and George Davis, Benton's partner, were frequent fliers. There was Agnes Flanagan, Marilyn Monroe's hairdresser; then Claudye Bozzacchi, Elizabeth's hairdresser; Gianni Bozzacchi, Claudye's husband, who became Elizabeth's personal photographer; Gaston Sanz, the bodyguard and driver; as well as Bob Wilson, Richard's dresser from Broadway. There were four kids and four to ten dogs, depending on who had had puppies. There were *no* cats.

For a while there was Sarah, a nurse, to whom Elizabeth gave a sable coat in a moment of feeling sorry for her having given up her personal life to fly around the world for a year carrying Elizabeth's pill bag. It was the '60s and Doctor Feelgoods gave her wake-up pills for jet lag, go-to-sleep pills, pain pills, act-outraged pills (for intense parts), and pills to sleep off hangovers to be mixed with Bull Marys. We all got to share the pills, too.

Generally, we were companions to gossip and play Scrabble or do crossword puzzles with to fill up the hours between scenes in the dressing rooms and the long nights in strange hotels. Elizabeth's favorite pastime was celebrity gossip. Her definition of celebrity included royalty, world leaders, writers, artists and musicians, and the occasional Greek billionaire. Elizabeth needed gossip as fuel to shock at dinner parties. She had to know who was sleeping with whom, who was great in bed and who was not, and who was well hung. The gay secretaries were especially good at collecting that necessary information, and Richard Hanley's years at MGM made him a sexpert on the entire film industry. Richard Burton did not partake in the gossip; his nose was always in a book if he wasn't writing in his diary. Occasionally he would chuckle, especially if the stories concerned English royalty.

I was able to add bits about models and musicians, and I had to keep up with the latest about her two favorite male actors, the twin sexpots Marlon Brando (who I assume slept with Elizabeth, Marilyn, and everyone else) and Warren Beatty (who tried), both of whom she demanded as her leading men if Richard did not suit the part. Elizabeth wanted people around, and she got them. Stars of the '30s, '40s, and '50s were "studio owned" and lucky to get their favorite hairdresser for a film. Elizabeth spent her entire life as a celebrity. At sixteen she was already the most photographed movie star in the world. The knowledge of how the old system worked, plus her wild, independent nature, allowed her to envision a new way to live as a celebrity. She would find all her favorite people in each category—hair, makeup, etc.—and travel the world with them in tow, and whenever she could, she'd have the producer of the film pay for it all.

Did she *like* being holed up in enormous hotel suites with all her favorite food and wine and her favorite people being flown in from all over the world to be at her beck and call? She *loved* it! The children were in their suites when out of school; one day we got a phone call from Richard Hanley because Ron's son, Craig, who was thirteen and on vacation at the Dorchester in London, was ordering a dozen oysters from room service for breakfast each morning with his eggs and mimosas.

Often Elizabeth's brother, Howard, and his family stayed in the suites, too, and there was the occasional Jenkins, Burton's Welsh family, or a best friend flown in to spice up conversation. Dinner would be room service, everyone ordering what they pleased, eating on tray tables, lying on couches or beds. Rarely was there a formal sit-down except for holidays, birthdays, or funerals.

Photographers have been around since the camera was invented, but it wasn't until 1959 that Federico Fellini coined the name Paparazzo for a photographer in *La Dolce Vita*. Soon after, in the '60s, groups of photographers stalking celebs became known as paparazzi. Elizabeth had her own paparazzi that shadowed her everywhere she went. The major pest was Ron Galella. Once, Richard had him arrested hiding in a tree in Puerto Vallarta. There were never fewer than four photographers or more than twenty every day. The paparazzi started in the middle '50s with Mike Todd's death and Elizabeth's Debbie–Eddie breakup. I think she was relieved when Jackie Kennedy came along and they could share the spotlight and Ron Galella.

At night, however, when Elizabeth went out to make an appearance, it was always in a major gown and Richard in a tux. She went the whole nine yards—diamond tiara, necklace, three bracelets, five diamond rings with major stones, sables, couture gowns, and killer makeup. Going out was a performance and would be recorded in every paper. In those days there were only a few movie magazines. It was Elizabeth and Jackie Kennedy who aroused the public's interest in off-screen celebrity lifestyles. Fashion trends would be launched from the way they tied their Hermès scarves. Grace Kelly was also a target of paparazzi, but her husband ruled Monaco and he wanted Grace to become low-key after their marriage, so she was not bothered as much.

By the time I joined the entourage full-time in 1966, Elizabeth no longer had any sense of the real world, especially of finances. Once she handed me a hundred-dollar bill to buy a bikini on the beach in Rome and sweetly asked if it would be enough. The price of a good swimsuit then was $10, and from a beach vendor half that. She could have been robbed blind by the entourage, but we all loved her and would never have done it. She never minded the vast hotel or dinner bills as long as everyone was happy.

Elizabeth's favorite pastime was eating and drinking on the set in a private dining room or in the hotel suite. Special guests were brought in for lunch or dinner. Everybody who was anybody on the planet wanted to meet her, so it was not unusual for luncheon guests to include Valentino, Yul Brynner, Maria Callas, Princess Grace or Princess Margaret, heads of states like Marshal Tito of Yugoslavia or the duke of this or that, jewelers like Gianni Bulgari, the musicians André Previn and Tom Jones or the writers Gore Vidal, Graham Greene, and Kenneth Tynan. English actors who were in town would come over to take on Richard. Michael Caine, Richard Harris, Peter O'Toole, and Burton would make fun of each other's Shakespearian accents as they ripped apart other actors. Elizabeth's lunches were eating marathons often lasting three to four hours, especially in Italy, where chefs at the studio invented dishes to please her.

To Elizabeth, from what I saw, the things that mattered most were:

- Being Earth Mother to her loved ones

- Sex

- Food and drink

- Helping the unfortunate (humans and animals)

- How much money she was being paid to do a movie, and what jewelry was offered by the producer for the "end of the movie" gift

Her fame and beauty did not matter very much to her. She was never one to worry about herself as much as she worried about others. She really didn't pursue the film career she might have had. Her financial interests were nil. She never counted her money or cared, wanting only to know that there was enough to pay each vast hotel bill, one of which amounted to a few hundred thousand for a multiweek stay (it would be $1 million today).

The reason she wanted the world's top salary (she was the first actor to be paid $1 million for a movie) was that she loved to "mess" with producers. Having been given a hard time early in her career as a child star by Louis B. Mayer (who owned every actor at MGM), she never looked back once she was free from his clutches. She was always an activist.

When Ron did the makeup that won an Oscar for *7 Faces of Dr. Lao,* his boss at MGM, Bill Tuttle, got the award because his name, not Ron's, was on the screen. In early Hollywood, only the head of each department in the studio got screen credit. The actual person who did the work never got credit. When Ron mentioned this to Elizabeth, she screamed, "Not fair!" and, ever the activist, she got the Academy rules changed. Ron was the first actual makeup man to get credit for a film he did. Ever since *Who's Afraid of Virginia Woolf?* the individual makeup and fashion designers get the credit, not just Bill Tuttle or Edith Head. Thanks to our dearest Elizabeth.

I know Elizabeth really loved Richard, just as Louis loved Mia, in spite of the fact that they were total opposites. She loved the challenge of being married to an intellectual and a great actor and a big star. Their marriage was like taming a wild horse. Richard hated everything she loved, except food, drink, and sex. His idea of happiness was to be alone with a vodka tonic, reading a good book or watching a rugby match. Every morning he would get up early and type in his diary. Sometimes he would copy what he wrote and give it to one of us. He addressed one beautiful poem to me, starting with the line, "Licky—Sticky—Vicky."

He'd begin his day reading one of his five books—one in the car, one on the bedside table, one on the living room table, one in the studio dressing room, and one in the loo. Each book stayed in its proper place. The reading material was always poetry, a biography, a mystery, a current novel, and a script. His taste ran from his favorite authors Dylan Thomas and Hemingway to the poets e. e. cummings and Keats (whom he was always quoting) to biographies of world leaders such as Winston Churchill to Ian Fleming's James Bond novels. If Richard liked a living writer, he would summon him or her for a visit. Elizabeth had twenty pieces of tapestry luggage filled with clothes; Richard had no clothes but two trunks of books. Richard was a lifelong scholar. Elizabeth learned to enjoy mystery novels and became a fan of John D. MacDonald.

Unlike Elizabeth, who gave away everything and discarded lovers and husbands, Richard discarded nothing. He had an ugly green suit from his Oxford acting days. It must have been almost ten years old, and he carried it around, along with an ugly green typewriter also from his old student days. He also had an ugly green Rolls, his first nice car. Richard liked everything basic and old and green, and hated change. I'm sure he would have kept his ex-wife, Sybil, too, had he been able, before the press got involved. Richard hated to see anything he loved go!

Once Elizabeth and Richard were married, and with her newly acquired intellectual confidence, she set out to mingle with the nobles of Europe. Once she was invited by Baron Guy de Rothschild and his wife to their country home, Château de Ferrières, for their yearly ball. Jacqueline de Ribes was to accompany them to the château. It was the late sixties fashion look: Rusty browns, leather, fur trim, and riding boots were the craze with Yves Saint Laurent's fall collection. Fur and suede layered over culotte skirts. Country chic.

Elizabeth dressed for the château in a pink and purple geometric print Pucci minidress, Pucci print panty hose, and Pucci print boots to match, with giant diamond and emerald rings on each finger except her thumbs! Around her neck was her emerald drop.

"Elizabeth," I said, "that doesn't look like the French countryside."

"Oh, I'll liven things up," she answered. "I'm going as a rich hippie!" She was a big hit. As Richard complained to me when they returned, all the Frenchmen formed a circle around her over cocktails like Scarlett O'Hara at the Twelve Oaks barbeque, when she arrived all Puccified.

Elizabeth was no snob. She truly felt all humans had the same value in society. She preferred to befriend cooks, housekeepers, and secretaries rather than their bosses. She hated snobs almost as much as she hated cheap producers.

Once, while she was in Rome, French *Vogue* sent a team to the De Laurentiis Studios to photograph Elizabeth wearing furs. She was to get a free fur for the shoot. The studio dressing room was very small and crowded and had lots of newspapers on the floor with yet-to-be-cleaned-up dog pee. Her dog just wasn't used to going out, since he was usually cooped up with the entourage like the rest of us.

The self-important fashion editor and weary assistant waltzed in with a rack of ten furs. They were horrified by the dog pee and the décor, and started to complain and act like prima

donnas, everything Elizabeth hated. I could see her anger growing, and I knew she was going to play with them.

"Well, Miss Taylor," the editor said, "perhaps we could visit
another day, in a more convenient environment."

"Oh, hell no," she said. "This is how I live everywhere! Champagne and poop."

"You understand," he replied icily, "you were going to get one
of these coats for free."

Smiling graciously, she waved her hand to dismiss the fashion editor. "Oh, never mind, sugar!" she said. "I already have
one of each of these furs. Thank you very much. Bye now!" (If she
didn't like someone, she wouldn't want his gifts.)

Elizabeth loved losers as friends. The bigger the loser, the
more she loved him. I think this softheartedness explained many
of her marriages. She was a sucker for a sob story; she believed
everyone. She once confided in me that her childhood was lonely: no friends, no boyfriends, no high school proms. "I wasn't
allowed to date," she said. "As a result, I had no real inner self-
confidence." I was astounded! The most beautiful woman in the
world admitting her own insecurity.

Elizabeth's warmth was contagious, and to know her was to
love her. All my preconceived ideas of her being the untouchable
movie star were forgotten. I had drawn her at fifteen in art class
as my favorite movie star. Now this down-to-earth woman was
my friend. Elizabeth's generosity was her foremost quality, and it
shined in her love for all her friends and extended family.

LESSONS I LEARNED FROM ELIZABETH

- Don't take yourself seriously, and don't take anyone else seriously (except doctors).

- If you are really important, a really "big star," you'd better be nice to all the little people who got you there. Every time she met a stuck-up movie star or socialite she would call them a "B ACTRESS."

- Be happy with your own face. Don't wear makeup at home. It clogs up your pores and is bad for your skin.

- Always have sex with your husband—or someone else will.

- Always be kind to and approve of any friends your children bring home. You have only a few people who are truly yours forever: your kids and family. Don't risk losing them!

- Train your lovers or husbands to buy jewelry for all your gifts. Help them by pointing out pieces you love throughout the year. This prevents receiving gifts you can't use.

- Be responsible for your own menus. You can never bring enough of your own food with you when visiting a third world country.

ELIZABETH TAYLOR'S TYPICAL DAILY MENU, 1960s

BREAKFAST

- Mimosa: Combine equal parts Dom Pérignon champagne, fresh-squeezed orange juice, and vodka. Pour into an extra-large crystal cognac snifter over crushed ice.
- Crisp bacon and scrambled eggs
- English muffins (from England) with English orange marmalade

LUNCH

- Peanut butter (smooth) and bacon sandwich on French baguette; scoop out the extra bread inside
- Château Margaux 1945

COCKTAILS

- Jack Daniel's on the rocks in a chilled glass
- Homemade potato chips with sea salt

DINNER

- Crispy fried chicken
- Mashed potatoes and gravy
- Corn bread
- Biscuits and gravy
- Fresh green peas
- Chilled Sancerre rosé or Fontana Candida Frascati
- Trifle

- Italian espresso
- Sambuca, with an uneven number of coffee beans (three or five) for good luck

Richard Burton .. A Man Apart

Richard Burton was the man responsible for my dressing Elizabeth for more than twenty years. It wasn't Ron, who was still hiding our relationship. One day Richard walked over to me outside *The Sandpiper* shooting stage in Paris. He grabbed my arm and a shiver went through me. He was electric, with piercing green eyes the color of a tabby cat's. I was confused. He picked up on my nervousness and laughed. "Hello, luv, just wanted to tell you you look delicious. What have we here, a night-gown?"

I explained I was wearing a minidress, the latest fashion I created to show the legs and thighs. "Oh my, must have one of these for the missus. Let's keep it a surprise. Our wedding anniversary is coming up in November. She loves pearls, cover it with pearls."

I worked hard on the design and made the "missus" an ivory crepe mini with pearls on the edges of the neckline, hem, and sleeves. I added a surprise: ivory lace panty hose with baby pearls embroidered every few inches. With love and care, I beaded them by hand.

Elizabeth adored the outfit and ordered more of my designs, all minidresses. Slowly we became friends: I visited her on the set as her new designer, still hiding my relationship with Ron. Elizabeth actually was extremely puritanical. Her mother, Rose, had kept a constant eye on her and brought her up to be a nice girl, much like Debbie Reynolds, her classmate at the MGM school for child stars.

In Elizabeth, Richard had met his match in power and charisma. When he met her he was still married to Sybil, and he was having a serious affair with Claire Bloom (who was married to Rod Steiger at the time), his costar in *Look Back in Anger*, his breakthrough film. Plus he was having another hidden affair with the also very married (to director Richard Brooks) Jean Simmons, his costar from his earlier film *The Robe*, while at the same time having miniaffairs with Susan Strasberg and many of his other leading ladies. Unlike all the rest of them who had succumbed to the Welsh charm, Elizabeth was no easy prey. If Richard wanted to bed her regularly, he would have to wed her just as in *The Taming of the Shrew*, a film they would eventually do together. Elizabeth married all the men she loved. Nobody had yet to refuse her, but dominating Richard would be a constant battle and most likely a losing one, which intrigued her even more.

Ruggedly handsome with a pockmarked face from childhood smallpox, Richard's skin had the texture of rough-cut stone. His yellow-green eyes were fierce. His voice was so deep and so well trained that he could outyell anyone in the room with only a whisper. He would often entertain guests at dinner by reading the telephone book. He could make you laugh or cry just by pronouncing the most common names. There were few people on earth as mesmerizing as Richard Burton. If they had his deep Shakespearean voice, they didn't have his sexy looks. If they had his looks, they lacked his wit and Oxford education. Richard loved to seduce women, either in person or in an audience, with very well-thought-out words perfectly pronounced. He would hold them spellbound and truly conquer them. Playing Alexander the Great and Marc Antony must have gone to his head!

It was once written by someone who it would seem never knew Richard Burton that he was bisexual, and it was implied that he had slept with English actors who adored him during his rise to fame and fortune. In their *wildest* dreams did they sleep with Richard Burton! If Richard said that he tried it and that he didn't like it, that would just be his "Oxford" way of putting his gay friends off.

Ron and Richard were together for more than twenty years and as close as any two men could be. If Richard had slept with a man, it would have been Ron, the stud of MGM, and there were not two more seductive men in the film industry of their time. I was not yet married to Ron, but we were living together and my antennae were always up when it came to women who were after my man. Richard was a target as the male in a superstar couple. Every woman on the planet would have loved to bed him and show up Elizabeth. Many women tried their best. Especially the costars. It was often comical.

Only once did Elizabeth and I arrive at such a low point of self-confidence and bad character as to become lady detectives. During the filming of *Anne of the Thousand Days* in 1968, during the dark, foggy English winter, Burton filmed alone at Shepperton Studios. Richard's costar, Geneviève Bujold, was determined to conquer one or both of our husbands. I don't know if it was the weather and the season causing the gloom, but our men were pub-hopping after work and not coming home.

As fledgling detectives, Elizabeth and I would show up for

lunch in my bright-colored culotte dresses with Cossack boots and afterward pretend to leave and go shopping. In reality, we would visit other sets—everyone welcomed Elizabeth. At five P.M., when Richard and Ron left work in the dark in their green Rolls-Royce, we would discreetly follow them in our Silver Cloud Rolls as they pub-hopped all the way home. We knew their route and wanted to be sure they were in pubs and not some women's beds. Gaston, Elizabeth's faithful chauffeur, would pull up behind the pub and Elizabeth and I would slip out, pull down our Russian Cossack hats over our heads, and hide our bright outfits under fluffy brown furs with only our bright red lips visible on faces otherwise covered with extra-large Ray-Ban dark glasses. We would peer into pub windows and check on our boys. Fortunately, the current fashion was influenced by Yves Saint Laurent's brown Russian collection and we went unnoticed if we had to pop into a pub door or two. Once we caught Richard and Ron drinking in a pub with Geneviève Bujold. We trailed them all back into the city, where the boys dropped her off and came home.

Thus ended the spying careers of Elizabeth Taylor and Vicky Tiel.

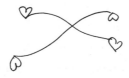

Mother Knows Best

London, 1964

Even though Ron told me over and over that his marriage was over, it clearly was not. He was still living with his wife and two children in Malibu.

Of course my mother repeated the age-old wisdom: "If he'll do it to her, he'll do it to you." And, of course, I ignored her. I was madly in love. I had every little girl's dream romance in Paris. We went to all the romantic spots: moonlight walks along the Seine, dinners at the Crazy Horse saloon, dancing every night at Castel's or New Jimmy's, the world's first discotheque. Everything was perfect until it was time for him to go back home. *The Sandpiper* was finished.

He had been living in the Hôtel Montalembert, where all the cast and crew were housed. There was a party to celebrate the end of filming, and Ron invited me to attend it with him. We were accompanied by Charles Bronson, a bit player in the movie, along with his date, Enid Stulberger, who later dumped Bronson before he became a superstar and married the singer Donovan. At the party, Ron and I kissed in front of everyone. I felt that this openness meant that we were officially a serious couple. He said, "Wait for me! Elizabeth's next film will start in Europe in a few weeks."

He was wrong. Two months passed. I worked with Mia on new

collections and our contracts. I went on a ski holiday at Cortina d'Ampezzo and skied and danced a lot but missed Ron terribly and stayed true. Yet there was no news. No calls. Eventually I read in the papers that the Burtons were in London and living at the Dorchester. Then the phone rang. It was Ron calling from London. Richard was to shoot a movie based on *Faust* in Oxford and Ron asked me to meet him there as soon as they started shooting. He said he'd call when he knew when. Then I read in a French newspaper that the filming had already begun in London and the cast and crew were staying at the Europa Hotel.

Unable to wait for Ron's phone call, I flew to London to surprise him. I marched into the Europa and told the front desk I was Mrs. Ron Berkeley. I went up to the room and knocked on the door. The door opened just a crack, revealing Ron's horrified face.

"Sweetheart," he pleaded, "whatever happens, please remember I love you!" At that, a very tall, muscular black woman flew out the door, screaming at Ron. He explained, "She's a dancer in the film, pay no attention!" I was in shock. Even with all the commotion, I thought Ron seemed glad to see me. We went downstairs to the bar to celebrate our reunion. As soon as we sat down, the hotel manager came over. Apparently, the exotic dancer had also registered as Mrs. Ron Berkeley, and now there was another Mrs. Ron Berkeley calling on the phone from California. I knew I should have been in tears, but I couldn't stop laughing.

"Sir," said the manager in his finest English accent, "we must ask you to leave. This is a family hotel!"

Elizabeth's Caftan

Not wanting to be left alone all day in the romantic penthouse suite of the Dorchester Hotel, Elizabeth decided to join the cast of *Doctor Faustus* and created a small but visible part for herself as Helen of Troy. I was still in London, hiding out with Ron in a mews apartment in Mayfair just behind the hotel. Ron had rented it by the week for my visits. Elizabeth asked me to design her gown for the film. We met in her hotel suite and together created "Elizabeth's caftan."

It was a giant rectangle in matte jersey doubled over with two small slits for sleeves and one large slit for the head. Although the rectangle was large, the matte jersey draped sensually, clinging to the body, especially the breasts. The caftan was covered with ostrich feathers down the arms and was sprinkled with crystals for an ethereal quality.

Ron did Elizabeth's makeup, covering her eyelids in tiny faux diamonds and painting her face in gold lamé. Alexandre, her Parisian hairdresser, flew over with a tall headdress filled in with flowers and jewels. Elizabeth was so breathtakingly beautiful that the photos of her taken by Norman Parkinson for *Vogue* are all that anyone remembers from the film. Elizabeth has lived in her caftans ever since.

Nearby on Ebury Street were the offices of John Heyman, the Burtons' agent. I found him movie-star handsome and just as clever. I sweetly asked if he could be my agent for movies. He had never represented any costume designers, but he quickly agreed—Elizabeth's Helen of Troy outfit was getting so much press that Mia and I were hot commodities. He soon found a job for Fonssagrives-Tiel in L.A. working on *Eye of the Devil*, with Kim Novak. Mia agreed to watch over the orders in Paris couture.

I could now follow my lover to his hometown and see if he was sincere. Was this a fling, or a real love story? The truth could also be somewhere in the middle, but I wanted to know either way. I didn't have any experience at twenty-one with married men, and being "the confident cheerleader" I was probably no match for Hollywood Ron. But I believed he truly loved me, and when I told him about my job in L.A., he smiled and grabbed me and said, "Great, baby."

Kim Novak, An American Geisha

Culver City, California, 1965

Man eats woman, and woman eats man; that's basic.
—BETTE DAVIS, in the movie *A Stolen Life*

The bartender asked the blond woman sitting on a bar stool next to me, "Did anyone ever tell you that you look a lot like Kim Novak?" She laughed and said, "Yes, all the time!" Without makeup, the healthy-looking woman in a striped

T-shirt and jeans did bear a slight resemblance to the glamorous star of *Picnic* and *Vertigo*. In fact, she *was* Kim Novak! Sitting together in the bar that night, we shared our life stories. We were taking a break from working on *Eye of the Devil*.

After I'd worked alone on the set of *What's New Pussycat?* Mia suggested that I stay on the sets of the film in California while she produced our next collection in Féraud's Paris workrooms. She was working, modeling, continuing to get all the free publicity we were still generating. The press couldn't get enough of her. I could be near Ron and she could be near Louis. We had come to the conclusion that my fearless personality could not be intimidated by movie stars. Mia remained shy and loved to look at the world from afar, a bit more like Lisa.

We established our costly daily routine. Every morning at five I would wake up in L.A. and call Mia as her workday ended in Paris. Our first minutes were all pure gossip, the details of Ron and Louis and how the previous night with them had been, what our plans for the day were; then the work details. We got together every six weeks, alternating between L.A. and Paris. The film with Kim was being shot at MGM studios in Culver City.

The studios had tried to create a new platinum blond Jean Harlow in Kim, dressing her up in silk and satin bias-cut gowns with no bra, like the stars of the thirties. In person, she was more of a nature girl. Harry Cohn, fabled head of Columbia Pictures, fell in love with her and made her one of his stars. Kim told me that in 1957 when she fell in love hard with Sammy Davis Jr., Harry Cohn threatened to have Davis killed if he married Kim. America was not ready for a biracial love affair between their stars.

Now, I could tell by the way he acted that Marty Ransohoff, the producer of *Eye of the Devil,* was also in love with her. Kim refused to be under his control and had just run off and married Richard Johnson, her costar in her previous film. Marty suddenly canceled all her expensive costumes that I had designed. He told me, "Take her to the May Company [a low-priced department store] and get her some clothes off the rack."

Kim and I were meeting to decide what to do. We talked about men and their love of power. I told her to let go of Marty and accept his stupid idea of dressing her from a department store. I would buy some classic solid jersey dresses and "sex up" some trench coats, tied at the waist to show her no-bra look, and recut the store-bought clothes in Paris to show off her fabulous body. I said, "Don't dance with the devil, or a devilish ex-boyfriend producer!"

One night years later, much to my surprise, Louis Féraud spoke of his love affair with Kim, before he met Mia.

"What was she like?" I asked.

"Ah, she was always barefoot. She was a geisha. A barefoot American geisha!" He went on to describe how Kim would have a cocktail ready for him when he came home. She would have a hot bath all prepared with aromatic salts, and soft music playing. Kim, wearing a sexy nightgown (dinner already prepared), would help Louis into the tub and rub him . . . everywhere! After the bath, she would wrap his body in a towel, dry his back, then dress him in a kimono and lead him into dinner. Every two weeks she would give him a manicure and pedicure followed by a cream rub. A domestic goddess. No wonder producers hated seeing her go.

But the truth was that Hollywood and Kim just did not mesh. She was a free spirit who told me she just wanted to be barefoot in the hills of Big Sur, where she had a home on a cliff overlooking the sea. She wanted to retire there and paint. The life of a movie star held no attraction for her.

Fortunately for Kim, Marty transferred his attentions to his other leading lady, beautiful blond Sharon Tate, in her first role. Later during the filming, Kim was replaced by Deborah Kerr. Marty told Kim, "You're finished in Hollywood." It was music to Kim's ears, and she couldn't have been happier. After that, she worked on film or TV only on her own terms, when and if she wanted to. She married a veterinarian she met when he came to her farm in Big Sur to call on her sick horse, and they are still living happily ever after somewhere in the northwest, where she can look out over the sea.

WHAT I LEARNED FROM KIM

- Never wear a bra if you don't need one, especially if you have beautiful nipples.
- Find a color that represents you and is your trademark. (Kim's was pale lavender.)
- Follow your own path. Go barefoot and feel the earth between your toes. (I always do *whenever possible*.)
- Treat your man like you're his geisha.
- Learn to give a good manicure and pedicure and a creamy foot massage (and a good whatever he likes most), while wearing sexy see-through lingerie. The foot is a hot plate for sex.
- It's not demeaning to do things like this; just consider it all part of the sex act!

Living With Lolita

Hollywood, 1965

In 1965, when I was the ripe old age of twenty-two, Paramount decided to buy our life story: two American girls who take on Paris couture! This amazing deal was thanks to John Heyman and Ron Leif, my new agent in L.A. Ron Leif's father-in-law was Lew Wasserman, the most powerful man in Hollywood at the time. Ron's commission was 15 percent. My lawyer, Allan Sussman, who was also Marlon Brando's lawyer, got 10 percent. Whatever was left was then divided between the writers, Arnold and Lois Peyser, and Mia and me. Suddenly we had $80,000. We were rich!

With our check in hand we ran to the bank on Sunset Boulevard and put $40,000 away for our dream shop in Paris one day. Mia then flew back to Paris to prepare our first solo collection. We planned to show during couture week at an art gallery on Faubourg Saint-Honoré, when *Eye of the Devil* was over. I was also supervising the film of our "life story."

The proposed film was to be called *The Ye Ye Girls*, a name the Parisian papers had given us, based on the Beatles refrain, "She loves you, yeah, yeah, yeah" (and pronounced the same in French). I flew to Hollywood when Ron flew home from Massachusetts and I moved in as a houseguest with the Peysers for several weeks while we were working on the "Ye Ye" script and I was doing the costumes for Kim Novak.

"Ye Ye Girls" was given to Gene Nelson, a tap dancer turned director. The choice of director should have been a red flag that the project was doomed. The casting was just as bad, with Sandra Dee chosen to play me and Nancy Sinatra to play Mia. We were to dance and sing our way to the Paris collections, à la *Funny Face*.

Then Howard Koch, the producer and the head of Paramount, got fired. All his projects were shelved. It was just as well. The movie would have been a stinker. But the good news was that Mia and I got to keep the bundle of cash the studio had paid for our story! This experience taught us that getting a film made is a crapshoot.

But none of it mattered. I was in Hollywood, with money to burn. The first thing I did was try to acquire what I thought was a "Hollywood lifestyle." With my fat wad of cash, I bought a yellow Morgan convertible with bright blue leather interiors. Then I moved in with Sue Lyon, the blond baby doll who at seventeen had appeared in *Lolita* with James Mason and *The Night of the Iguana* with Richard Burton. Richard had suggested I call her when I arrived in L.A. He knew we had a lot in common. We met at the Daisy, a nightclub, the hangout on Rodeo Drive: She was nineteen, I was twenty-two, and we both loved to dance.

Sue and I were perfect roommates. Both of us were in love with married men. I felt I needed to be close to Ron, who was still promising to leave his wife and marry me. Sue was in love with a young lawyer turned movie producer she called "Schwartzy." We both were hiding out in a love shack in the canyon above Beverly Hills. The wooden shack was on two levels. Sue would meet her sweetie on level two with the view of the mountains, and I would meet Ron on level one in a cozy log room with a wood-burning fireplace.

Come nightfall, we would go out to the Daisy with "escorts." Sue pretended to be dating Burt Sugarman, and I was "dating" Aaron Spelling (Tori's dad). They both seemed happy to have arm candy, two babes with hair longer than our pastel ruffled mini-dresses. The appearance of being our boyfriends was enough for these businessmen.

The Daisy was the top place to appear after dinner; it was the place to be "discovered." Many waitresses became actresses or rich Beverly Hills wives. It was a discotheque launched by Jack Hanson, creator of Jax slacks (skintight pedal pushers in soft pastel cottons with no side seams and a tight butt fit). Jack's club was filled with '60s movie stars, notably Natalie Wood and Warren Beatty, who really made the place with their love affair, after she divorced Bob Wagner for Warren.

Lunches were another time to meet our married boyfriends. I'd leave MGM, where I was still working on the costumes for Kim Novak, and drive to Warner Bros. in the Valley, where Ron was working. We would meet at the Retake Room, a dimly lit bar across the street from the studio. Every booth was filled with Hollywood "secret" lovers. The bartender was paid to keep reporters out. One day Ron told me to meet him on my film set at the MGM soundstage after lunch. He said he would be next to the Coke machine near Stage 8. I obediently went to the designated spot and waited, as told, wearing my new look, sideless hot pants and boots. Suddenly I heard a very familiar voice saying, "Vicky, can I buy you a Coke?"

I turned around to see, in the flesh, Elvis Presley! He was alone. I was frozen with fear and awe—it was ELVIS! I couldn't move and my mouth was hanging open. Words simply would not come out. Elvis burst out laughing and Ron appeared from around the corner.

Elvis had that effect on every woman. Time stood still. He was bigger than life. It wasn't always so. He came to MGM in 1956 to do *Jailhouse Rock*. William Tuttle, head of MGM's makeup department, and Ron, his assistant, took one look at Elvis's dirty blond hair and decided to dye it blue-black, with eyebrows and sideburns dyed to match.

Ron said that in all the films he did with Elvis until 1966, when Ron quit MGM to work full-time with Richard and Elizabeth, he never saw Elvis abuse drugs or alcohol. Elvis loved Coca-Cola and his mama's cooking. Years later Ron said that Elvis and his mother died at the same age, forty-three, both very overweight and bloated. Elvis had inherited his mom's genes and short life span. Elvis was brilliant, very well read, especially in the occult and Eastern philosophy. He was articulate and, according to Ron, just about the nicest guy in show business. Ron was one of ten guys Elvis gave a motorcycle to at Christmas and we rode it in the mountains and canyons behind Sue's cabin.

From Ron's perspective, all the mess at the end of Elvis's life was a mystery. His theory was that Priscilla broke his heart when she took up with his karate instructor, and it all went downhill after that. Elvis was a conservative Southern boy and wanted his family intact. Who could believe that a great night for Elvis was at home with music, a good book, home cooking, and a pretty girl seated nearby wearing a sexy dress, tons of jewelry, and a lot of makeup, all for him. If Elvis was in a great mood he would play the guitar or piano and sing just for her. But this much is certain: The real Elvis Presley was comfortingly, boringly normal.

I was thrilled that Ron loved me enough to surprise me with

an introduction to my childhood hero. Elvis grabbed Ron's neck with one arm and grabbed around my neck with the other and sweetly knocked our heads together. The King approved!

Ron told me an intriguing story about Elvis. It seems one summer Elvis asked Ron to rent him a beach house in Malibu for him and his buddies, and Ron rented them the house next door. Knowing Elvis blistered and burned, Ron asked, "Why the beach?" Elvis replied, "The boys want to swim and play on the sand. I took it for them." One day Elvis was sitting inside watching "his" boys play on the beach, and he said to Ron, "I love this place, especially at night when I can walk all alone on the beach and look out to sea." Ron asked him, "What do you see, Elvis, when you look out there?" He answered, "Maybe someday I'll see where I'm going."

What It's Like to Be A Mistress on Location

South Hadley, Massachusetts, 1965

During our summer vacation in August when Paris shuts down, I joined Ron during the filming of *Who's Afraid of Virginia Woolf?* directed by Mike Nichols, and starring Richard Burton and Elizabeth Taylor, with costars George Segal and Sandy Dennis. Mia stayed in Paris working on a collection for Paraphernalia, a new fashion company that had hired us and Betsey Johnson for its first collection, called Youthquake.

This time I wasn't being a costume designer. I was playing the now familiar role of the makeup man's mistress. Ron invited me to stay with him during the location filming at Smith College in South Hadley, Massachusetts. He was still promising to leave his wife any day, get divorced, and marry me, and I hadn't given up hope. However, he told me we had to keep a low profile, even though being "on location" with him was considered okay. (As time went on, I was to learn a lot more about the Hollywood traditions of "being on location.")

I was instructed to hole up in a motel, the Towne House Motor Lodge, where the crew members were staying. The stars got to live in great old country homes on the Smith campus, which was closed for the summer.

Also at the motel were the producer's "wife," the director's "wife," and the set decorator's "wife." These ladies became my friends. We called ourselves "the Wife"—that is, until the actual wife showed up!

Since the atmosphere seemed so relaxed, I decided on the first day to make a surprise visit to the set. Ron had told me to be careful and avoid the set, that Mike Nichols was a very serious guy and took the project much too seriously for Elizabeth Taylor's taste. But it was his first movie.

I rented a moped from a nearby shop and took off with confidence, wearing my lemon yellow Jax slacks and matching ruffled blouse. I had ridden on motorcycles with the best of them, so a puny little moped should be no problem. Trouble was, it didn't stop when I got close to the set. I hadn't learned how to brake the thing, and I could see them shooting right on Main Street in front of a big house. Richard Burton was sitting on a swing on the front porch, doing his famous monologue, and I crashed right into the set, knocking down cameras, lights, and everything. I was in *big* trouble.

I wasn't good at playing the mistress, and Mike Nichols never spoke to me again. But Elizabeth just laughed. She thought I was hilarious and invited me to come inside her dressing room, and that's when we really became friends and I was no longer just her dress designer. She always loved the underdog and finally realized I was there with Ron. It had been more than a year since Paris when we all had met in the commissary.

Our time in the Berkshires was Ron's and my first vacation as a couple. We had been outed. Ron rented a giant Harley and we biked all over. It was before helmets, and my long brown hair flew into his new French-style long blond hair as we held on tight. Symbolically, at last, we were one.

I was formally invited by the Burtons to their rented farmhouse on a lake. Each Sunday there were family fish fries with all four of her kids. Elizabeth actually fished for her own dinner with a rod and a worm as bait. She caught three or four catfish while wearing a crisp pair of blue jeans and a plain white T-shirt. She did not go as far as wearing tennis shoes but instead wore silver thongs with diamond straps between her toes. She did not "do country" as far as her feet.

With her approval, I wasn't banned from the set in the future—but they did take away my moped.

The Beverly Glen Motorcycle Gang

After I had been living in California for six months with the occasional trip to Paris and New York, Ron was still saying that he was going to get a divorce and marry me, but now I was getting impatient. He could visit me only on weekends for sex and a sandwich or meet me during the lunch hour. Some nights when I missed him, full of angst, I would sneak up on his private beach and have a kiss as he walked his dog. The loneliness crept in. Was the divorce a lie or wishful thinking? It was time to take some action. I knew that halfway up Beverly Glen Canyon on the left-hand side was a small nondescript ratty old bar. In the 1960s, beginning in the early fall, every Sunday morning a group of motorcycle riders gathered there.

Parked outside were some fairly nice Triumph 750s and Benzes, some new Harleys, and a few custom antique Harleys. Inside the bar were Clint Eastwood, Paul Newman, Steve McQueen, Lee Marvin, Donald Sutherland, Dennis Hopper, Peter Fonda, and a few other macho types, including Ron. Whoever got there by nine Sunday morning got to go on the ride. The guys departed together, taking it easy up the canyon to Mulholland Drive, turning left and then taking a lazy drive through the mountains, each time taking different trails behind the Malibu hills, coming down through Trancas, and ending up at a producer's shack in the Malibu Colony for cocktails and lunch.

Not a single wife or girlfriend knew about the motorcycle gang. They had no idea where the men met or where they ended up. If word got out, the women would have flocked there in droves with the paparazzi close behind. These were the most gorgeous alpha male movie stars of the decade, having their private Sunday escape from the world.

I had moved out of the Beverly Hills canyon cabin and to Malibu to be closer to Ron's house on Topanga Canyon Beach. I rented an apartment across the road from the beach, on the Pacific Coast Highway south of the Malibu Pier. My apartment had a large picture window overlooking the highway and the ocean. I filled it with my newly acquired 150 cc cherry red Suzuki motorcycle. Having a ground-floor apartment allowed me to roll my bike inside and park it in my living room by the big glass window. Ron could drive by and see if my bike was there, meaning I was home. He lived a short ride away and could be at my place in five minutes.

Our romance had continued through the summer and into the fall with a promise that by Christmas he would tell his wife and get a divorce. The bike was a way of proving my love to him, that I was his kind of girl—a biker's babe! I created an appropriate outfit and Mia sent it from Paris: a black granny flowerprint biker jacket and lime green leather miniculottes, with lime green leather boots with matching black granny flower-print tops so my inner legs would not get hot, and a matching flowerprint aviator's cap to wear over my long hair.

The only problem was that I couldn't ride a big bike. Actually, I could ride it, but kick-starting it was impossible. I needed a guy to do it for me. So the first Sunday morning after the purchase, my next-door neighbor (a nicely built fireman) agreed to jump-start my bike. I was out to follow Ron and meet up with the motorcycle gang.

Off I went. Ron was easy to follow since the traffic up Sunset

Boulevard was slow. I followed him up Beverly Glen to the bar and surprised him inside. It was nine forty-five and the guys were about to depart. I entered and joined them all at the bar. Needless to say, my motorcycle babe outfit was a big hit. I pretended not to know Ron and eventually struck up a conversation with Paul Newman, a gracious gentleman. I found him immensely masculine and even more attractive in person, with startlingly baby blue eyes set off by a deep tan and beautiful strong brown arms. He took off his Windbreaker and laid it on my bike. He wore a white undershirt. Seeing I was a novice, he helped me kick-start my Suzuki, and as he did I could see his beautiful muscle tone. He told me to follow him, so he could look after me. If you insist, Mr. Newman!

We wound our way up the canyon. Since my bike was only 150 cc, I couldn't go very fast. Paul kept me company on his 750 cc and we fell way behind the group. Hours after the others, we arrived together at the producer's house in Malibu. Lunch was over. Paul and I walked down to the beach. He took all his clothes off for a swim.

Ron came over and grabbed me by the arm. "Where have you been?" he asked.

I looked stunned and rolled my eyes. "Riding with Paul."

We couldn't have it out on the beach that day, as all the guests knew Ron as a married man; many probably knew his wife. He looked hurt and disappointed as I walked back to the road and took off on my bike, having missed the chance for us to spend time together.

I felt the time had come to move on.

The next week I packed up all my stuff and cleaned out the apartment. I shipped my car to Paris and sold my bike to the neighbor. I returned to Paris without telling Ron.

He drove by and didn't see my bike. The phone had been cut off. A few weeks later, Ron phoned me in Paris. "I'm getting a divorce," he said. "I'll move to Paris as soon as I can."

When my friends asked, "How did you get Ron to leave his wife?" I'd answer, "A great outfit and Paul Newman." If you can't get Paul, get a good substitute. Being a mistress was no fun. I was over hiding out. It was too hard. It must have been just as hard for his wife hearing all the lies. My advice: Give an unhappily married man *one* year to leave his wife, and then you split, for real.

A Hollywood Job Interview

Plaza Athénée Hotel, Paris, 1965

Trying to decide if we could become full-time costume designers or try to do both films and couture, I flew back to Paris in a hurry when Ursula Andress urged us to meet Harry Saltzman, producer of the James Bond movies. She thought we could convince him to let us design costumes for the upcoming *Thunderball*. Mia designed a one-piece suede catsuit with boots, similar to the one we had designed for Ursula in *Pussycat*. She wore it to the interview at the Plaza Athénée Hotel. I wore a plaid microminikilt with pink lace panty hose and pink satin mules. We went into the suite for the interview, and found Mr. Saltzman . . . quite naked!

Actually backside up, being massaged by Fred, the masseur to

Hollywood royalty. Fred had claimed to be Hitler's masseur and, even more impressive, Jack Warner's.

Harry Saltzman gave us both a warm hello. "You're here for *Thunderball*. Wow! You girls look great! Please walk up and down across the suite."

We did.

"Turn."

We did.

"Come closer and let me see your faces. Now profile. Now smile."

We did and did and did.

"Now take off your clothes."

We got down to our bras and panties, and I pulled out the black diamond string bikini we had created for the film. "I wonder, Mr. Saltzman, do you interview all costume designers like this?" I asked.

"Oh, shit!" he said. "I thought you girls were actresses. Sorry about that . . . hmmm . . . You'll be fine for the clothes. I plan to do a few more James Bond movies. My secretary will give you a call."

With that, he turned over, full frontal, and yelled, "NEXT!"

Claudine Auger, the *Thunderball* girl, wore our diamond string bikini and black cover-up on the pages of *Look* magazine to publicize the movie.

Mr. Saltzman and our agent could never come to terms for a movie contract, and the costumes for the next James Bond movie were designed by Anthony Mendelson. Years later, I told this story to Edith Head over dinner in Rome.

She had sponsored me into the film union in 1966. Edith was not a type to take off her clothes for any producer. Edith was all business. She ran the Paramount costume department for years. During her reign, every film made at MGM, whether she actually designed the clothes or not, trumpeted, "Costumes by Edith Head, Hollywood."

Hollywood was run by the department managers, and I was lucky that Edith liked me. We were the same small size, with brown hair, brown eyes, and long bangs. She lived with her beloved husband, the art director Wiard Ihnen. They never had kids; instead, they had movies. She tried to become a retail fashion designer, but her collections failed to sell. She warned me that Adrian, the other major Hollywood costume designer, had also tried to do both movie costumes and retail design and failed.

"Vicky," she said, "You can't do both. You have to choose."

EDITH HEAD'S LIFE LESSONS

- Develop a signature look as an artist and don't change it. She had big glasses, bangs, and hair pulled into a tight bun. With her Chanelish suits, she could be recognized on the set in an instant.

- Narrow your niche. You have to choose!

- Become indispensable at work. Keep ahead of the producer.

- Get along with the crew. Be a peacemaker.

- Keep your private life private. Don't oversocialize. Be mysterious. Go home to a nice home life and husband. Recharge your batteries.

Oscar Night

Villa Fiorentina, France, 1967

The house was unbelievable. Many people claimed that it was the most beautiful spot on earth. In 1917, Villa Fiorentina, a copy of a Palladian villa, was built. In 1940, it was bought by the most beautiful woman in France, Enid Cameron. Her son Rory decorated it with antiques and art in the classical Roman style. The gardens were his joy and he built them on three hillsides leading down to the sea. The villa took up the entire point of Cap Ferrat. Great writers and poets often gathered there. Somerset Maugham was a neighbor and David Niven lived nearby.

In 1967, with his mother gone, Rory Cameron rented La Fiorentina to the Burtons. (Later, in 1970, he sold it to Mary Wells Lawrence, perhaps happy to keep the home still inhabited by one of the world's great beauties.) Elizabeth loved the pool that clung to the hillside, overlooking the Mediterranean. Her dogs could roam free, as the place was gated, with the only escape the rocky cliffs hanging over the sea. La Fiorentina had seen many dazzling parties, adding to the glitter of the Côte d'Azur.

Elizabeth and Richard were both nominated for Oscars that year. *Who's Afraid of Virginia Woolf?* had been a critical success, and Mike Nichols was nominated for best director, too. Elizabeth and Richard were shooting *The Comedians,* based on the novel by Graham Greene, in Nice and were unavailable to attend the Oscars in Hollywood.

The press expected Richard to win. Everyone in our little group was *certain* he would win. Nobody thought Elizabeth had a chance. She had already won an Oscar for *Butterfield 8*, playing Gloria, the call girl. Besides, many critics had slammed her performance in *Woolf*. The public was not used to seeing her so unlovely, fat, and overbearing. Some said her acting was over the top in the role of Richard's nagging wife, Martha. Richard played the introverted professor whose wife ate him up alive, and he had to summon all his skill as an actor for that role, since at that point in their relationship he was winning the war of "Who's on Top?"

The evening was long. Because of the time difference, we waited and waited and played gin and drank and champagne until three A.M. The men's acting award came first. Richard lost to Paul Scofield in *A Man for All Seasons*. There was a devastating hush in the room. Everyone expected Elizabeth to lose next. We were all prepared to go to sleep and started to say our good nights when they announced that Elizabeth won. The look on Richard's face—he was furious! Years and years of teasing Elizabeth about her acting, her grammar, her voice. And she beat him at what he did best.

Even though they stayed married for many more years, something changed that night. Elizabeth was upset for Richard. She showed no joy in her own award, only unhappiness that her beloved genius husband was robbed. She never even smiled. She took her dogs for a walk alone, said good night, and went to bed.

Richard never got over that loss, nor his childish jealousy toward Elizabeth. He was nominated for five more Oscars, seven in all, and tied with Peter O'Toole for being the most nominated actor never to win.

The dress I had made for Elizabeth to wear on Oscar night (if she'd been able to go), a pink pleated chiffon multitiered gown, was cast aside and given to her secretary to wear to the gay drag festival in Beverly Hills!

A Mexican Standoff

Salzberg, Austria, 1967

I had been traveling with the Burtons for two years, partially hidden in the entourage, and now suddenly I was out in the open. Ron had returned to California for another "divorce visit" and to pick up his son, Craig, now twelve, and enroll him in the posh English boarding school Millfield (not far from Berkeley Castle) with Elizabeth's sons, Michael and Christopher Wilding. Ron came back with no divorce—Lea still refused to sign—but he now had custody of Craig. That was proof, he told me, of his good intentions. "We will have a ball together," he promised.

At last our parents could meet; they stayed together in Villefranche at the Hotel Welcome at the end of filming *The Comedians* in Nice. Over drinks in the old port with the Burtons, my mother swooned sitting with Ron, Bunny Berkeley, and Burton. "Forget Modigliani and Clark Gable," she told me later.

After filming we flew to quaint Salzberg at the foothills of the Alps. Richard left Nice without an Oscar and Elizabeth with her second Oscar. The entourage now consisted of twelve people. We had a *lot* of luggage.

Richard was to shoot *Where Eagles Dare* in Austria. The World War II location scenes were to be shot first. The action took place in the snow high in the mountains above the picturesque town and the Österreich Hotel on the river's edge, where the cast and entourage stayed.

Clint Eastwood, Richard Burton's costar, did not have an entourage. In fact, he came entirely alone. Eastwood had become known for Italian spaghetti Westerns. The clever producer Elliott Kastner figured him to be a future star. When Richard met Clint, he said to Ron, "He's the next Gary Cooper."

Actors work on instinct and are excellent judges of who has the power on any set. Richard admired Clint and the two began to hang out together. Richard and Clint had lots of action scenes up and down the mountain. Richard was accustomed to climbing mountains in Wales and had no problem with balance, but Clint kept falling down. Richard got a kick out of the fact that Clint, the action star, could not walk up or down the mountain in the snow without taking a tumble. The two became quite good friends. Opposites attract. As much as Richard could chatter on any subject, and all the more over cocktails, Clint was quiet and poker-faced and happy to listen and learn.

One night, cocktails included a group of five: Burton; Eastwood; Burton's dresser, Bob Wilson; Brook Williams, the actor son of Emlyn Williams; and Ron. They were seated by the hotel's fireplace and were joined by an odd Englishman who was sitting nearby. At one point, the very drunk Englishman got annoyed by Richard's teasing wit. He suddenly said, "I don't like you very much." At which point, he pulled out a loaded gun.

I was upstairs just waking up from my nap. It was nine P.M. I left my room and leaned over the balcony, just above the hotel lobby. "Ron, where are you?" I called out. "Come upstairs!"

"Later, honey," he answered back.

I walked back to my room in a huff and slammed the door.

At ten o'clock I went out again and heard Elizabeth yelling, "Richard, come to *bed*!"

One hour later, still with no Ron and no dinner, I fell asleep again. I slept through all the excitement downstairs.

Elizabeth, unable to get Richard upstairs by screaming over the balcony a few times, went down to the lobby wearing a see-through white chiffon nightie and matching robe. She walked right up to the odd Englishman who had apparently been holding a gun in Richard's face for the past few hours.

"Put that thing down!" she said and grabbed the gun.

The startled man, seeing Elizabeth in the flesh, in all her bosomy glory, handed her the gun without a word.

She placed it on the coffee table. She then grabbed Richard's arm and said, "I want you to come to bed *now*, buster!" and off they went.

The Englishman was later arrested.

Clint was in shock, as were all the others—but we were all used to Elizabeth. She was not afraid; to her, all guns were props.

CAROLYN KASTNER'S PINK TUNA SALAD SANDWICH

Every day, Carolyn Kastner sent her tuna salad sandwich to her husband Elliott's office in Mayfair. Elliott produced some of the Burtons' finest movies, including *Where Eagles Dare*. When I finally learned Carolyn's secret ingredient, I taught her recipe to everyone, including Elizabeth, who then told everyone in Hollywood: "Carolyn Kastner puts ketchup in her tuna salad!"

MAKES 2 SANDWICHES

1 can white tuna in water
1½ tablespoons Hellmann's mayonnaise
1 tablespoon Heinz ketchup
1½ tablespoons sweet pickle relish
1½ tablespoons minced Vidalia onion (optional)
4 slices whole wheat toast
1 large ripe tomato, sliced

Mix everything together and put it on the toast, then top with tomato slices.

In the '60s, Hellmann's mayonnaise and sweet pickle relish were not available in Europe except at Fauchon in Paris. They had to be flown to Austria, Israel, Yugoslavia, and South Africa to make Carolyn's pink tuna sandwiches.

"Baby Doll"

London, 1967

The Dorchester in London was home away from home for the Burtons. They lived in the Oliver Messel Suite for many years. The first few years, Ron and I lived with them in adjoining rooms. Later we rented flats around Sloane Square in mews houses. *Secret Ceremony* with Robert Mitchum and Mia Farrow was shot in an art deco mansion not far from the hotel.

After shooting, we all gathered in the Oliver Messel Suite for cocktails, with Mia's future costar Larry Harvey; his wife, Pauline, an ex-model; and their baby daughter, Domino Harvey, who would later be the subject of the movie *Domino*, on her life and death as a bounty hunter. We were joined by the very young, almost bald Mia Farrow. I was looking forward to meeting her and hoping maybe to do her clothes for her next movie, as she was the wife of Frank Sinatra and a future star.

Mia Farrow had seemed disturbed during rehearsal that day. Later that night, in the Burtons' suite, she told us, "Frank served papers on me!"

Sinatra had filed for a divorce. When Mia married Frank, he had asked her to give up acting and she had agreed. Their May-December marriage had shocked Hollywood and the world. How could Frank be with a badly dressed "baby doll" after chic, glamorous Ava Gardner, a femme fatale in the same mold as Elizabeth? Impossible!

Did Frank marry Mia to get Ava jealous and push her buttons? Frank and Ava's fights and their amorous makeup sessions lasted almost twenty years.

That evening, Mia needed consoling. She sat on Burton's lap in a short, puffy baby doll dress and colored panty hose with flat shoes and lamented losing Frank. Elizabeth listened sympathetically and offered her pink champagne in a crystal flute. Mia went on and on, in grief, saying that Frank was the love of her life. Elizabeth had always had a terrific interest in Frank Sinatra stories, and she especially loved "sex gossip." Frank was known as Hollywood's premiere swordsman, reputedly blessed with one of the largest weapons in town!

Naïvely, Elizabeth listened avidly to every word and poured out advice to Mia from her heart: Never quit your career for a man. Mia should hang in there and maybe Frank would take her back. Seeing how much she loved him, he would realize his mistake but, if not, "Move on, baby."

Later that night, Richard confided to Ron that while he had been comforting her, Mia had taken every possible opportunity, whenever the guests weren't looking, to perform a subtle, but very deliberate, lap dance on him—he was certainly turned-on.

Three years later, Mia ran off with André Previn, her best friend's husband. She had been a frequent houseguest of Dory Previn's and decided to walk off with more than the towels. Karmic tables turn, and later another baby doll, Soon-Yi (the adopted daughter of Mia and André), made off with Mia's decade-long partner, Woody Allen.

Dory Previn remained discreet when she lost her man and at least kept her dignity.

But not Mia. She told the world her story, and the world—at least for a while—turned on Woody.

ELIZABETH TAYLOR'S BAKE-OFF

Every year in Europe on Thanksgiving we had a bake-off at the Dino De Laurentiis, Shepperton, or Victorine Studios in the studio's kitchen. Each member of Elizabeth's entourage had to cook a complete Thanksgiving dinner and Elizabeth would award a prize (jewelry, furs, cars) in each category:

1. Bird

2. Stuffing

3. Mashed potatoes

4. Gravy

5. Vegetables

6. Bread

7. Dessert

The Thanksgiving wine was Bordeaux and the label Mouton or Lafite Rothschild. Now Elizabeth was friends with the Rothschilds, so their wine was preferred, but for Thanksgiving we also drank the three other grand cru, always '61 or '64, her favorite years.

Everyone's favorite dish each year was Agnes Flanagan's stuffing. Agnes, in her seventies, had been Marilyn Monroe's hairdresser before becoming Elizabeth's.

AGNES FLANAGAN'S STUFFING

1 cup pork sausage meat
1 cup veal sausage meat
1 large red onion, diced
butter
1 loaf white bread, crusts cut off, toasted and cubed
2 cups corn bread, crumbled
2 cups cooked chestnuts (available at specialty food stores
   or over the Internet)
1 tablespoon fresh chopped sage, or ½ tablespoon dried
salt and fresh ground pepper

1. In a frying pan, sauté the sausage meats and onion in
   butter until the sausage meats are cooked through.

2. In a large bowl, use your hands to mix together the
   cooked sausages (including the butter it was cooked in)
   and the remaining ingredients. If the stuffing seems too
   dry, add some stock. Stuff in bird.

The Making of Boom

Hotel Capo Caccio, Sardinia, 1967

CAST OF CHARACTERS

Elizabeth Taylor	*Flora "Sissy" Goforth*
Richard Burton	*Chris Flanders*
Noël Coward	*Witch of Capri*
Michael Dunn	*Rudi*
Tennessee Williams	*Playwright*
Joseph Losey	*Director*
John Heyman	*Producer*
Norma Heyman	*John's wife*
Joanna Shimkus	*Model turned actress*
Michael and Christopher Wilding	*Sons of Elizabeth Taylor and Michael Wilding*
Liza Todd	*Daughter of Elizabeth Taylor and Mike Todd*
Maria Burton	*Adopted daughter of Richard Burton and Elizabeth Taylor*

O n location, almost every actor, writer, producer, hair-dresser, set dresser, and even the key grips go nuts and fool around, generally with each other. Behind the scenes, the cast and crew can begin to resemble one big dysfunctional family. The making of *Boom!* is a perfect example of Hollywood gone wild.

Boom! was the film version of Tennessee Williams's play *The Milk Train Doesn't Stop Here Anymore.* Elizabeth played the aging beauty, Sissy Goforth, in a Sardinian hillside mansion overlooking a steep cliff. Burton was her "young" lover, in an affair that ends tragically and melodramatically. The movie was a disaster, according to the critics, but they didn't know the half of it. The Italian fashion house Tiziani was the official designer for the film, but Elizabeth got to wear the large square chiffon beaded jersey caftans that I had created for her life in hotel rooms, which worked out perfectly as the film went on and on in the sultry heat.

For five long months, everybody involved in the movie lived in the Capo Caccio hotel on the western coast of Sardinia. The filming had started, but had stopped when the sets were blown off a hilltop during a strong storm. Richard MacDonald, England's Oscar-winning set decorator, had to rebuild sturdier sets that could withstand the gale-force winds blowing in from the Mediterranean. The cast and crew decided to wait it out in the nearby luxurious Capo, which was closed for the winter. Elizabeth and Richard bought the 165-foot *Kalizma,* named after their three daughters, Kate, Liza, and Maria. They were among the first of the exclusive few who owned yachts longer than 100 feet and "cruised the Med." They moored in the ocean just out of sight of the cameras on the set and came to work each day on yacht tenders.

During the hiatus, a few romances developed, including between producer John Heyman and the twenty-four-year-old ingénue Joanna Shimkus, who had a role in the film. The only problem was that John's wife, Norma, was Elizabeth Taylor's best friend.

One morning at dawn Norma Heyman caught her husband coming out of Joanna Shimkus's room and all hell broke loose. John Heyman had been Elizabeth's agent before becoming a producer and he, Richard, Norma, and Elizabeth had created a tight unit, having been friends for years. I was stuck in the middle. Being both Norma's and Joanna's friend, I couldn't help. A few days later, Norma herself got dramatic, and climbed up an ancient Saracen stone tower on the grounds of the hotel and would not come down. This got everyone's attention, since everyone's little children were there. All four of Elizabeth's children, as well as Norma's two children and Elizabeth's brother Howard's four children, were there. There was bedlam below the tower. Would "Auntie Norma" jump?

It all eventually worked out for the best. Norma negotiated a great divorce settlement. She got a three-picture deal as a producer, a house, and a new Jaguar car every year. Best of all, many years later their son, David Heyman, a clever Westminster and Harvard graduate in his thirties, read a first-time novel by an obscure Scottish writer before it was published and persuaded Warner Bros. to advance him the $50,000 required to take an option out on what has become the most successful franchise in movie history, the Harry Potter series, by single mum J. K. Rowling.

John got engaged to the beautiful Joanna but, before their scheduled wedding day, Joanna ran off with her costar, Sidney Poitier, in her first major role in an American film called *The Lost Man*; Sidney and Joanna married, had two children, and have lived happily ever after. John and Sidney became close friends, and John has always been grateful to Sidney for making it possible for him to marry his beautiful wife, Nizza, and to have two more beautiful children. John's daughter, Gabrielle, is close friends with Sidney's and Joanna's daughters.

Tennessee Williams, whom we called Tom, and his boyfriend, Bill Glavin, were a couple of romantics who had a daily routine. Tom would write the movie script from early in the morning until noon. Then he'd start drinking, and by afternoon he was plastered. Bill, all six feet of muscle, had to load Tom up and carry him piggyback up to their room, along with Tom's little bulldog, who had to be carried piggyback on top of Tom.

The hotel bar was never without action, either comic or tragic, from four to seven in the afternoon. One day, while having cocktails standing at the mirrored bar with Burton, Noël Coward kissed my lover Ron full on the lips right in front of me. "You may think this was a perfunctory kiss, young man," he explained, "but actually, it was riddled with sex."

The little person Michael Dunn played Elizabeth's bodyguard in the film, guarding her with two black rottweilers. The problem with Dunn was that he was almost always drunk and couldn't control the two dogs on the leash. One day, during the filming, the dogs took off and practically dragged him across the moun-  taintop over the cliff at the same place the original sets had gone.

Noël and Tennessee were very competitive with each other, especially once they were dressed in tuxes at the bar each evening. Often they sang "big" Italian love songs, played at the disco bar. They usually sang to an empty room, however. There were no guests in the bar or in the restaurant, just the Italian singer and the piano player. The hotel was completely empty except for our cast and crew. Picture Jack Nicholson in *The Shining* and snatch the locale from New England to the Mediterranean Sea, and you can picture the Capo.

As for Michael Dunn, one night he invited Noël Coward

and Tennessee Williams to a nightclub in Alghero. They traveled there on motorcycles, with Dunn's legs flying out straight behind. At the bar, Dunn met a tall redheaded showgirl and fell instantly in love with her.

A few days later, back in the Capo bar, Dunn assumed he had been elevated to the status of Noël Coward's pal and drinking buddy. He tried to keep up with Noël's enormous capacity, but got in over his head, so to speak. We all gathered at one end of the cavernous barroom and watched the spectacle of the two of them downing drink after drink. When Michael got down on one knee and started to serenade Noël, Noël sighed and without a blink said to Michael, "It must be terrible, terrible, terrible being a midget, but being a midget and a bore . . ."

But maybe Dunn got the last laugh. He surprised all of us when we later read in the Hollywood gossip columns that after a whirlwind courtship he married the glamorous redhead from the Alghero bar.

A Shop of Our Own

Rue Bonaparte, Paris, 1968

Spring was in the air and one beautiful, sunshiny Saturday morning, Mia and Louis married at the mayor's office of the eighth arrondissement with tearful models in attendance and Louis's associate, Guy Rambaldi, as the best man. Mia and I both wore conservative short romantic dresses from our closets. There was not enough notice to make something special. Louis's surprise gift to his new bride was a duplex apartment outside Cannes with three giant terraces hanging over a cliff above the sea. The décor was minimalist with the apartment mainly set up for indoor-outdoor oil painting on large canvases. Louis began a series of nudes of Mia, à la Picasso, but in brighter, more lyrical and fashion-inspired colors.

After the wedding, Ron and I took a vacation together on the isle of Corfu in northern Greece. Mia's marriage had put pressure on Ron to convince Lea to agree to a divorce. She was holding back even though they hadn't seen each other in two years. The trip to Corfu was consolation. He had finished *Oedipus the King* in nearby Dodoni, with Orson Welles and Christopher Plummer and without the Burtons, who were still in Sardinia, on the *Kalizma*. We rented a villa high on the cliffs overlooking Paleokastritsa, the town the writer Gerald Durrell describes as the most beautiful place in the world. The only problem was the most beautiful place in the world had no telephone and I suffered. I couldn't call Mia every morning. Ron and I were almost never alone except in bed. We preferred a crowd or a cocktail party.

After a few days I rented a donkey, having been told there was a phone in a café in a village on top of the mountains. So I donkeyed up the cliffs to have my daily call to Mia. Ron couldn't take my fretting about Mia anymore, and to my surprise he had secretly donkeyed up to the café himself and called Féraud, who arrived the next day with Mia in tow, to share our villa and prolong their honeymoon. I couldn't live one day without talking to Mia, both to gossip and discuss dresses. I missed her so.

After the honeymoon and a lot of scuba diving, Ron and I rejoined the Burtons in Rome after the shooting of *Boom!* The Roman fashion house Tiziani had designed the costumes for *Boom!*

Karl Lagerfeld had begun his career at Tiziani but Evan Richards, the owner-designer of Tiziani, decided to take over as the sole designer so Karl moved on. Evan was a very grand sort of fellow from Texas, his clothing not completely Elizabeth's style, a little more tailored and less sensual than ours. One day on a visit to the set, Evan asked Elizabeth for backing.

Elizabeth was noncommittal. Then, once he had left, she turned to me and said, "Vicky, why don't *you* open a shop in Paris? We'd rather back you and Mia!"

I was shocked and thrilled. Our very own shop. It was a dream come true! Once I got over the initial surprise I called Mia with the good news. We faced the challenge of finding a good spot. Louis Féraud warned us that there are bad sides of the street in Paris and good sides. For mysterious reasons, people choose to walk on the good side and avoid the bad side.

"Make sure your shop is on the good side," he said. He also said there are bad locations, haunted by spirits. "Don't take over a shop that is already failing. It might have a bad omen on it. And whatever you do, do not go around anywhere to buy real estate looking rich!"

Following Louis's advice, Mia and I set out to go boutique shopping. We decided the shop had to be on the Left Bank, with its less traditional atmosphere. We wore faded jeans and granny ruffle print blouses. We rode bicycles to be sure to cover all the streets of the Left Bank.

Eventually we found an abandoned shop that was used as storage space for a well-known antiques shop. The street was rue Bonaparte. It had no fashion shops, only antiques shops, but lots of traffic on our side of the street. It was a major bus passage from boulevard Saint-Germain to the Seine, one block away. It was at the back of a cobblestoned courtyard with two charming large carved wooden windows covered with vines under a nineteenth-century awning. The shop had once been the prison of the church of Saint-Germain-des-Prés at 21 rue Bonaparte and was a historical monument. Best of all it was just one block away from Carolyn Tyson's Fischbacher, a good omen.

Mia and I visited Mr. Schruber, the owner of the shop. He wanted $40,000 for the boutique. We told him we would take it and handed him a down payment check for $10,000. The next day the French newspapers broke the story: "Elizabeth Taylor to open fashion house in Paris."

Poor Mr. Schruber. He called Mia screaming in French, "You have ruined me! Now my wife thinks I'm a fool. I thought two poor little Americans on bicycles wanted a store. Now it's Elizabeth Taylor. How could you?" Mia said, *"Je regrette"* (the famous line of Alain Delon), and Louis was very proud of his Mia.

In six months, the shop was finished and decorated with the help of the American hippie artist Ed Baynard. The look was young and trendy mod, and all the fashionable crowd appeared for our opening. Then, two weeks later, the 1968 student protests and general strike broke out all over Paris. The students demonstrated, broke shopwindows, and turned over cars. The police teargassed them. The National Assembly was dissolved, and de Gaulle took refuge at an air force base in Germany. The whole government seemed about to collapse. Our beautiful new shop was filled with wounded students. We had to close the ancient carved doors to our courtyard for a month during the riots and never sold one dress.

Elizabeth, however, was not one to let a collapsing government stand in her way. She was blissfully planning our opening

BLOOMIE DRESSES *to choose from*

FOR COCKTAIL

fashion show and sketching out some of her own top designs.

Elizabeth wanted our opening fashion show to be at Maxim's. It was her favorite restaurant, resembling an art nouveau museum, and made famous in the movie *Gigi* starring Leslie Caron. Since the 1890s it's been

the place to see and be seen in Paris. Every Friday night there was ballroom dancing to an orchestra with women in gowns and men in black tie. The dance floor would be a perfect setting for our show, and the models would be up close to the audience in the gilded mirrored ballroom. We planned a show that would put Paris fashion in a spin. Fashion shows traditionally end with a

wedding gown, and Elizabeth designed it, of course: a caftan of tulle covered with white roses over a white catsuit. Her sketches of it ran in all the newspapers before the show.

Where to get the models? Elizabeth insisted that we hire the world's most exotic and beautiful women from a variety of countries. She wanted Richard to drool! He had never been to a fashion show before ours, and he never went to another one again.

At the time of our opening, the world of models had begun to change. The first ethnic model I can remember was Hiroko, who was Japanese, Pierre Cardin's model in the late '50s and early '60s. Until Hiroko, Parisian models were mostly lily-white; black models were unheard-of.

Hiroko's Dutch bob matched Cardin's geometric designs. But a new linear modern art look had begun in Paris. Jean Shrimpton, with her long straight hair and long bangs, was in perfect proportion to show off the minidress, as was Twiggy, who, with her pixie hairdo and little-boy look, was the first androgynous model.

But sticklike waifs were not going to look right in our designs. We showed bikinis with bare bottoms and real diamond clasps just above the derriere crease. One swimsuit had a million dollars' worth of diamonds at the crotch, courtesy of Harry Winston. Louis sent us three of his most beautiful models.

Hebe Dorsey, fashion editor of the *Herald Tribune*, called to say, "There's a new model in from London, a long-legged blonde, you must have her. Her name is Amanda Lear, she is sexually ambiguous. She'll flirt with Richard Burton, and it will be fabulous." We hired her and had her model the swimsuits. Richard did, in fact, drool. The show was a huge success and made the international press in every country. A photo of the five of us ran worldwide—Elizabeth, Richard, Louis, Mia, and me, all crying and hugging at the show's end. We presented the world's first wraparound dress in panne velvet—which we showed on Gaby, a blond Swedish model who later had an affair with Thierry Roussel, Christina Onassis's husband—and jersey gowns that were the shape of things to come, all clingy, body draped, and see-through, highlighted by major diamonds as the only accessories.

Our models were absolutely the most beautiful in the world, and they all married well. Luana, from Brazil, was a Naomi Campbell look-alike. She married into one of the most aristocratic families in all of France and became the Countess of Noailles.

Erkiana, the other Brazilian model, also part Indian, married a rich Parisian businessman. Jacqueline, another black beauty, married the legendary Eric Tabarly—known as the father of French yachting—who crossed the Atlantic solo in his sailboat. Toukie Smith, sister of the designer Willi Smith, was the long-term partner of Robert De Niro, with whom she had twin sons.

It was the late 1960s and ethnic was novel and in. European playboys suddenly wanted exotic wives. These non-Caucasian women opened up the private clubs and broke down the racial barriers in European snobby society. After all, who could refuse the Countess of Noailles?

But the best of all was Amanda. She became a great pop singer in France. One day, Amanda walked into my shop with her "boyfriend of many years," Salvador Dalí.

"Where have you been, luv?" I asked.

"I'm pregnant," she said, *"et voicì mon mari!"* pointing to Dalí, who was wearing a black cape and top hat in the daytime.

I squealed congratulations and gave Amanda a great big hug.

She and Dalí roared with laughter, since I could never remember that Amanda was actually a man. At least that was the rumor—with surrealists and transexuals you never know for sure. Over the years Amanda has given many contradictory stories of her past and her sexual identity.

Dalí bought some trinkets from the shop and we went for drinks at the Hôtel Meurice, where Dalí lived in Paris. Amanda had been living with Dalí (and his wife, Gala) in Spain, where he had painted Amanda's reputedly hermaphroditic body for the last two years. She became known far and wide as Dalí's muse.

Years earlier, when her agency had called to arrange her interview for our opening fashion show, they explained she was from London, formerly called Peki d'Oslo, a popular female impersonator who was now modeling and known as Amanda Lear. The agent asked me if I had a problem with Amanda's ambiguous gender.

Paris was the city of liberation. I said, "As long as she looks great in the clothes, she has a job!"

Since our show, and her years with Dalí, she's had a long career as a painter, novelist, composer, singer, lyricist, media personality, and gay icon. Today there are many Dalí paintings of beautiful Amanda's nude body with the female parts on top and a large male part on the bottom. She fascinated Dalí and all the rest of us. A-man-da was the best.

WHAT THE FIRST SUPERMODELS IN PARIS TAUGHT ME TO EAT

Models and Frenchwomen don't diet. They live and eat this way every day.

YOU ARE WHAT YOU DRINK

- Absolutely no carbonation ever. It puffs you up. Drink nothing labeled "diet." It makes your stomach puffy and lumpy, and who knows what they put in there?

- Say *oui* to water.

- Say *oui* to freshly squeezed fruit juice. No high-fructose corn syrup or artificial fruit drinks. Of course, it's best to eat fresh fruit whole.

- Say *oui* to coffee and tea with no sugar and no artificial sweetener or creamer. Use skim milk instead.

- Say *oui* to red wine, in moderation. No more than seven glasses per week for a woman. Too much white wine gives bad dreams.

- Say *non* to fake anything.

NO CARBS AFTER SIX P.M.

- Avoid white food. Eat brown rice instead of white; yams instead of white potatoes; whole wheat pasta.

- Eat what is natural: no processed or packaged food except semolina pasta and healthy, crunchy brown rice. Eat plain yogurt and cheese (but each of these before six P.M.).

- Eat mostly fruits, vegetables, nuts, berries, and tea.

- Eat red meat rarely; eat only fish and free-range chicken if possible.

- Never eat "diet" food. Just eat less of the real food you like. Avoid food in plastic packaging.

- Always eat a sturdy breakfast and lunch for energy and so you burn calories during the day. Eat a smaller dinner.

- Say *oui* to fresh food cooked with little or no salt. Cook with olive oil, pepper, and herbs. Do not use salt substitutes; use sea salt.

- Say *oui* to fresh-baked bread. If you are buying or making bread that stays fresh more than two days, it is the wrong bread.

- Say *oui* to nonprocessed, spreadable cheese, preferably goat cheese.

- Always eat vegetable and fruit skins; they contain the vitamins.

- Don't forget a few pieces of 70 percent cacao dark chocolate, for happiness.

Victory for Nudes

Headlines in the English papers read, "Victory for Nudes: Match Won!"

From the *Daily Express*, December 31, 1970, "Two young nudes have succeeded where others have failed . . . to get into the pockets of Paris. For the first time in French history, Parisians can now take out a book of matches, strike a light, and gaze upon the cover bearing a picture of two naked ladies."

It took a long deliberation by a government commission before a photo of Mia and me in our all our naked glory was passed as art fit for the morals of French smokers.

In 1968, with the opening of our shop and all the international media attention, *Playboy* called and asked, "Would the two hip fashion designers be willing to be shot nude?"

"Well, Mia," I said, "it's the sexual revolution! Brenda Arquette was photographed nude and she went to Boston College. It's okay with me; we went to fashion school."

Herman Leonard, the ace photographer from *Playboy*, was sent to photograph us. Then an English writer doing an art book called *The Birds of Paris* asked to include us in a book featuring the "it" girls of Paris. We agreed.

To tell the truth, we actually wanted to be shot nude. The photos were incredible, and we used them on shopping bags and calling cards. Then we thought, why not make them into matchbook covers and distribute them to all the cafés and restaurants in Paris? The matchbooks were confiscated at the Brasserie Lipp, where the politicians habitually eat lunch. We hired a lawyer and a lobbyist and eventually we won our case.

Shortly afterward I went to the Yves Saint Laurent boutique opening at place Saint-Supice near our shop on rue Bonaparte. The entire wall opposite the door was a ten-foot-tall photo of Yves, nude, sitting exactly in my pose as seen on the matchbook covers.

Designers don't just copy dresses.

A Mysterious Girl

21 rue Bonaparte, Paris

Where's the man could ease a heart like a satin gown?
—DOROTHY PARKER

Fabled beauties walked into our shop every day in the late sixties. Our boutique was the talk of the town—everyone coming to Paris had it on her must-see list.

One girl who walked in was different: outrageously beautiful, yet strange and mysterious and calm. She looked Brazilian but said she was from Nicaragua. She bought a few elegant suits and blouses and handed me a check. It was from a man I knew in London. He was a friend of Ron's, a movie producer. The check was blank but signed. The bank was British.

I said nothing, filled in the pound amount, and never thought I would see this beautiful creature again.

A year later, she came in and bought the most expensive dress in the shop. She guiltily handed me a check, this one signed by Michael Caine. I said nothing, smiled, and said, "Thank you. Hope to see you again soon!" And I did. She became a regular client.

About two years later, she walked into the shop again and carefully selected the most offbeat modish gown, unlike anything she had previously purchased. Smiling humbly, she handed me another check from a British bank. It was blank, as usual, but this time it was signed by Mick Jagger.

The mysterious girl was named Bianca, later Bianca Jagger.

At her wedding to Mick Jagger she wore my white silk Marilyn Monroe–style halter dress with green polka dots and a big straw hat.

She knew what she wanted and she knew how to get it. I've seen women get men to come in and waste whole days watching them trying on dresses and hoping the checkbook would come out.

Bianca never had to worry about a silly thing like approval. Later she used her tremendous personal powers to help organize fund-raising for needy children and other worthy causes.

How the French Are Different

Moving back to live in France permanently in 1968, having given up the long film shoots in the States because of our shop, I experienced a massive culture shock. I really began to live with the French and learn what made them tick. To the French, the most important things in life, after family and God, are the following:

1. Food

2. Sex

3. Vacation

4. Style/fashion

5. Work/career

6. Money

Americans set their priorities like this:

1. Money

2. Career

3. Sex

4. Food

5. Style/fashion

6. Vacation

When I arrived in France in 1964, not speaking French well, I listened and learned. In school we were taught *"Bonjour, comment allez-vous?"* But *"Ça va?"* is what people actually say, both as a question and as a response. Watching French TV really helped. The TV was owned by the state, so instead of sitcoms, the French were given cultural programs or movies. The movies might last one and a half hours, but the post movie discussion often went on for three hours. Experts were brought in. Everyone debated, and to me it seemed that they beat each subject to death. "Real life" in Paris was the same way.

Outdoor cafés hugged every street corner. The evening social ritual was meeting friends for coffee or wine and talking for hours and hours until bedtime. Frenchmen seduced women with conversation. American men used pickup lines and then proceeded with brute testosterone. From my experience, New Yorkers came closest to the French in attempts at conversation, but I believe that verbal seduction must be taught young.

While American children went to gym class every day, French children were taught poetry and romance. Rimbaud, Voltaire, and Baudelaire were taught at eight years old. In France, school lasted from eight to five on weekdays, and Saturdays until noon. History, geography, literature, and art were more important than sports, home economics, and even math. The French considered themselves the world's elite intellectuals and were determined to pass on an appreciation for all things fine and worthy.

Salons de coiffure were everywhere. Every street in Paris had at least one. Frenchwomen rarely washed or colored their own hair. Legs, lips, bikini lines were waxed, bodies creamed, and hairdos changed weekly. It was not unusual for a Frenchwoman to have a new hair color every month. Light blond, red, brunette, streaked—they never shied from trying the latest "mode" to excite and bewilder the men in their lives.

Today the French are still ruled by the Napoleonic code, the Americans by English law. "You are guilty until proven innocent" keeps French criminals off the streets. Legally, you can kill your wife and her lover if you walk into your home and catch them in the act. The same goes for the wife who discovers her husband being unfaithful. This has led to the creation of the permanent mistress who has her own convenient apartment, away from the gun-toting wife. The French may also rent a *chambre cing à sept,* an afternoon apartment for the biweekly rendezvous. In fights, the person who strikes first goes to jail. This prevents barroom brawls and means that Frenchmen will yell insults to each other but seldom get physical.

The family member who earns more money gets the children in case of divorce. This often prevents divorce, since most men do not want to raise children alone. Women prefer keeping their mouths shut and staying married even when mates are unbearable. If the husband has a mistress, she takes a lover and doesn't risk losing her family. She has the attention of another man, who is often a cheating spouse, too, so everyone is safe.

Then there are professional mistresses. My excellent former patternmaker was one of these. She had her high-paying job, a devoted Yorkie dog, and a loving family that gathered on Sundays. She did not want the responsibility of being a wife. She was *la maitresse* of our dentist for twenty-five years. He visited her two nights a week and Saturday mornings.

During the four-week August vacation, the dentist, his wife, and his mistress all moved to the beach town near Biarritz, where they had *maisones de vacances* five miles apart. The two-nights-plus-Saturday-morning routine did not change. Every July, when his wife left for one month alone at the beach before her husband joined her, my assistant would move into the "family" apartment in Paris. In the morning, the female concierge would greet her with, *"Bonjour, mademoiselle,"* acknowledging the relationship. She never told the wife, and the wife never came up from vacation with a gun. The French don't own guns except for *"la chasse."*

The biggest difference between the French and the Americans is their relationships with their dogs. In France, a dog is a family member. The French take their dogs to restaurants, but never their young children, who are not as well behaved. Dogs sit on chairs at the table if they are small, and large dogs are served under the table. Meals for dogs are free. Dogs' names are remembered and they are treated like paying customers. They are well behaved in hotels, in restaurants, on sidewalks, and in cars. Certain cabdrivers do not allow dogs in their cabs. That's because they already have their own dogs riding shotgun.

My dog Wuffles and later my dog Chi Chi both lived the good life in France. Augusto, my driver, kept Chi Chi on the front seat as he did his deliveries. When I was out of town, he kept Chi Chi on her daily routine, picking her up at ten A.M., driving her to the boutique, going to the café for sugar cubes dipped in coffee, and keeping Augusto company on his rounds. Then in the evening when the shop closed, he would drive Chi Chi home to the apartment for a chicken and rice dinner, and off to bed.

Je Regrette

Mexico City

The biggest media love affair in Europe in the sixties was the romance of Romy Schneider and Alain Delon. The two superstars had fallen in love, helping to unite post–World War II Europe, since Romy was Austrian and Alain, French.

The French people accepted Romy, with her amazing beauty, as one of their own. She became the face of Coco Chanel and was seen wearing only Chanel designs. Romy invented the idea of a star promoting a single designer.

In the 1960s, Alain Delon was considered the best-looking man in Europe. The movie *Rocco and His Brothers* catapulted him to superstardom. Men and women alike couldn't collect enough of his photos, and he became a media sensation. When he met Romy, sparks flew and they fell in love immediately and caused an even bigger media sensation. Eventually the beautiful couple had a public engagement, with rings exchanged, and everyone buzzed with discussions of the upcoming wedding.

Like Richard Burton and Elizabeth Taylor, or Brad Pitt and Angelina Jolie, the chemistry of a few select couples is able to ignite the public frenzy, and every single moment of their lives is forever analyzed and archived.

It was too much for Alain. In 1963 he went to Morocco for a film and met a beautiful local script girl named Nathalie Canovas, who wore not Chanel couture but sexy shorts and skimpy tops. When Alain falls, he falls hard. Within weeks, while engaged to Romy, Alain and Nathalie married while the film was still shooting. The next day, in Paris, Romy received a single red rose with a card inscribed with the simple message, *"Je regrette!"*

Eight years later, Romy and Alain were reunited to do the film *The Assassination of Trotsky*, shot in Mexico with Richard Burton. It was the story of Trotsky's last days in Mexico before his murder. Alain was to play the murderer. Romy would have loved to murder Alain.

His marriage to Nathalie lasted only four years. They had a beautiful son, Anthony Delon, an actor today. Nathalie left Alain for a famous French director just like Alain left Romy. Romy, never having completely gotten over Alain, could not stop quizzing Ron on the set in Mexico. She wanted to know what Nathalie had that she didn't have.

He'd answer, "She had a perfectly symmetrical face."

"Ah," Romy said, "so her face is perfect—that's why? It's not making any sense. What else?"

Ron would then explain, "Well, she was very well read, quite intellectual!"

Romy remained unconvinced and continued to quiz Ron on Nathalie's charms.

"Well," he said, "she's very determined!"

Romy had had enough of these less than satisfactory explanations. She stared at Ron with her big eyes, forcing him to fess up.

Finally he said, "Nathalie tells every man she sleeps with that he's the best in bed, the best she's ever had."

Romy finally had her answer. But upon hearing the report of this conversation, *I* had a brand-new question: How did Ron know what Nathalie says in bed?

I was reunited with Romy in the Middle East, shopping for Arab clothing. Never one to miss a bargain, I discovered Arab caftans in 1969 while making the John Heyman movie *Bloomfield* (*The Hero*), shot in Jerusalem and Tel Aviv. *Bloomfield* is the story of a soccer team and takes place in old Jerusalem. The film starred Richard Harris and my new best friend Romy Schneider. Caftans turned out to be perfect hippie evening gowns for international nightclub hopping in the late sixties, especially worn with knee-high boots.

A caftan is a rectangle of fabric pulled over the head (no zippers or closings) and can be decorated with color and embroidery. I made them in clinging silk jersey in all colors for Elizabeth, and made a new shape in chiffon with ten floaty bias points that I named "Liza" after Liza Todd found a hippie dress made of points in Antiquarius Market in London and gave it to me to copy.

In our free time, Romy and I discovered wonderful shops that sold old embroidered caftans, robes, blouses, camel saddles, and other Arab artifacts. We bought every robe we could find in the Old City Market in Jerusalem. On one of my trips home to Paris, I took forty robes with me to resell in our Mia-Vicky shop. Romy wanted the very best ones for herself. I bought some for Elizabeth and Liza Todd. Eventually, there were none left to buy. The robes were genuine Bedouin, often in black velvet with red and gold embroidery on the fronts, sleeves, and sides. Some were ornamented with real gold thread. The silk embroideries were priceless. I bought the robes for $20 to $40 and resold them in Paris for $400. They sold out overnight. Where could I get more?

The 1967 Six-Day War had put a damper on things. Bedouin robes were the last thing people wanted to talk about. In Jerusalem, while we were shopping in the market, bombs were going off only one block away. Two people were killed, at a time when the war was supposed to be over. The reign of terrorism had begun. Unofficial war. Death at our doorstep.

Undaunted by bombs and still wanting to buy more robes, Romy and I decided to widen our search. Since we had cleaned out Jerusalem and Jaffa (the Arab section of Tel Aviv), we felt we had no choice but to drive out of town.

On Romy's day off, we swiped a jeep from one of the drivers on the film and without telling anyone, and dressed simply in pants and T-shirts, we headed east to the edge of the Sinai Desert. We wanted to find the Bedouin women we had heard about from the crew. It was said that the women rode on camels and sold the robes right in the desert. We drove around until we found a group of them and immediately bought up every robe and camel saddle and trinket they had. Delighted with our purchases and very proud of ourselves, we hadn't noticed a fleet of dusty army jeeps approaching.

Large jeeps surrounded our car and armed men in robes and headpieces informed us that we could not leave the area. We had been so engrossed in our shopping spree that we hadn't noticed that we had ventured into Jordan. Besides, it was news to us that Jordan was still at war with Israel. We were captured as prisoners and instructed to follow the lead jeep to an army barracks, actually a small roadside prison. When we arrived, we managed to grab the large bags stuffed with our purchases. The soldiers led us to a small cinder-block cell.

Once we were locked inside the cell, we changed into two of the lovely new caftans for a more relaxed prison look.

The soldiers yelled at us in Arabic. We were terrified. While I had visions of chain gangs and horrifying executions, Romy got busy. Somehow, she rummaged through our bags, looking for some identification, and came up with an embroidered Bedouin mirror. The edges were hung with old coins and pearls.

Miraculously, one side had been decorated with a Chanel promo photograph of Romy; the other side was a mirror. The photo had been torn from a movie magazine and it showed her against a bright yellow background as Princess Elizabeth in *Sissi*, the film that had made her an international star ten years earlier. She showed the photograph to the guards, pointing to herself and to the photo.

"Ah! Romy Schneider!" one of them yelled. Then the soldiers began to talk animatedly in Arabic. I figured they were saying she didn't look much like a European film queen in her desert shopping outfit and with no makeup!

Once they recognized Romy, the soldiers graciously let us out of our cell and escorted us back to the border with Israel. Romy happily signed autographs for the soldiers. Before waving goodbye, the men reprimanded us for hanging out on the wrong side of a war zone.

In 1981, Romy and her husband, Daniel Biasini, rented Elizabeth Taylor's home in Puerto Vallarta. While on vacation, they got the horrifying news that Romy's fourteen-year-old son, David, had died in a freak accident. While attempting to climb a spiked fence at his stepfather's home, the boy fell and punctured his femoral artery. He died at the hospital.

Romy never got over it. The brave woman from the arrest in Jordan fell apart. She and her husband separated soon after. A year later she died from a bad combination of drinks and pills, leaving behind her daughter, Sarah, an actress who looks just like her, and who probably inherited her mother's beautiful antique Bedouin robes.

Jane Birkin Wore a Basket, Not a Birkin Bag

Paris, 1969

Castel's on rue Princesse was the world's first private club with a discotheque. It had a twenty-by-twenty dance floor in the "cave" basement and nonstop twist music. Régine, originally a *dame pipi* (collector of toilet tips) in Whisky a Go Go in Paris, eventually became an *animatrice* at the Whisky. There is no comparable word in English, but it translates as "she who ignites the party." Régine was the first to replace the jukebox with two turntables, for constant music. She also created the idea of flashing disco lights at the Whisky and at New Jimmy's, her own club, and so is known as the inventor of the disco.

Jean Castel, a handsome Corsican, came up with the idea of a private disco dance club and promoted the idea of the "beautiful people" crushed together on a tiny dance floor, hands above their heads, bodies writhing to the nonstop pulsating music.

My own contribution to this wave of innovation was dirty dancing. With my handsome surfer lover Ron, now long-haired and wearing a goatee, I would turn my backside to his groin and grind up and down, hands above my head while his arms encircled my hips.

One night in the late sixties, I had some competition on the dance floor. Jane Birkin was newly arrived from London, where she had just made her name in *Blow-Up* with David Hemmings and Vanessa Redgrave. Jane's first big movie scene was a nude romp on the floor with a fashion photographer, à la David Bailey. Her first exposure at Castel's was with Serge Gainsbourg, whom she'd met on the film *Slogan*.

Jane was a long-haired flower child and carried a large round picnic basket as a purse. Tall and very long legged, and wearing a micromini, Jane did a slow dance with Serge that topped anything seen there before. With their legs entwined, Serge's pelvis held tightly against Jane's thigh, they moved through the sensual dance like two bodies melted into one. Amazingly, their lips met in a kiss that lasted through the *entire* three-minute song.

Jane Birkin and I later appeared together in a French variety show where we were interviewed and the audience got to see our "new look." Jane wore a long granny skirt unbuttoned up to her waist with her white undies showing through and a white cotton tank top, nipples visible and pointed. She also carried her picnic basket purse. I wore a cotton granny print minidress with puff sleeves and knee-high lime green leather boots. Jane was the first woman I'd ever seen wearing a white undershirt with no bra as an outer garment.

Jane eventually moved in with Serge Gainsbourg on rue de Verneuil, two blocks from my shop. Their home has become a historical monument in Paris with graffitied love letters from Serge's fans covering the entire building.

Early on in her love life, Brigitte Bardot had a brief fling with Serge, and her heart was broken. She asked Serge to write her the most beautiful love song ever written. And he did: *"Je t' aime . . . moi non plus"* (the first version) was recorded with Serge and Brigitte making love to the music. It was explicit not only for the slow, rhythmic moaning sounds but also the words, which shook the French: *"Je te ferait amour mais je la rétienne"* (I will make love to you but I will hold back).

The version of "Je t'aime" with Jane Birkin, Serge's wife, is the one known worldwide today. When it was released in 1972, nobody knew it had originally been recorded with Bardot. The passion of Jane's moaning orgasm was the real thing, as was her passion for Serge on the dance floor. It took an English dolly with a picnic basket to shock and rock the French.

Caesars Palace

Las Vegas, 1969

We were holed up in a lavish red-and-white Valentine Suite in Ceasars Palace in Las Vegas while shooting *The Only Game in Town*. Elizabeth costarred with Warren "Beauty" (her name for him), and Richard was more than a little interested in his American male counterpart, the only actor to score more leading ladies than he did.

February 14 was approaching, and Richard had to prove his love with a jewel. This was one of Elizabeth's favorite indoor games: thinking of ways she could charm men into buying her gems. Mike Todd had trained her to love jewelry. He gave her treasures: a complete set of emeralds; a diamond necklace, earrings, and bracelet; as well as her 29-carat emerald-cut diamond engagement ring. What she didn't realize was that *she* was the one actually buying the jewelry. Mike Todd died owing several million dollars and Elizabeth spent years after her marriage to Richard Burton paying off every single Mike Todd debt.

Richard did not want to be outdone by a previous husband, even a dead one. At an auction in London at Sotheby's, he paid $37,000 for the famous La Peregrina pearl. In the mid-1500s, King Philip II of Spain had given this 223-gram (56-carat) pearl to his bride, Mary I of England. Virtually every painting of Mary shows her wearing this teardrop-shaped pearl suspended from a jeweled chain attached to a jeweled choker. (For Elizabeth, the chain and choker were redone.)

Now it was being brought to Vegas by Sotheby's jewelry director Ward Landrigan (who today owns Verdura, jeweler of Chanel's favorite Maltese Cross bangles).

We were having a pajama party in the Duplex Valentine Suite with room service fried chicken and champagne. The walls were hot pink. The carpet was four inches of white shag. Elizabeth's little white Pekingese dog, Ofie, looked like part of the décor. The couches were red velvet and the furniture was gold. A hot pink staircase curved upstairs to the bedroom, where Richard was fast asleep in a heart-shaped waterbed, dead to the world. His plan was to present the pearl to Elizabeth the next day, Valentine's Day. But Elizabeth managed to charm Ward and he agreed to leave the pearl in the suite so she could take a peek at it with her friends. He dutifully brought it to her and then retired to his own suite.

Elizabeth in her silk caftan had called for a girls-only party of three: her hairdresser Claudye Bozzacchi and me. We all took turns admiring the pearl, which rested in a black velvet box. We each put it in our hair, placed it over our pajamas, and then—reluctantly—put it back in the box.

At one point, we went to the door to let in room service. Three rolling trays of food arrived. We were wolfing down food and drinking champagne when we heard Elizabeth scream, *"Oh, my God!"*

La Peregrina was gone! Luckily, Richard still slept soundly upstairs and didn't hear the scream. At first we thought the room service waitress had stolen the pearl, but she had never been to the part of the room where the box lay on the coffee table. We then shot glances at each other, declared innocence, and promised it was no joke.

Down on our hands and knees, from midnight to dawn, we went through every inch of the white shag carpet until we were dead from exhaustion. With a little help from the champagne, we all fell asleep on the floor.

Richard got up at six A.M. to make coffee and write in his diary. We all pretended we were still asleep. How to tell him? Who would be brave enough to break the news, and who would take the fall?

Richard stepped right over the three of us lying on the carpet, walked into the living room, and went into the kitchen. He came right out again, woke up Elizabeth, and handed her the pearl.

"Here," he said. "I found your dog in his bed chewing on this!"

After more than four hundred years of queens wearing the world's most famous teardrop pearl, a little white dog's tooth marks will remain as a reminder of a different kind of queen.

Hanging With Miles Davis

Paris

Sketches of Spain was the single most played album in our college dorm in the sixties. In Paris, in the early sixties, Miles Davis was my client Jacqui Goldman's close friend. His first wife, Frances, and Jacqui had both been stars of the Katherine Dunham dance troupe, along with Julie (Mrs. Harry) Belafonte. Miles always visited Jacqui in Paris, even after he and Frances were long divorced.

Miles loved Paris and loved to perform there. A food and wine connoisseur, Miles, unlike most great African-American musicians, grew up rather wealthy in East St. Louis, Illinois, where his father was a dental surgeon. Miles appreciated all things beautiful and expensive, and women were no exception. Miles was considered a genius in his field, in his craft, and in his personal life.

One night I was invited to meet Miles at a party in his honor. Much to my surprise, I got to sit opposite him at the King Club on rue de l'Echaudé. I was wearing a clingy turquoise satin halter gown with a front slit for my large breasts. I sensed that Miles appreciated the quality of my gown as well as the plunging décolleté.

He turned his big smile of seduction on me and pleaded, "Baby, I need some new clothes. Would you make some outfits for me to tour in?"

His whispery rasp was unlike anyone else's in the world. I was intrigued and we made a date to meet in my shop the next day. I was feeling on top of the world. At that exact moment, the waiter brought my lobster bisque to the table.

The poor waiter. He seemed agitated and confused. Was it my exposed double-Ds or Miles Davis in person that threw him off? Who knows? But he stumbled while placing my soup and poured the entire burning orange concoction down my turquoise satin neckline—scalding my breasts! Miles had to pour water all over my chest and pat me down with ice.

The next day, we met at the shop under better circumstances. The shop was decorated in late sixties hippie décor, with a sunken area three steps down, making a large conversation pit—a place to hook up with friends and discuss the radical politics of 1968— filled with overstuffed Indian mirrored pillows and a pastel mirrored ball above. It turned with flashing reflections that floated across a cracked mirrored wall. The feeling was one of floating in time—all we needed was a bong.

Miles broke into a smile as soon as he walked in. Seeing the conversation pit, he grabbed my arm and whispered in his raspy voice, "Baby, I love holes!"

Jacqui Goldman told me years later that Miles had fallen for me at the dinner party, but I was faithful to Ron and still feeling a little scalded, so we just became "flirty friends." Keeping everything on a professional basis I made Miles some cool outfits. That week I designed two suits in velvet with long printed scarves for his tour. He loved to create his own fashion even more than he loved to follow it. He liked tight-fitting clothes and soft silk or velvet pants that showed off his well-tuned body. He also loved drugs and he loved the gym. He had a worldwide reputation as a fantastic lover and had a collection of women of all colors and creeds, with a preference for Jewish girls as lovers. When it came to marriage, though, he stuck with African-American women.

Over the years, I would meet Miles at Jacqui and Michael's dinners, especially parties in their *cave*. Miles loved to sit me in a corner all night and pour out advice along with the fabulous wine. He loved my designs and my latest style, which was now graphic jumpsuits, and he always encouraged me to express myself. Without fear.

Once I went to see Miles perform in Paris and was lucky enough to sit in the front row. The entire night, he played with his back to the audience. He finished each piece with one last note that just hung there unresolved, as if the song had not ended. After the concert, I asked him about it. He explained his musical philosophy in a nutshell: "Baby, always keep them wanting more!" (Good advice for all artists and lovers.)

The next time I saw Miles, I found him in an unusually sad mood. He had married Cicely Tyson. Soon after, they separated, and he went into a terrible depression. He was in his fifties and had a hard time with "getting old." He shut himself in his brownstone on Central Park West in New York for seven years. He never saw anybody, although he made an exception for Michael Goldman, who visited occasionally.

Michael said later that Miles told him he didn't have anything else to play. He had done it all and just wanted to stay home and do drugs.

After Miles died, Frances Davis, Jacqui Goldman, and I met for a drink at Café de Flore in Paris to reminisce about Miles, whom we all had loved. On the way to the café, the streets were erupting into a Bastille Day–like celebration; François Mitterrand, the Socialist candidate, had just been elected president.

The three of us got caught up in the street dancing and we celebrated Miles with the hordes of French students.

Later that night at Café de Flore, we shared our experiences of our beloved Miles. Frances, his first wife, was the beautiful woman on the cover of his albums *In Person at the Blackhawk*, *Someday My Prince Will Come*, and *E.S.P.* Though their marriage lasted less than ten years, it was during the critical time when Miles became a star. She had known him both "before" and "after."

Jacqui told Frances that she had always been the woman Miles loved the most. He had a crush on me only because I reminded him of her. He confessed to Jacqui that his marriage to Cicely Tyson was a problem because he was afraid of her. Once, when she was angry, he claimed she pulled out his hair extensions! She was the opposite of the petite, elegant, and gentle Frances, who inspired his greatest work. Still working at eighty-one years old, Frances has been a much-loved waitress at Hamburger Hamlet in Los Angeles.

Who knows . . . Would his life have been happier had he never lost his first love? Like his music, that last note remains unresolved.

MILES DAVIS'S LIFE LESSONS

- "Always leave 'em wanting more." As an artist, singer, painter, or writer, don't tell everything at once. Allow the imagination of the reader or listener to participate.

- Be Fabulous. Express Yourself. Develop a look that is recognizable. Create your own persona. With Miles it was over-the-top fashion and elegance.

- Always be creative and grow as an artist. Surround yourself with young people; change with the youth of today. Stay forever young.

- Travel, read, and learn. Miles was always following art, fashion, literature, new music, and travel. The world was his oyster; he could talk to everyone and learn something new to incorporate into his music.

- Bring creative people together. Be the nucleus.

Eating and Drinking Our Way From Paris to Rome

1967

Ron finally called his wife from Paris and insisted that she sign the divorce papers. I suppose she had held fast in the hope that he would come to his senses and come home to Malibu. If he didn't miss her, he should at least miss surfing. Instead, Ron asked me to celebrate our being together officially with a drive to Rome, where Richard Burton was starting to film *Candy*.

"How about leaving a week early, Vicky, and let's eat and drink our way from Paris to Rome? We'll eat in every Michelin three-star restaurant along the way!"

We hopped into Ron's navy blue Maserati convertible with natural brown leather interior and took off with Wuffles (dogs were allowed in every great restaurant). I wore my new multicolored pink wrap dress that had just been photographed for *Redbook* magazine. I would make the dress for *Candy*.

We drove south. We ate a picnic lunch of chilled Sancerre rosé and crisp baguettes stuffed with foie gras from the local charcuterie, lying on a blanket on the bank of the Saône and watching houseboats go by. Wearing a wrap dress was a smart choice. I could easily loosen it as I ate my way to Rome.

Day one: We drove to Saulieu and La Côte d'Or (today Bernard Loiseau), considered by many gourmets to be the greatest restaurant outside Paris. Our dinner was salmon trout, fried foie gras, and pear soufflé with hot chocolate sauce and macaroons. It was followed by a room to sleep off the two bottles of house champagne and Clos de la Pousse d'Or, a Pommard, the best wine I have tasted in my life.

Day two: A drive to the town of Roanne and a stop at Frères Troisgros. We lunched on the bank of the Rhône with a packed lunch prepared by Côte d'Or, consisting of ham and cheese baguettes with a bottle of Saint-Amour '64 "for the lovers." It was accompanied by grapes, cherries, and pots of crème brûlée, which we ate on the blanket at teatime near the Pont du Gard, a Roman aqueduct from 500 B.C.

Day three: fish soup, fava beans cooked in cream, dandelion salad with fruit, and profiteroles at Baumanière in Provence.

After a long night of sexy moves on four-hundred-thread-count Egyptian cotton sheets at Les Baux and a quick swim in the pool at dawn, we left Provence and crossed the Alps into Italy and sped down the Mount Blanc Tunnel at 100 mph only to have the Maserati's engine blow up on the steep incline into northern Italy. Ron fussed with the engine and was told to turn off at the first Italian exit in the Aosta Valley. There was a village with a great restaurant-hotel and the owner would get our car repaired. He had "resources," we were told.

We arrived at our hotel late at night. To our surprise, when we rang the bell, a smiling older Italian-American man opened the door. He had a Brooklyn accent. Ron told him about our car and handed him the keys. The place looked ordinary, with dark wood furniture, flower-printed Italian tile floors, and lots of potted plants.

The American owner sent up to our sumptuous room a complimentary vin santo from Tuscany, in crystal glasses on a silver tray with a cut-glass plate filled with delicious homemade cookies to dip in the port. This was a sign we were not in an ordinary restaurant-hotel.

The next day we stayed in bed frolicking until one P.M., then went downstairs to lunch to find the entire restaurant filled with some forty men wearing serious suits with wide ties. The men were all from America, Sicily, and Italy. They were enjoying a loud, rambunctious, cigar-smoking lunch. Not a woman was in sight. Our drop-by hotel was the secret yearly meeting place of the leaders of the worldwide Mafia. It was owned by the mob and not in any restaurant guides. There were no other guests.

We stayed alone together for three days while the car was being fixed and ate every meal there, the best northern Italian cooking and no pizza. Rare game, rare cheese, risottos with rare mushrooms and white truffles, and our desserts were the finest puffy creamy delights—pure poetry. I fell in love with the Mont Blanc: a hazelnut paste cream puff that Ron spoon-fed me. It is still my favorite dessert, after Lisa Fonssagrives's apple pie. Eating and drinking with the mob was instructive: Even if you run the world, your stomach comes first.

Candy, A Roman Orgy

Italy

With our international reputation of being sexy Ye Ye girls, Mia and I were hired by the handsome French actor Christian Marquand to design the costumes for the movie version of the novel *Candy* by Terry Southern. It's the psychedelic story of a teenage nymphette who seduces a series of exotic older men, played by Richard Burton, Ringo Starr, Marlon Brando, James Coburn, John Astin, Walter Matthau, and John Huston. The movie was shot in Rome in 1967. Christian Marquand was Marlon's best friend (rumored to have once been his lover) and the star of *No Sun in Venice,* one of my favorite French movies. The movie sound track, by the Modern Jazz Quartet, was Ron's and my favorite sexy background music for lovemaking.

After Fellini's *8½*, Rome became the sex-crazed playground capital of the world, at least in people's minds. Everyone wanted to make a film there and, of course, get invited to an orgy!

The first part of the filming process was known as the "Candy Contest" and involved choosing an actress to play the leading role. Each important male in the production had his favorite. The producer had his Candy, the director had his, and the financial backer had his. Eventually, after twenty to thirty blond "fifteen-year-olds" each took a turn on the casting couch, the men settled on the director's choice, Ewa Aulin, a Swedish model with a big pout who couldn't speak English, let alone act.

The producer's choice, an American, Sydne Rome, became the stand-in Candy. Sydne did actually become an actress in Europe and was later photographed on the cover of *Cosmopolitan* in my first bra dress, a lime green empire gown with a draped bra and halter straps.

Ewa Aulin, after such films as *Microscopic Liquid Subway to Oblivion* and *Death Laid an Egg,* eventually disappeared.

Mia flew in from Paris and we worked on the costumes. We put Candy in a mint green mini—wrap dress and white bunny fur minicoat. She is unwrapped by Ringo and escapes in her underwear. (Years later, Diane von Furstenberg "invented" the wrap dress. Actually, even before Mia and Vicky, Claire McCardell did a button wrap skirt without ties.)

Working with Marlon on *Candy* was probably the most difficult job I ever had designing clothes. How could I dress the man whose poster had hung over my childhood bed? The very man who awoke my first sexual desires at age eleven? And there was a tiny bit of "history" between us as well.

During my early Village days in 1963, I had been lucky enough to attend the premiere of *The Ugly American* in New York, invited by David Tyson. I had been so thrilled I skipped school and made a special outfit, hoping to catch Marlon's attention. I remember it well: a clingy yellow-and-white polka-dot jersey minidress that I sewed in one hour, topped off with my red fox chubby, huge hoop earrings, red fishnet stockings, and strappy red sandals. It worked. My dress had "magic powers."

When I got to the theater, Marlon was by the popcorn counter surrounded by photographers. He made his way over to me, gave me an intense glare followed by the sweetest smile, and whispered, "Meet me later. I'm at the Warwick Hotel."

I was only eighteen and too scared. Did he think I was a hooker? If so, could I live up to his expectations? I didn't go. It's one of the biggest regrets of my life.

Now, all these years later, I had to measure Marlon for his outfits, and he was in a bad mood, refusing to look at the costume sketches and not letting anyone, even the director, into his dressing room. After getting permission from the assistant director, I summoned my courage and gently knocked on the door.

"Mr. Brando," I said in my sexiest voice, "it's Vicky Tiel, your costume designer. I've come to take your measurements."

The door slowly opened and he let me in. He looked me up and down and, opening his arms, said, "Come here!" and gave me that big smile. He was so gorgeous I felt myself melting. He put his hands on the zipper of his tailored brown tweed wool slacks and spread his legs. "You can start by taking the inseam!" he said.

Since that is the distance from the crotch to the bottom of the leg, I gently placed the measuring tape exactly where I was supposed to, trying not to shake.

My hand was on his crotch. He looked down at me and said, in his soft Marlon-mumble, "Why didn't you show up at the Warwick?"

My heart was pounding so hard I was sure he could hear it. I didn't answer but quickly finished the other measurements and ran out of the dressing room and into my future husband's arms.

"How was Marlon?" Ron asked.

Ron and I rented the actor Mickey Knox's Rome apartment on the Via Sistina and cruised the outdoor café scene at night. One night, we ran into Rory Calhoun, the American movie star from the fifties. He invited us to dinner in his fabulous apartment on the Via Veneto, overlooking the city. Being busy with the film, we arrived late (and hungry) to dinner and walked in to find a long refectory table surrounded by the Beautiful People of the Italian film industry, along with a sprinkling of gorgeous *Vogue* models. The guests were already wolfing down dessert and seemed unhappy with us, the late arrivals. The waiters hurriedly plunked down large plates of spaghetti in front of us and ran off.

The host, unable to wait any longer, suddenly reached over to his dinner partner's strapless dress and gently plucked out an ample breast. He bent down, put his lips to her nipple, and then turned his head to one side long enough to declare, "Let the orgy begin!"

Ron seemed *way* too delighted and immediately dropped his forkful of spaghetti. But I was not one to share my lover with anyone. I yanked Ron's arm, wiped the tomato sauce from his mouth, and managed to pull him out the door and into the elevator. Without a word, I punched the Down button with a fury I didn't know I had. So much for Roman orgies.

But why had I bothered? The filming of *Candy* was more of the same. Sex was the subject matter, and nymphettes, drugs, and orgies ran rampant on the set. At night the cast and crew were welcome at Christian Marquand's home on Via Appia Antica, and everyone would get high on the local weed that grew in the mountains of Orvieto and drink the local Fontana Candida white wines.

Richard Burton was cast as MacPhisto (Mephisto), a character supposedly based on the poet Dylan Thomas. We dressed Richard in a ruffled shirt, velvet jacket, and long white scarf.

During the *Candy* orgy period, Elizabeth and Richard also had a home on Via Appia Antica and, when guests were invited over, their "orgies" were all about food. Elizabeth held her thirty-sixth birthday party for thirty of her closest friends in the Hostaria Antica Roma on the Via Appia Antica, the most exclusive restaurant in the Italian countryside. Each person had his or her own personal bottle of Château Lafite 1961 (a great year!) and an entire bottle of vintage Dom Pérignon.

The birthday dinner lasted six hours, until two A.M., at which point Ron and I, feeling no pain, took off in his Maserati and headed out toward the sea. Or so we thought at the time.

At dawn we awoke to find the pink-orange sun rising over a field of pine trees. Somehow, the car's engine was still running. Apparently, Ron had fallen asleep at the wheel and Somebody Upstairs had guided us quietly off the Via Appia Antica and into a small olive grove, leaving both of us alive and well. Neither one of us had a single scratch or even a headache.

Château Lafite 1961 was a very good year.

The Mill House

Normandy, 1968

S till not divorced, but now "committed," Ron suggested that we buy a home together—as "partners." We found our dream of a country house in a tiny peaceful village called Autheuil-Authouillet in Normandy (pop. 600), sixty miles from Paris, halfway between the capital and Deauville. Built in 1600 as a mill house for a member of the DuBarry family, it was constructed of board and bat siding on a small island in the Eure River. We loved the two hundred rosebushes growing wild outside and knew we had to buy it when we saw the walk-in fireplace in the living room. We filled the rooms with antique treasures from our travels. The house was three stories high and narrow, with the top windows overlooking the tiny picturesque village below. Autheuil was close to Elizabeth's friend Yul Brynner's farm, making it easy for the Burtons to visit us both.

Yves Montand and his wife, Simone Signoret, had made their home in Autheuil-Authouillet since the '50s. They lived in a showy white mansion on a hill, where they frequently entertained show business people, writers, and Communist leaders. The villagers told us that the famous couple kept to themselves and never participated in the traditional festivities in spite of their left-wing leanings.

Our village held an annual New Year's Eve feast that consisted of eleven courses, starting at eight P.M. and ending with breakfast at six A.M. Attendance was required if one ever wanted to be in the good graces of plumbers, electricians, and carpenters. We never saw the Montands there.

The French have the (in my experience, undeserved) reputation for being unfriendly to foreigners. But we didn't want to take any chances. Our village had eighty houses and three bars. One morning soon after our arrival, we entered our local bistro, Chez Denis, wearing plaid shirts, old pants, and large green gum boots, accompanied by a dog on a leash. For breakfast, Ron ordered *café calva*—coffee with a side of calvados—and poured the alcohol into the espresso and drank it at once like a shot of whiskey. Then he turned to the barman and said, *"Encore!"* Later that afternoon, he returned to Chez Denis and cried out, *"Une ballon rouge"*—"A glass of red wine." That did it.

Although the big mill wheel was gone, we could look down from our house and see the Eure stream by, full of the jumping trout we had placed there for easy catching. Ron loved to cook Dorian Leigh's Seven-hour Lamb, Lisa Fonssagrives's Glug, and Louis Féraud's baked potatoes in the fireplace.

We would take off to the country every weekend in the vintage black Thunderbird limousine Ron had received as an end-of-movie gift from the American producer of *The Comedians*. Ron sold his beloved Maserati convertible to buy our riverside house, a difficult sacrifice for any man, but especially for the stud of MGM.

Our Normandy home became a hangout for English-speaking actors shooting films in France. Besides Richard Burton, one could find Donald Sutherland; Faye Dunaway; the producer Ernest Lehman and his wife, Jackie; or the French actress Nathalie Delon and her boyfriend, the karate champion of France. Once Richard Harris stayed for weeks in the attic bedroom healing a broken heart after his divorce from his beautiful, aristocratic wife, Elizabeth, and claimed he saw the ghost of a little boy playing in the garden down by the river. We thought it was because he was Irish and Irishmen all see ghosts, but later we found out it might have been true! Before Ron and I bought the house, a little boy drowned in that exact spot.

At the mill house, I began to paint.

I first began painting in the attic bedroom. I painted everything around me: the countryside, my husband in the local bicycle race, and a red-and-blue hot-air ballon flying over our town at sunset.

Eventually Ron had the circa 1620 stone shed cleaned up and stored his new purchase, a black 1930 Citroën, on the lower level. He put hooks above the car doors and we hung our fishing rods so we could fish up and down the Eure. Later he built some small steps to a wonderful room with southern exposure so I could create my naïve paintings of our perfect life together in our charming village.

After a few years of painting, I asked Ron to widen the steps to my studio and add a railing so I could climb up easily when I was creaky-kneed in my eighties. I figured if Grandma Moses could paint the last twenty years of her life, so could I. I could easily see myself living out my older years in the mill house, walking to get my groceries at the market for exercise, a regular "character" in the village. It was the perfect house for my last hurrah—the perfect river for a summer dip, and my trout would multiply so I'd always have fresh fish to eat and my roses would cover the walls and cascade everywhere.

It was a lovely vision. But it would never come to be.

NEW YEAR'S EVE FEAST IN AUTHEUIL-AUTHOUILLET
This is done in many French villages in the town hall. Everyone comes, from grandmas to kids. Dinner started at eight P.M., and we all crawled home at dawn.

- *Amuse-gueule* (amuse your mouth; appetizer)—*tartlet de fromage au gratin*
- *Huîtres* (oysters) and champagne (Moët et Chandon)
- *Soupe froid* (cold soup)—vichyssoise
- *Truite aux amandes* with sautéed new potatoes
- *Coupe l'appétite* (to clean the palate)—champagne sorbet

- *Rosbif*—rare roast beef sliced thick with *pommes dauphinoise*
- *Salade de mâche*—green salad with clementines and *chèvre chaud* (warm goat cheese)
- *Fromage normandie*—Camembert and/or Pont l'Evêque, served with port wine
- Tarte tatin with crème fraîche or *glacé bûche de Noël* (Yule log), coffee, calvados, little coffee bean chocolates
- Four A.M.: *soupe à l'oignon* (onion soup), topped with bread and melted Gruyère
- Six A.M.: *petit déjeuner*—coffee and croissants

DORIAN'S SEVEN-HOUR LAMB

leg of lamb
olive oil
rosemary
salt and fresh-ground pepper
garlic, sliced
large brown paper bag
1 carrot

1. Get an early start. Preheat the oven to 175°.

2. Rub the lamb with olive oil, rosemary, salt, and pepper. Cut slits in the meat and insert garlic slivers (use lots of garlic).

3. Put the lamb in the paper bag, close the bag tightly, and place the carrot on top of the bag (really!).

4. Cook the lamb in a large open casserole, preferably cast iron, for 7 hours.

5. Let the lamb cool in the bag for ½ hour. Pour the sauce from the bag over the lamb. The meat will fall away from the bone.

In olden days in French villages, butchers would put the lamb in the bread ovens, after they had been turned off, early on Sunday morning to be picked up at one o'clock for lunch.
The carrot does something magical!

LISA FONSSAGRIVES'S GLUG

In Sweden, where it is very dark and cold, Lisa's family had a vat of Christmas glug going all winter.

    1 bottle aquavit
    1 bottle cognac
    1 bottle red wine (Beaujolais is perfect)
    3 oranges with whole cloves poked in all over
    2 cups white raisins
    2 teaspoons crushed cloves
    zest from 5 oranges and 5 lemons
    cinnamon sticks

Put all the ingredients in a big pot, covered tightly. Simmer over the lowest possible heat off and on for a week. Serve with a cinnamon stick as a "stirrer."

When the level of the glug goes down, add more alcohol and another clove-studded orange.

Louis Feraud's Fireplace-Baked Potatoes

L ouis Féraud's favorite way to cook food was in his fireplace. After work, his models and some good friends like Gilles and Christine Lambert (the food editor of *Le Figaro* and his wife, my former assistant) often gathered in Louis and Mia's large living room. He would throw steak rubbed with crushed garlic, very good olive oil, and herbes de Provence full of fresh thyme twigs into his fireplace to grill on a rack over hot coals. Accompanying the steaks were Louis's special baked potatoes.

LOUIS'S FIREPLACE-BAKED POTATOES

Cover 4 medium-size baking potatoes with olive oil and sea salt. Poke them with a fork. Put the potatoes on a rack in the fireplace—the flames cook them. Move them around to cook all sides. When the potatoes are almost cooked but not yet crispy, in about 45 minutes to one hour, put the steak on the rack. When the potatoes are super-crispy, in another 15 minutes or so, open them and top with a scoop of butter and two scoops of crème fraîche. Sprinkle with sea salt and fresh-ground pepper to taste.

Louis served dinner on a low table in front of the fireplace where his guests sat on big cushions. These simple, rustic meals were always served on fabulous (and rare) extra-large sixteenth-century earthenware plates in blue and white, from Assisi.

Once in a while during his cooking, Louis would turn to Mia and say, "Don't forget, chérie, I have heed zee gold bars inside zee fireplace walls, as I built zee fireplace myself."

Louis hated banks, hated taxes, hated stocks and investments. He liked property, and he *loved* gold.

He poked around in the four new fireplaces he acquired over the years as he built his extended apartment up and down faubourg Saint-Honore by buying maids' rooms. He told me, "I bought zem all, Vickee, to hide zee gold."

Louis's last party was a miracle. One day in the late '90s while in Paris, I became nostalgic and ordered a surprise birthday party for Louis and invited the whole gang from the '60s. Christine Lambert held the party in her house and served Louis steak and potatoes. We had not been reunited for more than fifteen years. Louis came with a young Russian model named Liouba (who later married Alec Wildenstein). We all told our crazy stories about the "good old days."

Louis and Jacques Schoeller, two of France's foremost playboys and storytellers, kept the table mesmerized. Jacques's brother was Guy Schoeller (who had been married to Françoise Sagan). The Schoeller brothers had seen and heard it all. Secrets, both political and personal, were divulged. It was a great night.

The following week, Gilles Lambert called me. He said, "I've just come from visiting Louis, and he's lost his mind."

Sadly, Louis had developed advanced Alzheimer's, seemingly overnight. He didn't recognize Gilles. I realized how lucky we were to have celebrated our little *"band d'amis"* with that great last meal together.

Louis died in 1999 and left his gorgeous home opposite the Élysée Palace to his only child, his daughter, Kiki. She looked for years—even pulled the walls apart—but never found zee gold.

Different Strokes

Normandy, France, 1970

Faye Dunaway was the girl of the moment. She had been elevated to superstardom by *Bonnie and Clyde*. Women everywhere were influenced by her sleek style—skinny jackets, long jersey skirts, boots, and a straight asymmetrical haircut topped off with the famous beret.

But on this day in 1970, Faye was sitting on the swing in my garden in Normandy, crying her eyes out. She swung back and forth, pumping so hard she nearly pitched over into the river. Appropriately, the swing was hung on a weeping willow tree. But it was a delicate old tree, and the branch finally gave way and snapped. She broke my tree! The heart of the tree cried out and cracked from the center.

Faye stepped off, oblivious to anything but her own pain. She had just broken up with her boyfriend, fashion photographer Jerry Schátzberg, then the love of her life. She had played the lead in *Puzzle of a Downfall Child*, a movie Jerry had written and directed, about a fashion model in New York. I had been doing costumes for *The Deadly Trap*, a film Faye had done in France with the great director René Clément. We had never discussed her personal life until that weekend in my country house. Faye was mysterious, quiet, extremely demanding, and very hardworking—a perfectionist.

"Why can't I have a relationship that works?" she asked me, not expecting an answer.

I wasn't sure if I should mention that I had dated Jerry, too. In 1964, as a young fashion student, just before I went to Paris, I met Jerry with Mick Jagger. Mick and I met at a party and he dragged me to another in Midtown Manhattan at Jerry's photo studio. Mick was almost unknown, with his first album barely out, and seemed very young and unsure of himself. He kept trying to phone his girlfriend back in London (was it Marianne Faithfull?), but it was three A.M. there and she kept hanging up on him. He seemed pathetic—agitated about his girlfriend, sad, skinny and, I thought, not attractive at all. I would never have predicted his rise to a strutting rooster of a superstar, with women lined up around the block and groupies everywhere fighting for a chance to be with him.

On the other hand, Jerry was my idea of a hunk: thin, sensitive yet masculine. A fashion photographer, Jerry would turn in a few years to films and make his name directing *The Panic in*

Needle Park with Al Pacino, a new talent. From what I knew of the New York fashion scene, where models took coke and speed to stay thin, a film about druggies would not be a stretch for Jerry.

Jerry and I had planned to meet in Paris during the upcoming collections. He stayed at the Hotel Crillon on the place de la Concord with the staff of *Glamour* magazine. We met at Lison Bonfils's home. She was a fashion editor, married to Didier Bernardin, whose father owned the Crazy Horse saloon. Lison was chic, tall, beautiful, and the first woman I knew who was able to cuss like a sailor with the grace and ease of a princess. The New York fashion contingent thronged her cocktail parties.

I told her, "I just arrived in Paris. I'm here to design couture, but I can't speak French very well. How do you think I can learn French very fast?"

Her answer was to the point: "Fuck Frenchmen," she said and hurried off to attend to her other guests.

I didn't follow her advice. I preferred American men (with them I *thought* I had a chance of fidelity). Jerry took me back to the Crillon for a romantic evening in a glamorous suite overlooking the place de la Concorde, a dream come true.

To my surprise, his gentle kisses were meaningless—he was *too* gentle and I was used to hot Steve and powerful Rainier. I thought Jerry was Prince Charming, but I was mistaken. I rushed out of there like Cinderella, trying to beat the clock. Somehow, the chemistry just wasn't there, for either of us.

I decided not to share my story with Faye. But her tears had a lasting impact on me. Here she was, Faye Dunaway, at the summit of her career, the most photographed woman in the world. Someone I had run away from very young was now breaking her heart.

Swinging London

Chelsea, 1969

London became *the* place to be in 1965. With The Beatles and the Rolling Stones came the "London look." By 1969, anything British was happening.

Carnaby Street, where the pop stars dressed, got all the acclaim. It was there that John Stephen's shop had started the shrunken-suit teddy boy look. The Beatles wore pin-striped teddy suits on American TV. Brian Jones, of the Stones, was the first singer to wear the dress shirt with four ruffles along with pin-striped dress pants in the daytime, and the dandy look was born. Young people everywhere who wanted to be hip or see what was hip got on a plane and headed for swinging London.

The real action was on the King's Road, winding across Chelsea from Eaton Square to Fulham. The far end of the King's Road over the bridge had shops like Mr. Freedom and head shops springing up next to hairdressers specializing in men's styles last worn in London by Beau Brummel.

A few private club restaurants, like Club Dell'Aretusa and Tramp, turned up on or near the King's Road. No one could get into these spots unless he or she was very famous or very fashionable. Before this moment, English restaurants had welcomed *any* paying guests. Private clubs, of course, were exclusive, but the idea of a restaurant refusing admittance immediately established

Aretusa as The Place to Be. It was a brand-new idea. Aretusa quickly became a private spot for rock/movie/fashion folk. Every movie producer had a table for eight that quickly filled up. One never saw a bill paid. They were sent to accountants with the wave of a hand.

Among the most popular film people in London was Gene Gutowski, a Polish producer who, like his friend Roman Polanski, ate lunch each weekend at Aretusa. Roman and Gene were to have lunch one bright summer Sunday in August with Ron and me, and Peter and Gail Katz. Roman never showed up, and then we all heard the news that Sharon Tate had been murdered.

Gene left the table to call Roman, then came back sobbing, "Sharon and the baby are dead. [Celebrity hairstylist] Jay Sebring, too. In [record producer] Terry Melcher's house."

Now, the crazy thing was Terry was Ron's cousin. Terry's father was Al Jorden, not Marty Melcher, who adopted Terry. Al Jorden, a lonely alcoholic jazz trombonist who was Doris Day's first husband, was Ron's uncle. Terry had been on drugs and had befriended Charles Manson and promised him a record deal, which never happened. Manson blamed Terry for the broken promise, put a curse on the house, and sent his disciples. They killed the wrong people. Ron thought Terry Melcher was supposed to be the victim, not Jay and Sharon, who had rented the same house in the hills.

Swinging London came to a halt. I consider the Manson murders to be the major turning point for many drug users in show business and the creative arts. People packed up their bongs and went straight. The parties stopped. The yogis came to London, and "Make Love Not War" took over. Sometimes it takes an earth-shaking drama like those gruesome murders to make a lasting impact. Drug culture and hippies went out of style and awareness and productivity began to blossom. The only problem was that there were still many people who found it hard to give up drugs.

Sharon had been a friend. I did her clothes for *Eye of the Devil*. The film was shot in France and Sharon had stayed in L'Hôtel, near my shop. She had the most perfect body and creamy white skin. She was sweet and wholesome-looking, yet she must have had a dark side. After all, she married Roman, who created such dark movies about death and horror. But opposites *do* attract. Roman also had been a friend of mine before he became famous.

We had met in 1961 when I was an art student at Pratt Institute. Roman had, as a young student, shot his first feature-length film, *Knife in the Water.* His cousin Richard Horowitz fixed us up. But we were not a match, he was *trop* petite and artistic.

The three of us had a wonderful time one snowy evening in New York. We all danced "Follow the Yellow Brick Road" from *The Wizard of Oz* up Fifth Avenue through Rockefeller Center. It was so corny. We stopped in front of the bronze Atlas statue holding the world on his shoulders and promised each other in the snow to "make it" one day. Roman proclaimed, "I am going to become a great director."

Ron told me after Sharon's death that he had been her lover before he knew me.

"Some small world," I told him, and added, "She's the most beautiful girl I've ever seen undressed."

Ron said she was so beautiful that when they had sex, she liked to watch herself do it.

I answered, "If I looked like her, I would, too."

Roman would never be the same. It was almost as if he were being punished for his avant-garde work, which many people considered sick. And Sharon was being punished for being too beautiful. But she was simply in the wrong place at the wrong time.

Hollywood took many years to get over the murders. From then on, people in show business locked out outsiders and bolted their doors.

We Wore Our Art

A work of art is a corner of creation seen through a temperament.
—ÉMILE ZOLA

In the beginning of "fashion," clothing from France was considered the ultimate for wealthy women in Europe, Russia, and even the United States. Printed catalogs would arrive from France in the American West, where dressmakers copied anything French for the ladies who entertained the cowboys of the plains.

The original couturiers, however, were simply unglamorous dressmakers. The dressmaker was a worker not unlike a cook or a maid, a have-not who serviced the haves of the world until suddenly, in 1911, a French dressmaker named Paul Poiret decided to become a have and join *"la societé."* Poiret became the Karl Lagerfeld of his day by becoming a media personality, the first designer-star. Poiret designed furniture, jewelry, rugs, and perfumes (the first designer to do so). His elaborate costume parties, on a houseboat on the Seine where he lived and entertained, were the social events of the season in the 1920s. Suddenly, the dressmaker was allowed to dine with the clients. Monsieur Poiret entertained to such an extent that he went bankrupt, a danger that has not abated in over a hundred years. Designers, unlike other artists, love clothing and love to wear their art.

Mia and I wore our art, too.

Arriving in Paris in July 1964, Mia and I went straight to meet Dorian Leigh, who gave us a complete rundown on how fashion worked.

Truly commercial fashion began in Paris in the 1950s, when the twelve major couturiers showed each year in late January and late July. Each couture house was owned by a designer with the bank as a backer. The couturier was able to design at his whim, but the practical side was there were five thousand customers worldwide who would pay $5,000 to $20,000 for a suit or a gown. This entitled them to five fittings before they received their garment. Of course, one had to fly to Paris for the fittings. Each couture house employed about 120 seamstresses, who produced two collections of one hundred styles each twice a year and then sewed all the orders. Each gown was ordered by several clients and the couture house made five hundred to six hundred pieces in six months. Each dress took from one to two weeks to sew. An elaborate gown, all hand beaded, could take up to three weeks, with many sewers working away, and could cost about $40,000, or the price of a two-bedroom Paris apartment or a small country manor home. No one got dresses free, not even movie stars.

Of the one hundred gowns presented, about three were for shock value and three were a new trend. The other ninety-four were just wearable.

When Christian Dior changed fashion with his midleg full-skirt suit (the "New Look") in 1947, and Coco Chanel and Elsa Schiaparelli became society darlings, the dressmaker-designers became accepted artists in France and were allowed to mingle with the aristocrats simply on the merits of their talent and fame. Suddenly, designers like Coco Chanel from very humble origins were elevated in status to that of their customers. Chanel became the long-lasting queen of fashion because she created so much newness: the short haircut, the use of jersey, the knit cardigan sweater, and the boxy hip-skimming jacket worn unchanged for sixty years.

By the '60s, simple Italian-born Pierre Cardin, whose father was a button maker in Genoa, became the newest French fashion leader. He dressed and dated France's leading movie star, Jeanne Moreau. Cardin invented licensing. He is probably, secretly, the richest man in France. Today, he owns the blocks of Paris around the Élysée Palace, along with hotels and restaurants, including Maxim's. He decided in the early '60s to "sell" his name for manufacturers to emblazon on products other than perfume; he was the first designer to put his name on ties, socks, and luggage.

I'll never forget Louis Féraud screaming, "Cardin has even put his name on chocolates!" Louis was competitive, but no one could compete with Cardin. He was all business, no play.

By 1965, each major couturier had an arrangement with a manufacturer in America (or Japan or Brazil) to produce a copy line of each collection for the public. These manufacturers paid a royalty on their total sales to the designer. This process was invented by Pierre Cardin and fine-tuned by the sexy and charming Guy Rambaldi of Féraud, who wooed and married luscious mannequins or other fashion-related babes six times. At one point in 1966, Louis had more than twenty-five licenses.

Fashion shows were always presented in the fashion house on models who at that time charged about the same as a good hairdresser. There was a showroom, often mirrored, with room for eighty to one hundred chairs. There were two opening shows: the first for the press, the second for the buying clients, including the department stores. The models' hairdos and makeup were specific for each outfit, and they often wore hats. Each model carried a card with a number to identify the outfit for ordering. The music, if any, was soft. Some shows, like Dior's, were completely silent. The models were beautiful, but they were not stars, except for Bettina, who dated Aly Khan and Porfirio Rubirosa, but even she was not a supermodel who earned millions.

Today, fashion houses are owned by huge conglomerates that don't want to sell couture. Out of every fifty dresses presented, only three are meant to be worn and forty-seven are for publicity only. Today it's *all* show.

Think Dirty

In the fall of 1969, Mia and I showed for the first and only time in the courtyard in front of our boutique on rue Bonaparte. We built a runway, had it tented with a green-and-white striped awning, decorated with pots of pink geraniums, and featured the most beautiful models in Paris.

The theme was jumpsuits and hot pants, and the bride with the bare bust closed the show. The clothes were over-the-top look-at-me on the runway, but after the collection of mostly jumpsuits showed, nothing sold but a "cock buckle" belt, a piece of sculpture Mia created herself in an artist's atelier. Even worse,

Pat McColl of *Women's Wear Daily* (a single lady we knew as our friend) wrote a terrible article with the headline "Think Dirty" and labeled us antifeminists!

Mia was shocked and disappointed. I wasn't. I tried to convince her to let go and move on, but the photo sessions stopped and I sensed her changed mood. Fashion had moved on but we had not. Saint Laurent was showing his Russian collection. Everything was brown and embroidered, and he dropped skirts to the ankle and called them midi lengths. Everything was new and oh so chic, and now we were being put down for being oversexed by a conservative journalist.

All the more, this journalist, like many '60s intellectuals, thought that overt sexuality equaled a loss of power for women, who then became "objects." As the powerful cheerleader (with emphasis on leader), I have always felt that clothing, as per Steve's chart, is part of the sex act and has nothing to do with equality or intellectual prowess. Being fabulously dressed also allows a woman to express herself as an artist as she paints her "self-portrait." Even the dress one wears to go shopping matters. You never know who you will meet on any given day.

But the bottom line was that Mia and I had had almost six years of glory—of being photographed and adored everywhere we went while we were young and beautiful—and now it was time to move on.

When the new designs didn't sell in the shop, I told Mia, "Let's create some very salable clothes and make some money."

WHO GETS THE IDEA VS. WHO GETS THE CREDIT

Just as Chanel had invented so much in the twenties, times were a-changin'. Mia and I hit fashion at the right time and came up with so many designs that would represent the modern sexualized woman. Others have taken credit for some of our ideas—especially the mini and the wrap dress. (We always get credit for hot pants!) The claims of who came first are endless.

One night before she died, Eleanor Lambert, the famous fashion publicist who established the Best Dressed List, sat with me at a glamorous fashion ball in New York (something I rarely do anymore; I like to start my day with the sunrise and close it with the sunset). Fortunately, this night the great fashion lady spoke.

Eleanor Lambert looked at me with her vivid red curls, white powdered face, and bright blue eyes and said, "Aha, Vicky. It doesn't matter who invented what, all that matters is that you're *good* and that you *last*."

THE STORY OF CREATION

The story of creation always swims in controversy. Not only the story of the Creation but also the creation of the first bikini or the first trench coat or the first pin-striped suit.

Having claimed the creation of the miniskirt with Mia, I was alarmed to hear Mary Quant claim it in the summer of 1964 (her husband, Alexander Plunkett Greene, was her fashion executive and publicist). Asked who made the miniskirt, I say Mia and me, but Mary Quant would answer she did.

Every good artist should be known for creating something. Look back in art history:

Rembrandt	Realist portraits with light on the face on a dark background
Braque or Picasso	Cubism
Mondrian	Squares

Fashion designers need to claim a garment. Think of the great ones:

Coco Chanel	Cardigan jacket and quilted bag
Christian Dior	New Look midcalf skirt
Charles James	Puff coat
André Courrèges	Flat boots and boxy geometric dresses
Yves Saint Laurent	Smoking tuxedo suit and the safari suit

I tell fashion students when I lecture that one must close one's eyes and conjure up visually what a top designer stands for. If there's nothing, he or she is a journeyman designer. If a designer has really created something, the signature silhouette should pop up in your mind.

On My Own

Paris, 1969

Thanksgiving night in 1969 found me with Ron at Michael and Jacqui Goldman's annual party in their triplex opposite Notre Dame. Jacqui had been a lead dancer with Katherine Dunham, and then a singer. She gave up a career with the Metropolitan Opera to follow her love to Paris. The day after our shop reopened after the 1968 revolution, she walked in and bought her first Mia-Vicky gown.

Michael, a wealthy wine collector, was the son of Nahum Goldmann, who, along with David Ben-Gurion, helped found the State of Israel. He was asked to be its first president but declined. It was Michael's father who met with Anwar Sadat and Menachem Begin in 1978 to negotiate the peace with Israel and Egypt. A natural peacekeeper and liberal thinker, Michael's father had blessed his son's marriage to the talented black jazz dancer.

Jacqui was wise from her travels with the Dunham troupe and was a fabulous cook, especially at making soul food. Great American cooking was hard to come by in Europe in the '60s, so every African-American celebrity in Paris who missed home cooking would be invited. Among Jacqui's frequent dinner guests were Sidney Poitier, Harry Belafonte, and Miles Davis. Her decorations changed with each party, and on this particular Thursday night the theme was Tibetan Thanksgiving, with prayer banners criss-crossing the beams above the table. The dinner was French soul food.

After living in Paris for five years, I had become a true French foodie. I could cook and shop the local outdoor markets for exotic spices like a pro. I fell in love with an extraordinary restaurant in the nondescript 17th arrondissement when I was introduced to Chez Denis by Michael and Jacqui Goldman. Chez Denis in Paris in the late '60s and '70s was the world's most expensive restaurant. The PR woman Yanou Collart organized a meal for two for Craig Claiborne that cost $4,000. He wrote about it in *The New York Times*. Denis got such press that the French claimed unpaid back taxes and Chez Denis closed.

Denis served Steak Denis, where he injected foie gras by syringe for the stuffing. There were no prices at Denis, only a staggering bill at the end. It was the favorite restaurant of Aristotle Onassis and Maria Callas as well as all the world's presidents and, of course, Ron and I when we went as guests of Michael and Jacqui Goldman. Denis also had a great collection of Bugattis, which he sold in order to retire.

GIGOT D'AGNEAU À LA CHEZ DENIS
prepared by Jacqui Goldman in honor of Clint Eastwood

leg of lamb
goose grease or duck fat (always keep in the fridge;
    you can also use it to fry potatoes)
2–3 carrots, diced

3 tablespoons minced shallots

2 leeks, sliced

1 tablespoon cold champagne or dry white wine

MARINADE

1½ tablespoons fresh lemon juice

1 tablespoon lemon zest

2 tablespoons honey

juice of 1 onion

salt and fresh-ground pepper

1. Combine all the marinade ingredients in a bowl. Marinate the lamb for 24 hours in the refrigerator. Turn the meat every 8 hours.

2. Preheat the oven to 275°.

3. Remove the meat and save the marinade. Wipe the meat dry and rub with goose grease or duck fat. Put the lamb, carrots, shallots, and leeks in an ovenproof casserole. Brown the meat over low-medium heat on the stove, stirring. Add the marinade and several tablespoons of water.

4. Cover and roast for 2½–3 hours, until the meat is tender but still rare.

5. Remove the lamb to a plate and cover with foil to keep it warm.

6. Whisk the marinade-gravy in the casserole. If necessary, use a blender or food processor to make it smooth. Mix in the champagne.

For Jacqui Goldman's thirty-fourth birthday party in her *cave*, Monsieur Denis cooked this dish and presented Jacqui with a magnum of Romanée Conti 1934. *Quel gentilhomme!*

JACQUI GOLDMAN'S FRENCH BLETTE (COLLARD GREENS)
  1 blette
  1 lemon (juiced)
  ½ stick of butter
  1 small garlic clove, chopped
  whole dried peppercorns, ground

Remove the large green leaves from the blette. Cut them up in small pieces and put them in a pan. Add lemon juice, butter, and garlic. Then cover the greens with the pepper. Stir-fry over medium-high heat until the greens are slightly undercooked.

You can save the white root of the blette and use it to flavor the soup.

The Goldman's party was also in honor of Clint Eastwood, who was returning to civilization after filming *Kelly's Heroes* in the mountains of Yugoslavia. Ron had been working on the film with Clint and Donald Sutherland, and they asked Jacqui and me to invite *lots* of beautiful girls. The guys (both of them married) had been staying in a tiny Croatian hillside village for five months and were starved for female attention. Mia and Louis were at the party, too.

Two long refectory tables had been set up in the fifteenth-century loft for the twenty guests. The room was enormous, with three-foot-wide wooden beams forming a *grenier* and two giant walk-in fireplaces with logs crackling brightly. Incense floated through the air. Tibetan prayer banners hung from the beams. The music was Diana Ross's "Ain't No Mountain High Enough" and Jacqui disco-danced around the tables in an elegant Ikat embroidered robe, bestowing blessings on us all.

Mia noticed a sexy-looking guy talking to Clint and asked Ron who he was. Ron said he was working with Steve McQueen. Mia was introduced to Sandy McPeak and I watched her follow him to the den to learn to read the *I Ching*. Louis was dancing with some young models and didn't notice Mia leave the room.

The party lasted all night. There were people floating around on all three levels listening to music and dancing, some still tasting the wine. I didn't see Louis or Mia leave.

The next day, while Ron and I were still in bed recovering from the festivities, the phone rang. It was Mia, calling from the airport—with Sandy McPeak.

"I'm going to L.A.," she announced. "I'm leaving Louis, and leaving Paris for good."

"Oh, my God, Mia!" I screamed. "What about our business? I love you, you're my best friend!" I had never gone a day without talking to her, no matter where we both were, for the last ten years.

She was matter-of-fact. "Vicky, you'll be fine," she assured me. "Your dresses sell better than mine."

"Mia, I love you. You're my best friend. *Please* don't do this."

She told me how great it was with Sandy. She confided that she had reached levels of passion in just one night that had been impossible with Louis, twenty-three years her senior. She added, "Vicky, it was too hard to keep track of Louis. Sandy's the faithful type. I'm leaving Paris." Did she see it all in the *I Ching*?

Though I knew I should be happy for Mia, I felt my world fall apart.

I had never dreamed of designing alone, let alone working without my closest friend. I waited for three months, hoping it was a passing phase. She never came back. She left all her clothes, her emeralds, even her precious dog, Snoopy. She had never been a day without him, either. She left it all, never to return—even to retrieve Snoopy, who became Louis's beloved dog and rarely left his side.

There *may* have been some signs that Mia was unhappy with her situation as Mrs. Féraud. Her marriage to Louis must have included moderate infidelity; Louis needed the adoration of his models. Louis also continued to work with his ex-wife, but perhaps even more than with Louis, Mia's problem was with me. Our store had now been open for a year and we could see the success of our individual designs. Although Mia was the more original artist and colorist, and her designs were more exciting to look at on paper, all my designs just sold and sold. My dresses were wearable. A dress design would pop into my head, I'd sketch it quickly on paper, and once sewn, the dress would fit and flatter the body in such a way that a woman could wear it year after year.

Mia seemed happy in L.A. with Sandy. Their next-door neighbors were Jane Fonda and Donald Sutherland, who lived and protested together.

Vanessa Mitchell, John Heyman's former secretary, called

me in France to keep me informed of Mia's status. She said, "Jane and Don sometimes share hot tubs with Mia and they are all one big happy family on the private movie star beach." Mia had all new friends, and I was the past. She already had an artist's studio and was producing beautiful sculptures sprayed with bright red car paint.

Mia wrote me a long letter, saying good-bye for good. She said she wanted to be a sculptress and she was going to show some pieces in a gallery in L.A. She sent me the brochure, and I saw her work was very simple and beautiful. I was impressed with how quickly she had succeeded in what she really wanted to do. She wanted a new life and nothing to do with Paris or fashion. I was in a state of shock but didn't have time to grieve. It was fall. I had a fashion show to create. I forced myself to move on.

I produced the show by myself at the Meurice Hotel in the grand ballroom. Peter Sellers, who had been in *What's New Pussy-cat?*, came as my guest of honor to hold my hand for good luck. Ann Keagy from Parsons New York was there in the front row. She had begged me for a seat. No more "F for Fashion," apparently! At the end of the show, as I was taking my bows, Mia entered the ballroom in the back. After the show, she came backstage to say good-bye in person. We hugged. I did not see her again for twenty years.

A year later, Sandy called Ron and me one night. "She disappeared on me, too!" he wailed.

Mia divorced Féraud and found the man of her dreams. She married a fabulously successful New York businessman and has never left him. She changed careers and became the famous sculptor her mother, Lisa Fonssagrives Penn, had dreamed of becoming herself. Mia also became a mother and a celebrated jewelry designer—living a fabulous life on her own terms.

(left) My dad, David Tiel, and mom, Ethel Kipnes, in Hudson, New York, 1943.

From the author's collection

(below) Aunt Dora.

From the author's collection

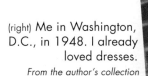

(right) Me in Washington, D.C., in 1948. I already loved dresses.
From the author's collection

(below) Bethesda Cheer Squad, 1961. (I'm in the front row, far right.)
From the author's collection

PARSONS SCHOOL OF DESIGN
410 EAST FIFTY-FOURTH STREET NEW YORK 22

Incorporated by the Regents of the University of the State of New York

ACADEMIC RECORD

Name **TIEL, VICKI KAY**
Permanent Address **3906 Montrose Drive**
Chevy Chase, Maryland

Date and Place of Birth **10/21/43 Washington, D.C.**

Country of Citizenship **USA**

Previous Schooling
HS **Bethesda** Yr. of grad. **'61**
College **Pratt Institute** Degree
Other

Name and address of parent, guardian, husband, wife
Mrs. Ethel Meisels, address above

Department **FASHION DESIGN**
Entered **1/31/62** Left **5/22/64**
Entrance status
If veteran, PL
Cert. of Grad. awarded **5/23/64**
Statement of Achievement awarded
Enrolled NYU for BFA degree ___ BS degree
PSD Scholarships

Other honors, awards

Course Number	Course Title	1st Sem. Grade	1st Sem. Points	2nd Sem. Grade	2nd Sem. Points	Total Points
	Advanced standing: (from Pratt)					
F 100	Art History				3	
F 123	Design & Pattern-making				3	
F 133	Fashion Fundamentals					
F 140	Basic Design				4	
F 170	Figure Drawing				1	
	Textiles				2	
	Physiology				2	15
	First year, 1961-62					
F 100	Art History			A	3	
F 123	Draping			B+	3	
F 133	Fashion Research			B+	1.5	
F 140	Fashion Illustration			C+	3	
F 170	Life Drawing			B-	3	
F 180	Model Drawing			B	3	16.5
	Second year, 1962-63					
F 200	Art History	A-	1.5	A	1.5	
F 223.1	Draping	B-	8.5			
F 240	Fashion Illustration	B	1.5	B-	1.5	
F 254	Pattern Drafting	C-	3	C+	3	16
F 280	Model Drawing	B	1.5	B	1.5	
F 210.2	Critic Problems			B	8.5	17
	Special Critic Problem			B	1	
	1963 EUROPEAN SUMMER SESSION			F		
	Third year, 1963-64					
F 331	Fashion Design	C	13	C+	13	
F 336.1	Textiles					16
F 340	Fashion Illustration	B+	3	B+	3	16

Three-year program for Certificate of Graduation consists of two 16-week semesters each year; 96 points required for graduation. Normal program 16 points each semester. 1 semester point = 1 hour/week of lecture courses. 1.5 semester points = 3 hours/week of studio courses. Statement of Achievement awarded to Special Students satisfactorily completing one year of study.

Grading: A 90-99, B 80-89, C 70-79, D 60-69, F = Failure. Inc. = Incomplete Work. + and — indicate upper and lower third within each grade range.

Graduation with Honors: Must rank in top 10% of class based on overall academic average.

Dean's List: Must have B + academic average.

Student entitled to honorable withdrawal unless otherwise noted. Transcript official only when bearing signature of Registrar and school seal.

(above left) My report card from Parsons School of Design. I was misunderstood there—look at my grades in pattern drafting and fashion design! *From the author's collection*

(above right) Parson's summer tour, Paris, 1963. Piscine Delight! Me (right) in a bikini I designed. *From the author's collection*

(above) My apartment, Greenwich Village, 1963. Peaches LaTour throws a costume party with Richard Horowitz (Roman Polanski's cousin). My sketches are on the wall.
From the author's collection

(left) Mia and me at my pink brownstone apartment, 7 Jones St., Greenwich Village—another party thrown by Peaches.
From the author's collection

(above) First photo with Ron Berkeley, December 1964. *Ron Berkeley*

(right) Mia and me with Wuffles, 1964. Wearing lace and our printed pantyhose and minidresses. *L. di San Marzano*

(top left) Peter O'Toole and Ursula Andress in *What's New Pussycat?*, 1964. Our first jumpsuit was in snakeskin cashmere jersey.
Metro-Goldwyn-Mayer Studios

(bottom left) Mia and me launch MADCAPS and bras and miniskirts, with Wuffles, 1965.
Paris Match

(left) *Life* magazine article, February 1965. The picture was taken on the balcony of our first apartment.
Paris Match

FASHION
Two American Girls Show Paris

If there's one place in the world where it would seem that two young, inexperienced American girls with aspirations in fashion design wouldn't stand a chance, it's Paris. But Mia Fonssagrives, 23 (*below, left*), and her partner, Vicki Tiel, 21, have the city of Dior and Balenciaga at their feet. After finishing at New York's Parsons School of Design, they took off for Paris last summer ("Send our diplomas c/o American Express!"). There they talked their way into doing two outfits for the young couturier Louis Feraud. Their brand of wacky chic— a combination of innocent seduction and clashingly compatible colors—was just what that yé-yé happy city wanted, and in no time they were the talk of the town. Now from their small apartment they find themselves in the enviable position of exporting their ideas back to the U.S. (*next page*).

(right) **Steve DeNaut.** *Don Hamilton*

(below) Ron and me, 1967. I'm wearing
a wrap dress Mia and I designed. It
appeared in *Redbook* magazine and was
sold at Bloomingdale's.
From the author's collection

(bottom) With Mia and Louis Féraud in
Corfu, 1968. *From the author's collection*

(top left)
Our shop's
opening
poster by Ed Baynard, Paris, 1968. Elizabeth
and Richard signed it for us. *Ed Baynard*

(top right) Mia and I launch hot pants, platforms,
and long sweaters in our sunken pit in the
boutique, 1968. *From the author's collection*

(right) The photo used on our shopping bags
and matchbook covers, 1968. My pose
showed up on Yves St. Laurent's
boutique wall. *From the author's collection*

(top) Our shop in Paris, 21 rue Bonaparte, 1968. *Paris Match*

(above) With Ron at a party in Paris, 1969. I launched the diamond bra. *Jack Nisberg*

(right) On the film set for *The Only Game in Town*, Las Vegas, 1969. Mia, Warren Beatty, and me on his knee getting a vibe. *From the author's collection*

(above) With Elizabeth and Mia on the set of *The Only Game in Town*. I'm wearing our mini wrap dress. *From the author's collection*

(right) Lisa Fonssagrives and Wuffles, my dog, in front of our shop in Paris, 1969. *From the author's collection*

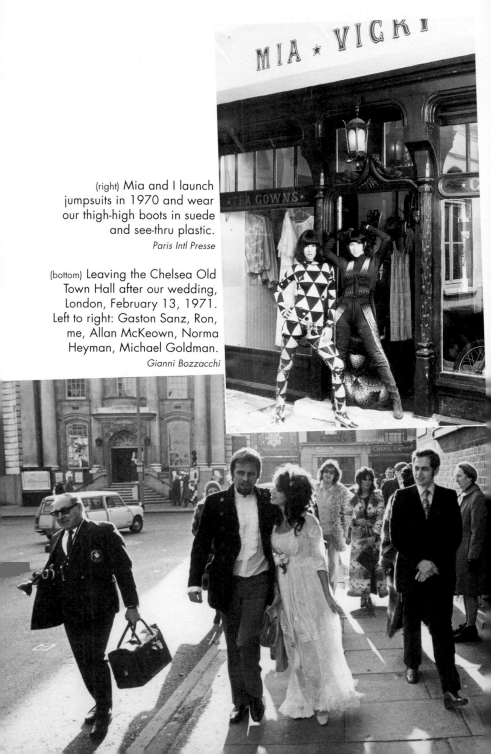

(right) Mia and I launch jumpsuits in 1970 and wear our thigh-high boots in suede and see-thru plastic.

Paris Intl Presse

(bottom) Leaving the Chelsea Old Town Hall after our wedding, London, February 13, 1971. Left to right: Gaston Sanz, Ron, me, Allan McKeown, Norma Heyman, Michael Goldman.

Gianni Bozzacchi

(top) Elizabeth with Ron and me
at our wedding reception.
Gianni Bozzacchi

(above) In 1971, Mia left the
business and Elizabeth and I
became partners. *Ron Berkeley*

(right) The *Kalizma*.
From the author's collection

(right) The Mill House, Autheuil-
Autheuillet, Normandy, 1972.
From the author's collection

(below) In 1975, nine months
pregnant with my son Rex, I go
out with Woody to a club and get
caught by paparazzi.
From the author's collection

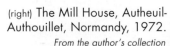

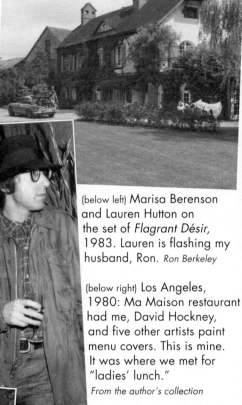

(below left) Marisa Berenson
and Lauren Hutton on
the set of *Flagrant Désir*,
1983. Lauren is flashing my
husband, Ron. *Ron Berkeley*

(below right) Los Angeles,
1980: Ma Maison restaurant
had me, David Hockney,
and five other artists paint
menu covers. This is mine.
It was where we met for
"ladies' lunch."
From the author's collection

(above) Me, surrounded by models, all in my designs, for an article in *People* magazine, September 1, 1986. *Barbara Bordnick*

(top) My sons, Richard and
Rex Berkeley, going to Camp
Kennebec, 1983.
From the author's collection

(above) Fishy with Mike.
From the author's collection

(right) With Aimee de Heeren,
Biarritz, 2003. She was 100.
From the author's collection

I hadn't spoken to her since receiving her "Dear Vicky" letter. Then in the midnineties, Fernand Fonssagrives had a large show in New York of his beautiful photos, including Lisa nude on the beach with a hat over her derrière—now selling for $150,000 per signed print. Tom Penn was there as well as David Tyson, the old crowd. Fernand had wanted to unite Mia and me—to have another hug before he died.

Mia arrived slender, silver haired, and so chic. I handed her a gift of my new fragrance, Originale, and mentioned I had sculpted the nude ladies myself and also that I was so proud of her and what she had accomplished as a sculptress. We hugged and spoke a bit about the old days and the fun we had had dancing all night in clubs wearing our outrageous outfits. And that was it. I will always miss her.

A Tie Salesman

Ralph Lauren breezed into my Paris shop one day in early 1970, right about the time Mia left. I had recently hired Suzanne White, an attractive American in Paris, to be my secretary-manager. Suzanne and Ralph were having an intimate conversation at my desk. It seemed they were casually dating whenever he was in town. He opened a large briefcase to show me his ties. They were thick Italian silk, solids and stripes, made in Italy, and they had a funny gold crest on them made to look like a tiny polo player. I was not impressed.

Suzanne left me to become a writer. She has written a dozen

books on Chinese astrology, which have sold millions of copies. She never had to work as a secretary again.

Ralph Lauren, of course, is no longer a "tie salesman." In the mideighties I befriended Buffy Birrittella, his chief designer (she's still there). Buffy was a friend of my client Andrea Dern, who was the wife of the actor Bruce Dern. Bruce had a fashion background; his family owned department stores in Chicago. During a party at the Derns' Malibu Beach Colony home, Buffy told the Derns some Ralph Lauren stories and I told mine. Buffy insisted I go to Ralph's next show in New York and surprise him, and so I did.

Buffy introduced me to Ralph, and I said, "Remember when you came to my shop in Paris with your ties?"

He turned his head and quickly walked away while he said, "No!"

"Hello Dahling"

London, 1971

Norma, now the former wife of John Heyman, was the original *Absolutely Fabulous* character played by Jennifer Saunders on the British TV show. She must have inspired the hit British show with her outrageous "champagne for breakfast, dahling" behavior, her lavender Jaguars, and her endless entertaining at home. She was the hostess with the mostest in London in the late sixties and early seventies and went on to a very successful career herself as a film producer after her divorce.

London had become mecca to Hollywood producers in the late '60s. Films could be shot in England very cheaply yet professionally at either Pinewood or Shepperton studios. Soon an expat American film community formed. Elliott Kastner, Peter Katz, Sandy Lieberman, and Marit Allen, who was also a popular film designer, all moved to London. Norma's huge drawing room off Sloane Square was a great place to gather and network. On Sundays, pubs closed at noon, so the film crowd would head for cocktails at Norma's with her boyfriend, the hairdresser Allan McKeown (who today is the husband/producer of the comic Tracey Ullman).

By 1971, Ron and I had been together for five years but were still not married. We were closer now that Mia had gone. One particular Sunday, Michael Caine, Elizabeth, and her current co-star Laurence Harvey were among the guests. I was at one end of the parlor talking to Norma's neighbor, a handsome young doctor. I mentioned that I had not been feeling well lately but I knew I couldn't be pregnant since I was on the pill.

Between champagne cocktails the doctor suggested a trip to the bathroom. We both slipped into the tiny powder room. He examined me very professionally, then announced, "You're pregnant, Vicky. About three months."

We emerged from the powder room and I ran over to Ron, who by then was fairly loaded.

"I'm pregnant!" I cried out with joy and then told him about the examination I had just experienced.

When told, Elizabeth Taylor declared, without skipping a

beat, "Well, Ron, you're getting married and I'm throwing the wedding in two weeks. You're all invited." She gestured to the room. The queen had spoken.

Ron looked at me sheepishly. He never got a chance to propose and he wouldn't dare disobey. The event was set in stone by Elizabeth, and that was that.

Fortunately his divorce was final and I could send for my dress, a little antique cotton voile and lace Victorian number I had optimistically purchased years before in a Parisian flea market. I'd figured that once the perfect dress was in the closet, the perfect man would come along.

I had the Beatles' Carnaby Street tailor make a black velvet double-breasted Edwardian suit with a white ruffled shirt for Ron to wear with pin-striped pants.

On the day of the big event, February 13, 1971, Michael and Jacqui Goldman, our best man and his wife, flew over from Paris and picked us up in Chelsea in Elizabeth's giant silver Rolls-Royce. It was ten A.M. Michael found Ron in the bedroom refusing to get dressed. I was in my 1890s ruffled lace gown with baby blue satin sash and cascading pastel roses, sobbing on the bed. It was a scene out of a Neil Simon play. Ron had emerged from the dressing room in jeans and cowboy boots. "I won't go out like a dolly boy."

I cried out, "I'm not getting married to you looking like you're looking. It's the suit and shirt I made for Burton to wear in *Candy*," I pleaded. "You can keep on your cowboy boots, darling."

Michael pulled the cork out of a bottle of Cristal champagne and walked Ron into the dressing room with two champagne flutes.

Just as his father had helped negotiate after the Six-Day War, Michael negotiated our fashion problem and a dashing Ron emerged from the bedroom wearing the velvet suit.

The wedding was held at Chelsea Old Town Hall followed by a lunch at San Lorenzo, followed by a dinner at Mimmo's, our favorite restaurant in London. Elizabeth invited eighty of our closest friends and most of the film crew, and I invited Louis Féraud (and my French friends). Louis showed up with a model in a see-through chiffon Féraud-tailored blouse (sans bra) and a long skirt. Obviously I couldn't object since I had pioneered the show-your-nipples look myself, but the problem was that her naked breasts somehow showed up in every wedding shot, so no photos could be released to the press except for the shots earlier at lunch at San Lorenzo, which Louis and the bare-chested model did not attend.

Ron, drunk from all the champagne and emotions, passed out before dinner was over and Larry Harvey politely helped me cut the cake. Mimmo's restaurant, forty years later, still had our wedding photos on the wall with Larry and me eating the cake as if it were our wedding. Later that night, when Ron came to and we finally left, a yellow MG convertible was waiting in front of Mimmo's on Elizabeth Street, a present from the Burtons.

We couldn't go on a honeymoon since Ron was shooting *X, Y and Zee* in London, so we spent all day Sunday with our wedding guests at our friend art dealer Lou Kaplan's town house in Chelsea. The house was filled with Lou's fabulous collection of William de Morgan art nouveau tiles and Lalique glass. The basement had a swimming pool and a sauna, and we continued drinking champagne in both. The wedding and the parties lasted an entire weekend.

On Monday morning I woke up at home and found the bedsheets red with blood. I was married at last, but I had lost our baby.

Surprise Party

Beverly Hills, 1971

I knew when I married Ron that he had a reputation in Hollywood as an expert "swordsman." I just never expected to have that reputation blow up in my face.

Once, during a stay in Beverly Hills, a friend of Ron's invited us to a New Year's Eve cocktail party to "celebrate our marriage." Mademoiselle Dove, the hostess, was a pretty thirtysomething girl around town. Her mother, Billie Dove, had been an old-time movie star and girlfriend of Howard Hughes. Our hostess was the daughter of her marriage to Robert Kenaston.

I wore a chic black 1940s cocktail dress, with diamond feather clips on my "belle décolleté."

The hostess introduced me to about six couples. With each introduction, I sensed a weird tension between the women and my husband. Was it my *poitrine*? Was my French chic too much for L.A.? Guess again, Vicky. I found out past midnight what the strange vibe was about.

The tipsy hostess pulled me aside and spilled the beans. "This party was a big joke on Ron," she said. "I invited everybody I knew who had slept with your husband, including me! I wanted him to see what he's missing, now that he's married."

I thought the "big joke" was funny and was amused by her

cunning. If her party was meant to upset me, it didn't work. I was in love. Ron was mine.

Champagne Overdose or Motherhood

1971–1975

Our baby had been the raison d'être for our marriage, but I figured that Ron and I had been together for almost seven years and the Burtons had given us a sports car as a wedding gift, and all of London and lots of Paris had flown over to the magical wedding, so I took the loss of the baby as *inshallah*—meant to be. The party continued.

I lost another baby in 1973, and the doctor (whom I saw less often than the vet) said, "Vicky, when you really want to be a mother, change your lifestyle." I guess he meant to stop drinking champagne and dancing all night at Castel's, Régine's, Studio 54, Le Club, Annabel's, Tramp, and Corsetti in Rome.

I took his advice, and in 1974 at the merry age of thirty-one I got pregnant and stayed pregnant—and stayed in bed for six months in Normandy. In 1975, baby Rex, named for Rex Harrison, his godfather, came into our life and the party was over.

After being bored with being pregnant for nine months and lying low, I went dancing at Castel's on rue Princesse until midnight and felt funny and went home, which was upstairs. Jean

Castel and Ron and I shared penthouses—his on the top of rue Princesse, ours on the top of rue Guisarde—however, both could be accessed by walking out Castel's back door into a small courtyard and up a private staircase.

No one, including Ron, had noticed I was gone. I had to call a friend to go to Castel's and get Ron out of a private room where he was drinking with his celebrity pals to come upstairs to take me to the hospital.

I had my last dance night on January 2, 1975.

Motherhood changed all that and more.

We moved to a huge apartment on nearby boulevard Saint-Germain at place de l'Odéon, a few doors down from Antonio Lopez, my school friend and now a world-renowned fashion illustrator. I moved my entire design staff of six women into the front rooms and we lived with fashion for ten years so I could be with baby Rex and, later, baby Richard (named for Richard Burton, his godfather).

The New York Times photographed me in bed with baby Richard in 1978 and wrote about my living in the atelier for a home fashion issue. The apartment was 1930s meets 1970—silver sleek, with zebra prints and mirror balls and large Antonio-framed black-and-white sketches. There were black mirrored tables and mint green couches, dogs, cats, babies, two nannies (one with a turban and the other, Madame Pomme, in a frilly French apron), a Portuguese driver, and Tunisian-Italian seamstresses.

The boys learned French, English, Portuguese, some Italian, and a few curse words in Arabic.

Being a mother changed my lifestyle. I focused on home and work, not parties. I decided to develop a strong couture business in the stores in America and soon had twenty-five accounts buying my handmade creations. I enjoyed being a hands-on designer like Coco Chanel—measuring and designing gowns for each individual woman, entering their lives with a special dress for a special moment. Bergdorf Goodman opened a Vicky Tiel shop on the second floor, where I introduced custom-made French gowns. I spent five days each month in New York, personally measuring my clients. Madame Pomme, the boys' baby nanny, watched them while I was gone.

Paris turned out to be a great place to raise the kids. Our home was a lot of fun for them, especially during the teenage years. We had *boums* for their classmates who weren't allowed to or couldn't afford to have big parties. Our thirty-foot living room with floor-to-ceiling windows overlooking the Seine provided a perfect backdrop for the *boum*, which is a blow-out sort of celebration, complete with nonstop DJ music.

I had a new ambition—to be known as a cool mom! My boys grew up going to regular French schools, not stuffy private ones. Their friends were the offspring of concierges, models, actors, and bistro owners. They learned proper French as well as the local argot. The boys had it made living in Saint-Germain-des-Prés and going to school one block from the Café de Flore and two blocks from my shop.

Rex's greatest moment was in high school, when his assignment (from me) was to help with the "next couture model" competition. At fifteen, he had to interview and measure all the girls in his high school who tried out. He had to determine who was 35–25–35, five nine, and had the right look. The chosen young lady would be the official Vicky Tiel model for the press. Rex and his friend Issam finally chose a beautiful classmate and soon her photos were seen all over the world.

With a father who was away six months of the year, shooting movies on location, and a mother who worked long hours five days a week, my boys learned to be independent. They won at sports and eventually evolved into creative, compassionate adults. They also learned the difference between rayon and silk.

Rex is still a great help with my business and is also a talented videographer and decorator. Richard works on films all over the world and speaks many languages including some Zulu. I am extremely proud of both of them.

WOODY'S REVENGE

Ron was away making a movie with Richard Burton and Rex Harrison. I was eight and a half months pregnant with Rex and fifty pounds overweight. Woody Allen was in Paris and wanted to go out to dinner. We were still friends, always happy to see each other.

Woody wanted to go to the opening of a new jazz club. I told him how big I was and he told me he didn't mind. As we left the club around midnight, a paparazzo photographed us. Woody had his hat pulled down trying to hide his face. His forearm was wrapped around me, hiding my big belly. Giant breasts were popping out of my panne velvet wrap gown. The look on our faces was shock and surprise. The photo appeared in the *National Enquirer* under this headline: "Vicky Tiel Is Carrying Woody Allen's Baby!"

My mother-in-law sent me the article from California in a plain envelope with no letter. I guess she sent her son the article as well, because the next night Ron came back early from filming with these words: "If that baby has red hair, I'm divorcing you."

I did not reply.

Rex, of course, was not Woody's baby, but he did come out with a full head of Shirley Temple red curls. Ron didn't divorce me.

I told Woody the story, and he was happy to get even. The next time I was in New York, we had dinner at Elaine's, and the next week, on Easter, I was photographed by Bill Cunningham kissing Woody in front of Bergdorf Goodman. It was printed in the Sunday *Times* Style section, in an article about Easter hats.

The Power of the Flash

In 1968, Richard Burton paid $180,000 to rent a boat on the Thames River in London for Daisy, Elizabeth's little black-and-white shih tzu. There was a six-month quarantine for all pets entering England. So while working on films in London, Elizabeth preferred to house her beloved dog on a boat rather than to lock her up. She had been staying in a kennel in Paris, where Elizabeth could visit her only on weekends. When we were in Rome, about to return to London, I made an offer I was soon to regret—especially since Daisy had just given birth to four puppies!

I told Elizabeth that I would smuggle the dogs into England.

The thinking went like this: "Oh, Elizabeth! I owe you this. You've been so wonderful to me and Ron. It's the least I can do!"

So I was at the vet's office in Paris with the dog and her pups, and I needed a plan. I decided that distraction always works. I would drive my purple Mini Cooper S to London via the boat ferry from Calais to Dover. I would hide the dogs in the car, under my seat.

I asked the vet to put a plaster cast on my leg. I then signed it with colored pens like graffiti to make it look very old. The vet gave me mild tranquilizers for Daisy and her pups and a stronger one for myself.

Ron's son Craig was the driver. The plan was to hide Daisy *et famille* under the floor-length silver-white fox coat over a white crocheted microminidress and my thigh-high cast. Because of the uncomfortable cast, I went out like Ursula: commando.

When we arrived at the hovercraft in Calais, Craig said, "My mother has a broken leg, and she can't get out of the car." The boat official agreed to let me stay.

The crossing went as planned. It took about two hours.

The mild dose of tranquilizers we gave the dogs worked. They were passed out under my car seat. We made it across the channel and onto English soil. The car left the ferry and proceeded to the dreaded customs line.

Then the unexpected happened. The line was way too long. We had to wait forever. The pups were trying to scamper out from under me. Daisy woke up.

As we pulled up to the booth for our inspection, the young customs officer asked me, "How much money do you have?"

Oh, my God! We had been so busy with the dogs that we'd forgotten about money. We had about $20 between us. The customs officer was stern.

"I can't let you in with that," he barked. "You need at least $200 per person to enter."

The officer came to my window. I opened the car door and swung out my leg in a cast ever so slowly to give the officer one giant flash. I got out beside him and smiled.

"Officer," I said, "don't you know who I am? I never carry money." I saw he appreciated the view.

"Oh, I'm so sorry, I didn't recognize you," he replied, confused, of course, not knowing who in the world I was. "Please excuse me. Go ahead!"

I never forgot the power of the flash.

The Power of the Poncho

Yugoslavia, 1970

John Heyman, widely credited with creating structured financing in the film industry, convinced Richard to portray Marshal Tito in a film based on a true incident in his life, *The Battle of Sutjeska*. The payoff was $1 million in cash from Tito himself. The hook was that we got to live in Tito's white marble palace in Kupari, south of Dubrovnik on the beautiful Adriatic coast. Tito had a great wine cellar, and we were told to help ourselves. Tito absolutely loved Richard Burton's voice and had chosen him from all the actors in the world to portray him. The film was for release only in the Eastern bloc, not for Western audiences.

The entire film was to be shot in the high mountains close to Mostar, near the beautiful Ottoman bridge that was blown up during the last civil war and recently rebuilt. The movie was mostly battle scenes. There was no place suitable in that hostile and almost vertical terrain in the mountains to live or eat. The Yugoslavian crew didn't mind sleeping in tents. But that wouldn't do for Richard.

He decided to stay at Tito's palace and be helicoptered up to the mountains each day from the coast. At five o'clock every morning Richard and Ron would be coptered up to the film location, a harrowing forty-five-minute flight through treacherous mountain passes.

At eleven, Elizabeth and I would copter up to join them for lunch. We would read books and sun ourselves all afternoon while our husbands worked. Then at four P.M. the copter would take us all back down the mountain.

There was no real reason for us to fly up the mountain every day. There were no women to worry about or spy on, since the cast was all male. There were no pubs to keep Richard and Ron out of. Our reason was pure boredom. It was more fun to fly helicopters to lunch. We would carry a picnic lunch for our husbands, with great wines and delicacies prepared by Tito's chef. It was more exciting than lying around the Adriatic Sea reading murder mysteries. Elizabeth and I were excitement junkies.

The only problem was that our constant flights were wearing out the creaky Russian helicopter from World War II. One day, we were flying up the mountain and I was wearing a red foxtail poncho. It was from Elizabeth's furrier Soldati, in Milan, and *very* well made. Suddenly the helicopter door on my side flew off, leaving a gaping hole. I started to get sucked out into the sky.

Mighty Elizabeth quickly grabbed me with both hands. She managed to grip one of the foxtails and then the poncho itself and slowly drag me back into the helicopter. For every second of the ten more minutes until we landed, Elizabeth held on to the poncho and kept me from getting sucked out again. Hooray for top-quality clothing—and a strong-willed woman who can save your life.

Another day, when I remained at the palace, a different helicopter returning from the film shoot broke down in the air and was forced to land in a farmer's field instead of Tito's private airstrip. Richard, Elizabeth, and Ron walked to the coastal road. They hiked along the road, sticking their thumbs out, and were soon picked up by some American tourists in a van.

Imagine their shock, running into famous movie stars hitchhiking along the highway. I love to picture Elizabeth sweetly purring, "Our helicopter broke down and we're terribly lost. By any chance, do you know how to get to Marshal Tito's place?"

Just before filming ended a helicopter finally crashed and tragically killed the pilot.

Thirty years later, I was at a posh dinner party in Bedford, New York, when the conversation about politics stalled. To liven things up, I mentioned I don't like politics because the political leaders are all power-crazy gourmands, and when I lived at Marshal Tito's house in the late '60s, although he was an ardent Communist, he had a marble palace with a basement full of the world's best wines and champagnes.

The next day when I called the hostess to thank her, she told me that nobody, including movie critic Rex Reed, believed a word I said.

I stopped attending fancy dinner parties. After years of living with Elizabeth Taylor, I couldn't relate to normal people.

Dinner with Coco Chanel

Paris, 1970

It is said that women dress for other women and out of a spirit of competition. This is true. But if there were no longer any men, women would not dress at all.

—COCO CHANEL

Coco Chanel had just designed Elizabeth's dress for the opening of the lavish cabaret Lido, a white crystal "Cleopatra" chiffon with a *plunging* neckline. It was scheduled to be the event of the year. The following week Elizabeth invited Alexandre, her hairdresser, and Coco Chanel to dinner.

The party was in Coco's honor and was to be held in Alexandre's mirrored penthouse overlooking the Bois de Boulogne.

To my surprise, I was invited. When I was a student, I had done a paper on Coco Chanel's life—how she loved to shock, how she invented sportswear, how she influenced women to wear pants, sweaters, short hair, and costume jewelry. My heroine!

Elizabeth knew this and loved the chance to introduce me to my idol. Lots of famous European socialites were invited. The Burtons, Ron, and I were the only English-speaking guests.

I felt I had to design something special to wear when I met the woman who had lifted the skirt to show the ankle and shocked the world. I decided to make a dress to represent the modern girl, but in the world's most expensive fabric. I went to Marie-Thérèse's shop on the rue de Bac. Karl Lagerfeld and I often fought over one-of-a-kind cuts left over from the 1920s and '30s haute couture samples. Marie-Thérèse would delicately unwrap each fabric, cut as if it were gossamer from the stars.

I selected one yard of a silver art deco lace in a spiderweb pattern with four delicate birds made of pearls flying across the front. Their beaks were rubies and their eyes were emeralds. The fabric was unique.

The dress was also utterly see-through. I wore a nude bra and panty hose, with mule slippers, and pearls. My jewel-necked dress stopped just below my crotch. When I entered Alexandre's penthouse, Richard Burton introduced me to Coco.

"I'd like you to meet my daughter," he said. "Vicky Tiel. She's a designer." Since there had been articles about me in the Paris press, she must have known about me and my miniskirts. She sat down next to me with a sour look on her face. Richard sat on my other side, and we all made polite conversation for a few minutes.

Then Coco turned to me and in a shrill voice asked, "What are you? A child or a woman?"

I took a deep breath and answered with a smile, "I am you— when you were young."

She stared at me, squinted her eyes under her white straw hat, and then smiled and went "Hummmmph!" It was a French "Hummmmph!" and it meant she approved.

I had never seen anyone like her: black crow eyes, black hair like a wig coming out of a straw hat. Her suit was white wool, all quilted, with a white blouse underneath and ten rows of white pearls draping her neck, and white ivory bracelets. White on white, with Chanel beige-and-black shoes. She was like a chic cloud.

She then turned on poor Maurice Chevalier, who had invited Mireille Mathieu, the French pop singer. Mireille came from the bad part of Arles. She was said to be the new Edith Piaf.

"Her parents are peasants!" screamed Coco, sending Mireille fleeing the party in tears, Maurice at her side. Coco must have forgotten that she, too, was born a peasant. The home she was born in had a dirt floor. I thought it was sad that she had forgotten her origins and she now was so hurtful to someone who shared the same heritage—poverty.

Coco was not a self-made woman. She started as a milliner (like Halston) in a small shop in Deauville and captivated a series of rich lovers who financed her shops. First Arthur "Boy" Capel, then Duke Dmitri of Russia, and at last the Duke of Westminster, the richest man in England, who met her in 1925. She opened her shop on rue Cambon three years later and it still stands there today.

They loved Coco, financed her, but never married her. In her time, rich men never married out of their class. Yet Coco was admired by all and had many friends in the bohemian arts community, such as Jean Cocteau, Sergey Diaghilev, Paul Iribe, and, of course, Igor Stravinsky. He adored Elizabeth and called her the most beautiful creature on earth.

Coco refused to speak a word of English. I spent the night translating. She spoke to me about her life, holding my hand, giving me some helpful warnings. "*Ma petite*, Vicky," she said, and instructed me never to sell my name or my perfume.

At the end of the evening, she gave me a hug, as if to send me off on my career. I like to think that she was tickled that someone actually stood up to her and reminded her, for a very brief second, what she had been when she, too, was very young.

One year later, when Coco died at her apartment in the Ritz Hotel at eighty-eight, someone came to her room before her body was discovered and stole all her jewelry. The thief was never caught, and the famous Verdura jewelry—those ropes of pearls, her gigantic pins, and all the beautiful jeweled ivory cuffs that she designed—were never recovered.

COCO CHANEL'S LESSONS

- Find a niche. She developed sportswear, separates, jersey as a fabric to wear, and the cardigan jacket (the Chanel jacket) worn by women for seventy years.

- Design something classic that you can wear forever.

- Find a signature style you can be known for. When a customer closes her eyes, your look should be able to come to mind immediately.

- Don't copy, be original.

- Always wear your own designs, never anyone else's.

- Network in life without shame. Use whomever you know to help you get ahead.

- Create your own fragrance and the bottle that represents you. My bottle has nude goddesses, which I sculpted. Coco designed hers.

- Never sell your perfume company. Don't sell or license your perfume name to anyone. Coco complained to me about her mistake in selling to Alain Wertheimer, who today still owns Chanel, and his becoming really, really rich on her creation.

Lunch with Dorian

Paris, 1971

One winter Sunday morning before noon, I got a phone call from Dorian Leigh. "Vicky, darling, I have a reservation for two at Chez Marie [Madame Cartet]. I waited for two months to get it. Can you join me?"

I said I would be delighted, as long as I could bring my two dogs.

Chez Marie, unlike Chez Denis, was not a real restaurant. It was an "upstairs wine cellar" with a couple of tables and a little French grandmother who could really cook. She did not serve dinner, only lunch three days a week. The price was fixed at $60 per person, which was a lot in 1971. The price included wine, but Dorian drank only pink champagne, and she brought her own Krug.

Lunch started at twelve thirty, and we ate for four hours. We began with homemade brioche smothered with Hungarian foie gras and ended with apple and apricot tarts swimming in crème fraîche. We ate and drank like fools.

Suddenly it was five o'clock and it was starting to get dark. I drove Dorian home in my new yellow MG. As we approached place Pigalle, there were barricades across the street.

"Darling," said Dorian, "please turn left. I must go down the street!"

I obeyed, and before I knew it, a policeman seemed to pop over the front of my car.

Did I run over him?

He limped to my door, sprung it open, and pointed a gun at my head.

"Vous-vous prenez pour James Bond!" Dorian exclaimed with glee.

We were both arrested for driving down a blocked road, hitting a policeman, and driving drunk.

It turned out that there was a demonstration against Prime Minister Chaban-Delmas, who had neglected to pay his taxes.

Dorian was wearing her long Russian sable and I was wearing my Italian foxtail poncho. Holding my Yorkies, Wuffles and Fang, we crawled into the back of the paddy wagon.

At the jail, Dorian and I were put in a large cage and my dogs in a smaller cage nearby. It was Saturday night and Place Pigalle jail was quickly filling up with hookers and thieves. There was also a sobbing woman who had stabbed her lover.

We had to visit the bathroom as a group, in one long line, and on the jail's schedule, not ours. The "toilets" were holes in the floor and we had to squat over them to pee. I managed to have some privacy with my poncho. Dorian's sable coat was too long and difficult to maneuver, however, and she had to hold it up.

At dawn, they let Dorian out of the cage. The guard laughed and told me I would get a year in jail for drunk driving. Around noon a well-dressed detective took me into a private room.

"Some phone calls have been received at the station," he said, "and unfortunately you are being released." He looked defeated. "I have to let you go."

Dorian had pulled some strings. Feeling guilty, she must have called some ex-lovers.

Years later, on vacation with Vivien Best, we were having lunch at a villa on the Côte d'Azur on a mountaintop in Èze. We were seated at an outdoor table overlooking the sea, with French "high society" and no Americans.

The host approached me and said, "Ah, Miss Tiel! I'm the gentleman who got you out of jail."

"Thank you, monsieur," I said demurely, "and how did you do that?"

"Madame," he replied, "I am the lawyer of the president, and I recommend you give up driving."

The Seduction of Warren Beatty

Paris, 1972

A sultry summer night found Ron and me eating dinner at the charming sawdust-strewn restaurant Bistro Julien. Ron whispered to me, "Tonight should be very amusing." Seated at our table were Warren Beatty, Brigitte Bardot, and a Frenchman we didn't know.

We wondered if Brigitte would be Warren's next conquest. Did this mean Julie Christie was being phased out? Warren had been coming to my shop since its opening, bringing his girlfriends along. Through Warren I had met and dressed Julie Christie, Michelle Phillips, and Goldie Hawn.

The tiny bistro was directly under Brigitte's apartment on avenue Paul Daumer. It seemed to be her hangout, since the waiters knew just what and when to serve Mademoiselle Bardot, who was wearing black hot pants, thigh-high boots, and a fluffy peekaboo lace blouse. A tight black belt cinched in her twenty-one-inch waist.

The waiters plied Warren, Ron, and the Frenchman with wine, champagne, liqueurs, and port. By one A.M., we had been drinking for four hours, listening to Warren charm Brigitte with his stories, his teeth, his hair, and those delicious dimples. It was clear that he was going to score with Brigitte on this, their first date.

Suddenly she exclaimed, in English, "Now you three men must race the elevator of my building up to zee sixth floor. Whoever wins gets to sleep with me!"

She was so beautiful, so blond, so . . . Brigitte Bardot that she somehow convinced even Ron to join the race. Brigitte and I took the old French elevator, and she smiled at me, close-mouthed, like a cat.

Poor Warren raced his heart out. Totally red faced, he won by a floor or two. My husband came in second. Brigitte dismissed the losers at the door and dragged Warren inside. The little boy in him glowed as he followed his prize inside.

Ron dropped his head.

The next day a joyous Warren appeared in my shop to announce he was throwing a party at l'Hôtel for Brigitte, Peter Ustinov, and Yul Brynner. Ron and I were invited to join the party in a private alcove he'd reserved. That night, we all waited for Brigitte.

Warren described how clever and interesting she was, and said they were a perfect love match. "Her English is so adorable, even her feet are beautiful. At last, the woman for me!" he boasted.

As the evening wore on, there was no sign of Brigitte.

A single Richard Burton joined the party and struck up a brilliant conversation with Ustinov and Brynner. All three actors were great storytellers, three jewelers with words, and had a wonderful time discussing politics and acting and reciting poetry.

Through it all, Warren remained sullen and quiet. Brigitte never appeared.

Later I learned from Nathalie Delon, another French sex kitten, that we had witnessed Brigitte's mating ritual. Every man she sleeps with must be able to drink until drunk, race up six flights of stairs, beat other men to the finish line, and then satisfy her in bed all night long.

So somehow Warren had won the battle but lost the war. The man who loved women had been defeated. Perhaps Warren hadn't been in France long enough to fully meet or even understand BB's challenge. Or maybe it's just that Warren was not really a drinker.

But what a couple they would have made!

"Happy Birthday, Elizabeth"

Budapest Hilton, February 1972

Grace is desperate to get out of Monte Carlo," Elizabeth told me. "She is *bored* up there in Monaco and wants to come and party without the prince. She loves to dance, and Rainier doesn't."

I knew Monaco. Mia and I had worked on the John Frankenheimer film *Grand Prix* and had lived in Monaco for a month in the Hôtel de Paris dressing Françoise Hardy in miniskirts and poor-boy sweaters. It had been a real dream. We got to meet Prince Rainier and Princess Grace, and Fred Chandon, of Moët & Chandon, the makers of our favorite champagne, Dom Perignon. When I was a Parsons student, I had visited Monte Carlo with my classmate Marty Ross, who had joined my German sweetheart (*my* Rainer) and me in Saint-Tropez. When it was time to return to the boat to take us back to New York, Marty and I made a quick visit to Monte Carlo, and we slept in a secluded doorway just down from the palace. We had spent all our money on Italian shoes, and I bought my first Jean Cacherel skintight striped blouse. The police came and arrested us and took us and our bags of clothes to a lovely antique jail so we could have a bed to sleep in. In the morning, they had prepared pan bagnat sandwiches for our breakfast.

PAN BAGNAT

This is the classic lunchtime dish in the Midi.

- ½ teaspoon Dijon mustard
- 2 tablespoons olive oil
- 1 tablespoon red wine vinegar
- 2 anchovy fillets, minced (optional)
- salt and fresh-ground pepper
- 1 long baguette, sliced lengthwise
- 1 can tuna, packed in oil, mashed with a fork
- 1 tomato, sliced
- 2 tablespoons sliced pitted olives, green, black, or a mixture
- ½ red onion, sliced
- 1 hard-boiled egg, sliced
- lettuce leaves
- 8 large fresh basil leaves

1. Put the mustard, oil, vinegar, anchovies, and salt and pepper in a jar with a cap. Shake until frothy.

2. Pull out some of the soft bread to make a cavity in the baguette. Layer the remaining ingredients (in any order). Top with the dressing. Press the sandwich together.

3. Wrap the sandwich tightly in foil or plastic wrap, and place it in a plastic bag. Put a weight on the sandwich, such as a cast-iron skillet topped with a filled kettle. After 7–10 minutes, flip the sandwich and weight it for another 7–10 minutes.

4. Cut the sandwich in half and share with a friend.

Elizabeth decided to throw a queen-size party for five hundred guests to celebrate her fortieth birthday. All the hotels in Buda and Pest were filled with family, friends, and just about anybody who had ever known Elizabeth Taylor and wanted to join the fun. Her guest of honor was to be Princess Grace Kelly of Monaco, Hollywood royalty. The two women had been friends since their early days at MGM.

Roger Moore and his wife, Luisa; Richard Harris; Michael Caine and his soon-to-be wife, Shakira; Norma Heyman; and Allan McKeown were all coming from England. Ron and I hung out with the English contingent during the festivities. Along with Richard's Welsh family members, our group partied the longest and the hardest.

There were three full days of events: breakfasts, lunches, dinners, cocktails, trips around the city, boat rides up the Danube. Budapest was a novelty destination, the Eastern bloc having just opened up. English and American low-budget films were suddenly being shot there.

We were there on the Buda side shooting *Bluebeard* with Richard Burton. I was doing the costumes for the various women Bluebeard/Burton seduced in real life as well as on the screen.

Nathalie Delon and Raquel Welch were both attempting (and somewhat succeeding) to get Richard into their beds, or as Nathalie told me, as far as her bathtub. He passed out in the tub from too much vodka and nothing happened.

Raquel and I were not close. She was known in Hollywood to be "difficult," but only off the set, for makeup artists and designers. I was to make her clothes in Paris and fly to L.A. for fittings. The measurements came, and to my shock she had my figure exactly, with two-inch-longer legs. We had the same exact bustline.

Raquel was ever the diva at Western Costumes in L.A., where the fitting was held in a giant dressing room. When Raquel tried on the dresses, her face revealed that she was waiting to start a "diva" routine. But . . . she was shut down. There were no corrections. The fit was perfect.

Stunned, she asked, "How did you do this, Miss Tiel?"

"Darling, Raquel. We have the exact same body."

She barely spoke to me again.

Lunch on a Hungarian film set was a cart carrying a pot of lard and huge round loaves of bread. The thick country bread was sliced and spread with lard and paprika sprinkled on top.

Elizabeth, of course, had exotic foods at her birthday celebration: Iranian gray caviar, Maine lobsters, champagne, Sancerre rosé and red Rothschild wines flown in for her party. Great local chefs were hired to prepare a feast Hungary hadn't seen since the revolution. As her favorite fried chicken was not possible, we had Hungarian chicken Kiev and five desserts, plus birthday cake.

We danced until dawn in beautiful gowns and jewels. The men wore black tie. At one point we had a conga line composed of Michael Caine, Raquel Welch, Ringo Starr, Liza Todd, Richard and Elizabeth, Alexandre the hairdresser, Welsh rugby players, Richard's eighty-year-old sister, Peter Ustinov, Richard's chauffeur Gaston Sanz, Ron, me, and of course, Princess Grace.

Princess Grace loved champagne. She was flying. At about four A.M. she was leading the conga line in a chiffon gown that flowed over tables and chairs. Her Alexandre hairdo was long gone and flying loose.

The next day Grace left, but not before thanking Elizabeth for the time of her life. Gaston, the chauffeur and the ex—martial arts champion of France, danced with Grace until the end of the party. He was the only one who could keep up with Her Highness.

Age forty was the turning point in Elizabeth's marriage to Richard. It was a milestone for female movie stars, and the leading lady parts diminished or dried up.

In the power struggle among leading ladies, one-upmanship is the name of the game, and Richard was the target. The Burtons' marriage couldn't survive Bluebeard's seven wives. Every one of the actresses—Raquel, Virna Lisi, Nathalie Delon, Karin Schubert, Joey Heatherton—had to seduce Richard on- and off-screen to show up Elizabeth. She fled to Rome. It was the first time I saw cracks in their "public" marriage. Their private, intense love and eternal interest in each other never diminished. She was his rock, his center, and she remained so until his death.

More BreakUps

Paris, 1975

One afternoon in Paris, Warren Beatty came into my shop and gave me a big long hug. "I'm at l'Hôtel shooting a film [*Shampoo*]. I'd like you to meet my leading lady."

I heard a familiar-sounding voice behind him saying, "Hiiiiieeeeeeee!" and Goldie Hawn waltzed in. "Warren has told me so much about you. I love your dresses—can I try some on?" Her voice had such a familiar ring.

"Are you from Maryland?" I asked.

"Yes," she answered, giggling. "How can you tell?"

"Because you sound just like me," I said. "Where did you go to high school?" It turned out she went to Blair and I went to Bethesda–Chevy Chase and we had both been cheerleaders. Our schools were archrivals. We had even cheered against each other the year B–CC beat Blair sixty-three to zero.

Goldie and I discovered we had a lot more in common, and a wonderful friendship was formed. I created a white draped jersey dress for her to wear to the Oscars.

Goldie had the ultimate big-blue-eyed-dumb-blonde look. But she was probably the smartest actress in Hollywood. At least the smartest one I had ever met. She seemed to have it all: brains, beauty, talent, friends, children, and business smarts. She was also just plain nice. A very unusual combination.

She would say to me, "You may think I'm the most together lady in Hollywood, but you're wrong. Meryl Streep is way above me in all categories. You just don't know her. Even Sally Field is a more 'together' person than I am."

I'd say, "Goldie, get off it! You are the best."

Later on, when our marriages were both in trouble and we both met other guys, I fell for a fisherman in Florida and Goldie fell for a Frenchman, Yves Rénier. So I saw a lot of her in the '80s when our kids were young; we were both "hot stuff" for being in our late thirties. We dressed in similar uniforms: tight jeans, antique T-shirts, and great belts we collected from our world travels. We both loved to go to flea markets and buy mirrored lamps, art nouveau statues of ladies, and embroidered linens and then we would sit in the outdoor cafés of Saint-Germain and gossip.

Yves Rénier was a TV star in France. He played the Don Johnson cop type, Inspector Moulin. The show has run for thirty years. A sexy, rugged, blond, blue-eyed, athletic hunk, Yves desperately wanted to marry Goldie, but a romance across the world was too difficult.

Yanou Collart was Goldie's publicist in France. Yanou told me that she would often be woken up in the middle of the night by a phone call.

The voice was Goldie's, saying, "Hiiiieeeee, honey, I miss you."

And Yanou would have to tell her, again, that she was Yanou, not Yves. In Goldie's address book Yves and Yanou were side by side.

Eventually, Goldie met an actor closer to home, and after a few years left Yves for an American version of the same rugged manly type, Kurt Russell.

Yves was despondent. He wrote a song called "PCV" about

losing Goldie and it became a French pop hit. He had taped her phone calls to him and her voice is the background of his song, with that same Maryland accent, saying, "Yves, I love you, but good-bye."

Goldie didn't know about the recording so I sent her a copy, with their breakup recorded on it for all posterity.

Goldie didn't get upset with Yves. She laughed her famous giggle. "Oh yes. Yves! He's so French, so dramatic!"

UTTER CONFIDENCE

Goldie Hawn told me she never manipulates men. She claims to have no seduction technique. Men must love her for herself. If they don't, then she says, "To hell with 'em."

Seduction is control, but control is not seduction. Controlling people are not seductive.

Every woman, except Goldie, has her own seduction technique as natural and individual as how she brushes her teeth. Beautiful women have perfected seduction. It comes from years of being finely tuned, like rare violins, on the men they practice on.

Goldie says, "I'm me, love me as I am." But that, too, is a technique. Utter confidence.

The majority of actresses are insecure, even—*especially*—the most successful and gorgeous ones. They are always worried about how long their beauty and their career will last. And while they last, what can they trade them for? Since actresses can act, they *pretend* to be secure and in control. This role is one of their best and it's almost as good as the real thing.

Seduction Hollywood Style

Seduction is the key word in the movies. The producer seduces the stars for his film, the stars seduce each other on-screen and off-screen, and hopefully the stars and film seduce the critics and the public all the way to the box office.

Seductive people mix control with ease. Of all the great seductresses I have known, Sophia Loren is nonpareil. Sophia has natural seduction and power. She could give lessons.

First of all, she's six feet tall with three-inch heels on and she *always* wears them. Most actors are short and their leading ladies have to match, head to head at least.

There is a famous photo of Sophia, newly arrived in Hollywood, at a table at a party eying Jayne Mansfield's enormous décolleté, checking out the competition. But no one came close to Sophia, and at almost eighty, she's still the most beautiful woman of her age in the world.

Elizabeth Taylor told me about a dinner party she attended after Sophia's jewelry was stolen in Paris. The two women had always been competitive. Wearing her emeralds proudly, Elizabeth said, "I'm so sorry, Sophia, to hear about the robbery. I see you are wearing no jewelry."

"No, dear," Sophia said, opening her arms to display her enormous bust and a low-cut Dior. "I'm wearing my skin."

The competition between the most beautiful American movie star and the most beautiful European movie star hit the jackpot when Richard and Elizabeth, vulnerable at forty, were house-guests at Carlo Ponti and Sophia's enormous villa in the hills outside Rome, preparing for Richard's next movie, *The Voyage*. Ron stayed there as well, in the huge guest villa by the pool. I arrived just after Elizabeth had left.

Sophia paraded around the pool in Carlo's pleated white men's tuxedo shirt, *rien* underneath, platform wedgies making her six foot three inches, the world's longest totally tan waxed legs visible up to her waist through the deep side slits of the curved shirt. Ron was *seriously* impressed as she bent over him and asked sweetly if she could cook him and Richard some of her homemade pasta.

MICKEY KNOX TEACHES ME SOPHIA LOREN'S PASTA SECRET

In the late 1960s, Ron and I stayed with Mickey Knox in a small apartment at the top of the Spanish Steps in Rome near the Hassler Hotel. All the American film community in Rome stayed at the Hassler. Mickey was an American actor of the '50s who left the States to coach acting in Rome. His pals were the "intellectual" Hollywood community that passed through. Mickey's dinner guests often included Gore Vidal, Eli Wallach, and Paul Newman. Mickey would serve Sophia Loren's pasta in his kitchen on a trestle table with Fontana Candida in a wicker-covered bottle.

SOPHIA LOREN'S PASTA

Pour 4 tablespoons of the world's best olive oil into a heavy iron frying pan. Add 6 minced garlic cloves and sauté until they are light brown. Don't let them burn. Add salt and cracked pepper, then pour over Italian spaghetti cooked al dente.

That's it. Of course, Sophia has fresh-made pasta from scratch.

Ron got into making fresh pasta with a hand-cranked Italian machine, and often our wooden kitchen table in Normandy had pasta hanging off the side in the afternoon. When it did, I knew we were going to eat Sophia Loren's pasta for dinner that night.

LE CHIC, LE CHÈQUE, OU LE CHOC

Here's a good bourgeois French expression taught to me by my friend Vivien Best Demonge: *le chic, le chèque, ou le choc.* The chic, the checkbook, or the shock (sex). Whenever we meet a couple, Vivien will whisper to me, *"le choc,"* or whichever describes the reason they married. Her intuition is superb.

Le chic enhances your lifestyle or position as viewed by others. It's marrying up, to someone with a name or a title or a high-powered job. Someone who will put you in nice surroundings: an exclusive club, good social friends, top-notch college, impeccable family backgrounds. Someone who will elevate you in the eyes of the world.

Le chèque provides money, period. He doesn't have to

have any class or style; money is the point. This is the shopgirl who marries her manager or the secretary who marries her boss. Usually, if the money is lost, the marriage ends.

Le choc is a great sex partner, a shock to the system. To Americans, this is "falling in love"; to the French, it's simply *l'orgasme spectaculaire*. It is sex you cannot live without. Often it wears out, but sometimes it doesn't, and couples who got together for *le choc* can have great sex into their nineties.

If two categories are combined to make one, it's heaven. I don't know anyone with all three, except for movie stars who don't have to work a lot. Generally, to have a lot of money, one needs to work all the time, and that curtails *le chic* and *le choc*.

The Last Supper

Paris, 1980

*The earth is the honey of all beings. All beings are
the honey of this earth.*
—UPANISHADS

Michael Goldman had put together the finest private *cave*—wine cellar—in Paris. Michael had even purchased much of Napoleon's wine cellar, along with his private stash of brandies.

From 1965 to 1980, Michael went to every major wine auction in Europe, buying the best bottles. His father had invested in real estate. Michael preferred to drink his money and invited many of the world's celebrities to drink it with him.

Everyone knew Michael Goldman—that is, everybody in the culinary world. Where else could you eat dinner in a musty fifteenth-century French cellar, opposite Notre-Dame, on a wooden plank table, sitting on wooden crates printed *Château d'Yquem 1927* or *La Tâche 1945*? They were the only seats and no woman cared if her stockings ran.

If any celebrities passed through Paris, Michael would throw a party and arrange to meet them. Then he would invite three-star chefs to come over and each cook a dish to accompany his great wines.

His wife, Jacqui, would hand-print a menu for each guest. The menus made incredible souvenirs.

Apéritif: Champagne Cristal 1959,
with foie gras and homemade buttered brioche

Corton-Charlemagne 1961, with salmon trout en croûte

Mouton Rothschild 1964, with coq au vin and potato soufflé

Château d'Yquem 1927,
with tarte tatin aux poires with hot chocolate sauce and macaroons
au cafe

French movie stars like Sophie Marceau, singers like Jacques Dutronc and Françoise Hardy, and actors like Clint Eastwood and Laurent Terzieff came to Michael Goldman's dinners. There was always the Prince de Paris or a relative of Winston Churchill at the trestle table. It was a true *salon* to rival that of Gertrude Stein on rue Lepic in the 1920s.

Michael actually bought the *caves* under all the houses on his street and had them connected underground, stopping only when he reached the Seine. François Mitterrand was Michael's neighbor, so there were always police outside to protect both the future president of France and Michael's wines.

Each of the five *caves* had two or three small rooms, and together they formed a labyrinth of a dozen rooms filled from floor to ceiling with every expensive wine Europe had to offer. There was a bottle of Hungarian Tokay from the 1920s worth $3,000 (in 1980). There were rooms full of brandies from the late 1800s.

Most of the wine-tasting parties involved deciding the best year of an individual wine. We *had* to test Château d'Yquem 1893, 1897, 1921, 1923, and 1945. We *had* to test Volnay 1959, 1961 to 1964, and we would test one Pommard against another.

Was Mouton Rothschild 1945 or Lafite Rothschild 1947 the better bottle?

As we all got drunk, opinions got stronger, and often there were great chefs there to declare a winner if there was a tie. In those days most three-star chefs in Paris were willing to turn their kitchens over to an assistant for the evening and run to Michael's *cave*.

Once during a wine tasting, Ron and I were sampling Courvoisier brandies and Cognac Napoléon. It was a Friday night. The 1940s were beating the 1890s, which the women found too strong. Suddenly we found ourselves in the last room, the farthest away from the entrance. People were leaving to go upstairs.

"Oh, my God, Ron, let's go!" I yelled. "We might get locked in here!"

The door was like a bank vault. Ron hadn't realized the possibility of being locked in the *cave* until that moment. I looked at his face and he grabbed me and put his hand over my mouth.

"Let's stay in," he said. He was already beyond a discussion.

Everybody else left. We were alone for a while as he continued to drink the rest of all the open bottles: 1918 . . . 1923 . . . 1937.

He was finishing the Grand Armagnac when I pleaded, "Please, Ron. I'm scared we'll be stuck here all weekend."

But *that* thought seemed to delight him all the more. Eventually, he began to get drowsy. It was two A.M., and we had been locked up for several hours. I managed to climb the old stones to a small hole near the ceiling that gave on to a street gutter. I screamed my head off.

Someone eventually called the police, who called the concierge, who woke up the Goldmans, who came down to let us out. Ron reluctantly trudged up the stairs. Years later, he would still get mad at me, telling other wine connoisseurs that he could have had a nice quiet weekend with a good excuse to drink himself to death on Napoleon's brandy.

All this came to a crashing end when Michael fell in love with Jacqui's secretary, a salesgirl she had plucked from the Saint Laurent boutique. Tall, skinny, redheaded, with a build like a high-fashion model, Martine was the opposite of black, curvy Jacqui. Once Jacqui discovered the betrayal, all hell broke loose. Remember, Jacqui was from Harlem.

Michael fled, leaving behind the triplex, the wine cellars, and his two kids. Jacqui was sad and furious. The kids were distraught. Friends speculated that Michael had to be on drugs, had gone mad, or had something else seriously wrong with him.

Why else would a man give up such a wine cellar?

Not one to wither away, Jacqui threw a giant celebration just before their divorce. She invited forty people, and all the great chefs of Paris, and their wives and her closest friends.

I asked Jacqui if I could bring a friend from America, since Ron was out of town and I would need someone to help me get home. I asked Wayne Rogers, the handsome dress designer.

We were allowed to go down in the cellar and take upstairs All the Wine We Could Carry. We could pick anything we wanted and stay until we drank it all. Some bottles were worth $2,000 or

$3,000 in 1980 or (about $10,000 today). I stuck with Château Palmer '61 and Haut-Brion '61 and hauled as many bottles as I could carry upstairs.

People were going insane. Wayne kept saying, "I can't believe this. I've got to call Lynne [his wife] and tell her." When he got upstairs with his wines, he called Lynne in Connecticut to share each divine taste with her.

People stayed all night. Early the next morning we crawled out, taking our empty bottles with us to prove that we had actually drunk these amazing wines. Jacqui plastered a wall in the kitchen with all the wine labels that were left.

Today Michael's *cave* would be worth a fortune: a case of Mouton or Lafite Rothschild 1982 is valued at $25,000. Michael sold it off slowly and wasn't crazy after all.

WHEN IN DOUBT, ORDER SAINT-JULIEN

Michael Goldman told me never to forget this lesson. After years of drinking in his *cave*, savoring his elaborate dinners and Chez Denis, I became a *connoisseur de vin*. After our wine tastings, I decided the greatest red Bordeaux wines were:

- Château Margaux 1945

- Château Palmer 1945

- Saint Emilion Grand Cru Cheval Blanc 1945, 1947

- Pomerol 1945

- Haut-Brion 1945

- Le Mission Haut-Brion 1945

- Château Pouillac 1947

The year 1945 was the ultimate of all time, and 1947 was right behind. It was very hot in the summer of 1945 until September 15, when the grapes were harvested. France rarely has hot summers.

The best years after 1945 and 1947 are 1959, 1961, 1967, 1970, 1982, 1986, 1990, 1994, 1995, and 1996.

My personal favorite is Mouton Rothschild, because we knew Guy and Marie-Hélène. They lived across the street from me in Paris, on the point of the river and Île Saint-Louis.

In white Burgundy, the best are Corton-Charlemagne and Puligny-Montrachet. In red Burgundy, the best is Volnay Clos de la Pousse d'Or served at Troisgros and Hôtel de la Côte d'Or in the French Midi, also Romanée-Conti and Clos de Vougeot 1978 and 1980.

Michael Goldman was in love with Château Petrus and Château Palmer. Of course, Château Palmer costs a fortune, so he always told me, "When in doubt in a simple restaurant, order Saint-Julien."

The Power of a Dress

THE TORRID DRESS LIVES ON

In the late seventies I concentrated on being a mom of two young boys and building my couture business in Paris and New York, at Henri Bendel's, who bought four collections a year. In 1980 Dawn Mello asked me to leave Bendel's for Bergdorf Goodman and offered me a boutique; and in 1990 I created a new custom couture department—made-to-measure gowns—exclusively with Bergdorf Goodman and Neiman Marcus that continues today.

However, my most famous dress was born one day in 1979, when Anne Parillaud walked into my apartment on boulevard Saint-Germain. She was accompanied by Olivier Dassault, the son of France's richest man, the aviation king Serge Dassault. (Contrary to popular belief, France's leading industry is not fashion or even food, but is actually aviation and weapons.)

Anne was barely twenty then, with long blond hair and the lithe body of a trained ballerina. She resembled an impish new version of Jane Birkin. She was appearing in her first film with Alain Delon, *For a Cop's Hide*. She came to me for something to wear to the Cannes Film Festival.

I created the Torrid dress for her, in filmy chiffon. It was a style similar to the clingy gown on the statue over the Barefoot Contessa's crypt, with a draped bodice and draped cap sleeves as well as a hip drape with a long scarf down to the floor. The Cannes cameras clicked away as Anne, in the lime green dress, was photographed against a hot pink background, an early indication of the '80s return to glamour.

A decade later, Anne had a worldwide hit in *La Femme Nikita* portraying a female "hit man" who falls in love with an innocent boy. In 2005, Anne married the devastatingly handsome musician and composer Jean-Michel Jarre, Charlotte Rampling's ex-husband.

In 1986, the Torrid (in white) was photographed in *People* magazine in an article that named me "Queen of the Bustiers." It was also worn on the TV show *Dynasty* by Joan Collins *and* Emma Samms. By now I was the main designer of gowns at Bergdorf Goodman and Neiman Marcus. They carried the Torrid in black, white, and gold. In 1988, after my photo spread in *People*, the costume designers for *Pretty Woman* got inspired by the red Torrid at Giorgio's Beverly Hills, and I made one in red for Julia Roberts to wear in her big transformation scene with Richard Gere. Since then, it has been called "the Pretty Woman Dress" instead of the Torrid. In 1990, both Ivana Trump and Goldie Hawn were photographed in versions of the Torrid.

In the late 1990s, the Torrid died down for a while until it was revived as "Sade" (as in Marquis de Sade) and later as "Sadie," Sadie-Lucky Lady. Chanel has her quilted handbags and trimmed cardigan jackets, both selling unchanged for fifty years. Torrid is now closing in on its thirtieth year—quite a life for a dress! For the last few years, these classic dresses have been selling in every color faster than we can produce them for the stores.

In 2008, Catherine Zeta-Jones bought one to wear to the Tony Awards. In 2009, Jill Biden bought Sadie in red to wear to the inaugural parties in Washington, D.C. In 2010, Mindy Hall wore it to the Academy Awards, where she received an Oscar for Best Makeup for her work on *Star Trek*.

Women try on the Torrid/Pretty Woman/Sade/Sadie and now call it the "Wonder Dress." Suddenly their bodies look twenty pounds slimmer. They often hear, "You never looked so good, darling."

What is the secret? Inside the bodice are twenty-four curved bones that become a hidden corset. You don't need underwear! The corset gives you the body you've always dreamed of, and the draped hips inspire lust. Such miracles, however, don't come easy. It usually takes two people to zip it up, and only one man to unzip it.

When my son Rex was married in 2005, the long Sadie in mint green with a silver beaded midriff was my choice. Rex chose to be married "at home" at a château on a hill in Autheuil, overlooking our village and the Eure River, even though the mill house was no longer ours. His beautiful bride, Ani, wore a beaded, fringed corset top in peach and a full nude and peach tulle skirt.

After the wedding, we drove by our mill house and visited our local café, where Madame Denis cooed in admiration, "Oh, Vicky. What a dress! You never looked so good."

The Motivated Heart

Connecticut, 1980

By the summer of 1978, I had completed ten naïve paintings of life in Normandy. One of them was of the town square in Autheuil. A houseguest, Patrick Terrail, nephew of Claude Terrail, the owner of Tour d' Argent, saw it and said, "Vicky, I'm getting David Hockney to do a menu cover of my new restaurant, Ma Maison, in Beverly Hills. Would you consider doing a naïve menu cover 'portrait' of our restaurant?"

I agreed, and the painting was a huge success on the menu. I had a bright idea: I called Yanou Collart, France's greatest restaurant press agent and friend of restaurant critic Gael Greene, and said, "Let's do a coffee-table cookbook of all the French country inns and I'll do a naïve portrait of each restaurant. We'll do each province of France and I'll do a painting of each section's finest restaurants: Brittany, the Loire, the Rhône, the Alps . . ." I loved the idea of a cookbook as I was an early foodie and we could eat great meals in all these restaurants.

Yanou agreed to get the recipes for the book. We went to visit Random House in New York and were told bluntly, "Coffee-table cookbooks do not sell."

Suffering from rejection, I went to Westport, Connecticut, for a rest-and-recuperation visit with my friends Wayne and Lynne

Rogers, of the wine-divorce night. Lynne is the perfect beautiful blonde. Everything she does is perfect. Do not try to play tennis, golf, Scrabble, or tiddlywinks with her—she will win every time. Once she decides to become something, a golfer or decorator or beauty queen, she will master the art of whatever it is within days.

Lynne had suddenly decided to become a caterer. Her cooking was renowned. She was the first person I ever heard of who spent $25,000 on a kitchen renovation in the early '70s.

Lynne had a sweet little neighbor who also wanted to cater. She was another beautiful blonde, named Martha Stewart. One evening while I was visiting Lynne, I told Martha that Random House had rejected my idea of a coffee-table cookbook.

Martha told me, "What a great idea! I'll do it."

Andy, her publisher husband, said, "What a great idea."

"Be my guest, Martha!" I replied.

Martha lived in a quaint old house in the middle of residential Westport. She had been a model and a stockbroker, and now was a determined homemaker. Her family was her everything, and she worked to provide them with an "old-fashioned" lifestyle: homemade breads and cookies, fresh-grown vegetables, flowers on every table, and a house decorated in a time warp, when people were kind and gentle. Her conversations centered on her husband and daughter. Her interests did not go beyond Westport and Turkey Hill Road. Martha was a happily married woman with a dream family and a dream husband.

Martha, like Lynne, decided to cater for a few wealthy families in Westport. When I was opening my first shop at Bergdorf Goodman, I asked Martha if she would cater my opening. She served sushi.

On the beach in Westport, Lynne Rogers soon got bored with

catering. She built a tennis court and got into playing tennis and beating the men. Lynne threw wonderful weekend parties and devoted her energies to becoming the perfect hostess. Of course we could all learn to copy her recipes, as her cooking was easier to prepare than Martha's. People would fly in from the Hamptons in helicopters and land on her lawn. Lynne threw a Gatsby party and we all wore white. Lynne and I often played tennis with the Wall Street moguls who told us what stocks to buy so we could make money to buy more diamonds.

But Martha was too busy to come. She was content to watch the helicopters landing while she corrected the proofs of her book *Entertaining*. The book was published along with a video on how to do parties. She wore my lace evening gown on the cover of both.

Martha worked and worked. Maybe she was too busy to notice what was happening to her marriage. Martha's world collapsed when she found her husband cheating with her young assistant, Robyn. He left Martha, married Robyn, and a new creature emerged. The new Martha had a motivated heart to show Andy, and she did.

I truly feel her drive was born of the need to let him know what she was capable of and make him sorry that he had left. Just like Mia leaving me, Andy's departure created Martha. She learned to stand alone and find out what she was worth. America and Martha both benefited.

The creative world is so small. Martha even hired my old friend Dorian Leigh to teach her her food secrets.

My home has all her products. The porches have Martha deck chairs and umbrellas, the hammock has a Martha bedspread and pillows, and every week we switch on the TV to let Martha tell us how to live the nice old-timey way.

Lynne Rogers moved on to decorating in L.A. She sold her home on Beachside Avenue in Westport to Phil Donahue and Marlo Thomas. It was the most beautiful family home I had ever seen anywhere.

Marlo Thomas gutted it.

MARTHA STEWART'S LIFE LESSONS

- Life can have two acts.
- You can develop any persona if you believe it yourself.
- Learn to speak correctly and beautifully, and you can become anyone you want.
- If you can get up at four thirty every morning, you will outwork the competition and achieve all your goals. When I visited Martha the Mogul in East Hampton, I got up at five and found Martha already out walking her dogs.
- Turn a failed marriage into a good thing.

A Little Corner of Powerful Women in Paris

After witnessing Martha's success, I realized a new woman was emerging: the '80s power woman, the ultimate achiever.

New designs would have to be made for this woman to wear,

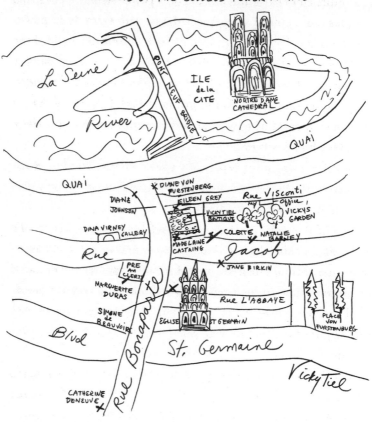

A Corner of Powerful Women

THE WOMB OF THE GODDESS POWER IN PARIS

the female dynamo who wanted it all: motherhood, career, and sex. I was one of them. The emergence of the power woman led me to two major inspirations.

First, I decided to reevaluate my marriage and seriously investigate Ron's rabbit behavior. (I'll explain later.)

Second, I wanted to design a new nonmasculine uniform for the '80s sexy power woman besides the party girl, fun-first minis, shorts, and jumpsuits of the '60s and '70s. This suit had to represent the new type: I can work, I can lead, and I'm all woman.

I returned to Paris and worked on a power suit. It was a fitted hourglass suit, almost a two-piece dress, with extra-large power shoulder pads that were inspired by Joan Crawford's suits of the late '40s, often designed by Adrian. I sold some of these suits to actresses in *Dynasty* and *Dallas*. But unlike the male designers' bulky, large-shouldered suits, my suits had draping, tucks, or some bust interest. They were always feminine and we wore them with sleek high heels or boots.

In Paris, I was at the center of a power vortex. Number 21 rue Bonaparte, the building that housed my shop, took up the entire block between rue Jacob and rue Visconti.

Two of the world's most celebrated octogenarians were the key residents. Madeleine Castaing, one of France's leading decorators and antiques dealers, owned the boutique that dominated the ground floor on the corner of rue Bonaparte and rue Jacob. She became a close friend when she discovered I made sexy leather jumpsuits that fit well. She bought a red one and a blue one and wore them constantly. She was eighty.

Madame Castaing's interior decoration was a mix and match of Directoire, Louis XIV, and Napoleon III, with leopard rugs and pale gray-blue walls known as "Madeleine's Blue." The overall effect was known as the famous "Castaing Look." Her style was so fashionable in the '60s that Jacqueline Kennedy hired her, with much controversy, to bring French style to the White House.

Madame Castaing was also a femme fatale. Among her famous protégés was Chaïm Soutine, the Russian painter of the 1920s and '30s. She proudly showed me the sealed window in her guest bedroom on rue Bonaparte where she hid Soutine, a Jew, during World War II. She also befriended Modigliani and Picasso.

On the other side of the courtyard, Eileen Gray, born in Ireland, exemplified the opposite style with her austere mannish look. She had been France's leading furniture designer in the '20s and '30s. (In 2009, her "Dragons" armchair sold for $28.3 million.) Her minimalist décor contrasted with my new boutique's pop-hippie style celebrating the '60s with Indian mirrored pillows and patchwork cracked mirrored walls. Whenever she passed by my outdoor potted red geraniums on her way to the stairwell, she pulled them out! When I went out in the mornings, I would repot them in their gold-trimmed wooden window boxes.

At precisely twelve thirty every day when the shop closed for lunch, I would go to my local café, Le Pré aux Clercs. I would be seated next to the neighbor who lived above the café, Marguerite Duras, the writer and film director who wrote the books and screenplays *The Lover* and *Hiroshima Mon Amour*. Neither of us spoke or even nodded to each other as we lunched side by side for twenty years. Number 21 rue Bonaparte had other centurions. Above Madame Castaing on the top floor was a Chinese woman who lived to be 102.

The story goes that Madame Castaing, who hated to pay taxes and was continuously in trouble with tax collectors (much like Dorian Leigh), had asked the last inspector for a dispensation as she was over ninety and still working. The man answered that almost every woman in the building was over ninety and that she was no exception. He said, "There is something curious going on in this building—maybe the water?"

Rue Jacob also had its powerful women. At number 28 had lived Colette, the iconographic French author who wrote *Gigi*. At number 20 lived Natalie Barney, the celebrated American playwright and novelist who was a "hostess" for over half a century and ran a salon for the "beautiful people." She entertained Jean Cocteau and Truman Capote and hoped to open a school for literary lesbians. (She was also a lover of neighbor Eileen Gray.) She lived to be ninety-five.

There was also Simone de Beauvoir, author of *The Second Sex*. She lived at the top of rue Bonaparte with Jean-Paul Sartre near the Église Saint-Germain-des-Prés.

More recent, Diane von Furstenberg moved to rue Bonaparte near the quai and the Seine. Diane Johnson, the American author of *Le Divorce* and *Le Mariage*, moved in next door.

France's leading actress, Catherine Deneuve, lives at the top of rue Bonaparte near place Saint-Sulpice, and Jane Birkin lives on rue Jacob, where she still walks around with a basket purse—not a Birkin bag.

Rabbits and Non Rabbits

After years of analyzing the love lives of my friends and clients, I have come to a conclusion. Men are divided into three categories: rabbits, nonrabbits, and snake rabbits. They cannot and will not switch categories, even with therapy.

There might be exceptions, but the exceptions will simply prove the rule. The most important thing is to discover if the man you are with is a rabbit.

THE "NEW" RABBIT TEST

Take your man to a restaurant where there are lots of attractive women coming in and out. They are usually to be found in the high-priced eateries, but it's worth the investment. As the lovely ladies saunter by your table, see if your man turns his head around to look.

· If the head swings completely around, he is a big rabbit.

· If the head swings a little or he slyly glances, he is a basic rabbit.

· If he never notices, he is a nonrabbit (or possibly gay!).

Do your best to marry nonrabbits. I've had both and, trust me, nonrabbits are better. I admit that the rabbits can be fun; just don't count on them for something as binding as marriage. Most women can put up with a lot, but please—not chronic infidelity. Rabbits don't change—they only die or leave you. A nonrabbit can make a mistake—let's call it a "slip." A slip can be forgiven. (In time, dears, in time.)

Note that a big rabbit not only cheats but often accuses *you* of cheating to shift the attention away from his own lapses. Big rabbits believe that everyone is as insatiable as they are and dismiss their sins with, "Everyone cheats!"

So forget a rabbit and get rid of him quickly. Introduce him to someone you can't stand or, better yet, to the au pair, if you have one. Rabbits always go for au pairs.

The snake rabbit, luckily, is fairly rare, but it's an extremely dangerous reptile!

- He seems to be the perfect husband.

- He never looks at another woman at any time.

- He never gives you any reason to distrust him.

- He always provides whatever you ask for.

- He always sits for hours, patiently watching, while you choose dresses or diamonds or furniture or art.

Is it because he is so devoted to you? No, it's because he has another honey, a full-time second relationship that takes up so much of his life that he can barely think.

This is the very worst rabbit, because if and when he finally goes off with his other woman, he will do the same thing to her. He is a serial-relationship rabbit.

If a man tells you that he has a wife or a mistress—or both—and he wants to leave them for you, *run* to the nearest exit and don't look back!

You've just evaded a snake rabbit! If you do find yourself married to a rabbit, consider this:

Frenchwomen and rabbits are a perfect match. They make an "arrangement" and take on lovers. The women make their husbands use condoms and they suddenly appear with a new hairdo and a radical change of clothes. Both spouses have a dazed smile at night when they return home for dinner from their afternoon *cinq à sept.*

A lot of commotion was made over Tiger Woods cheating on his wife, the former au pair of another golfer. She must have known before she married him, as I did with Ron, that she was marrying a snake rabbit. What did she expect?

Sandra Bullock married a man who had been married to a

porn star, just as Steve had married a nude model. Jesse James wasn't Peter Pan.

Is the Frenchwoman's solution to a "rabbit marriage" much better? Keep the charismatic rabbit and family intact, and girl-rabbit yourself.

Disturbing Photos

1983

How do you know when your husband has been rabbiting around? We all have clues. We can choose to ignore them. I did.

Ron would come back from film locations, his jacket pockets containing matchsbook covers or business cards with female names and numbers scrawled on them, never male names. Frequently the stories about where he had been didn't make sense. I looked the other way.

Marrying into the movie industry is like marrying into the incest industry. The cast and crews live together for at least three months on any movie and become a "family." They slip in and out of each other's hotel rooms like a game of musical chairs.

It is not unusual for a "production secretary" to be passed from director to star to director in one film. I was not ready to accept this Hollywood custom although I had been there myself at twenty.

One night Ron came home from the set of a quick French

movie, *Flagrant Désir*, with supermodels Lauren Hutton and Marisa Berenson. He left a whole roll of film on a table in the hall, and I had it developed. Men *always* do this kind of thing on purpose. So you'll find out without them having to tell you face-to-face. On the roll was a photo of lovely Lauren Hutton, with her trademark gap-toothed grin, shamelessly flashing the photographer, my husband! The funny thing was that Lauren had first been photographed in my dress for a Bergdorf ad. Did she know Ron was my husband?

I decided not to show the pictures to Ron and then have to listen to one of his implausible explanations. I put them away for safekeeping in my memory box.

One Red Leather Jumpsuit

New York

The first catsuit ever made in snakeskin cashmere was for Ursula Andress in *What's New Pussycat?* This one-piece pant-combined-with-top garment later was named a jumpsuit by the fashion press.

I had recently designed a red leather one and Barbra Streisand tried it on in the dressing room at Henri Bendel in my boutique in New York. Barbra was the reigning Diva. If she decided an outfit was suitable for Her Highness, the word was out: Jumpsuits are in.

From 1972 on, instead of carrying just evening gowns and

cocktail dresses at Bendel, we added leather clothes and especially leather jumpsuits. I got a red jumpsuit for myself and wore it on the set of *X, Y and Zee* in London.

"Oh, please, Vicky!" squealed Elizabeth, "make me a red one, too! Red is the color of the dragon on the Welsh flag, and it would really please Richard."

The idea of Elizabeth encased in red leather and crushed underneath a giant zipper was hard for me to imagine, but I told her, "No problem. I'll send you one as soon as possible."

I never saw her wear it in public, but Richard made comments about it to Ron. "My wife's gone kinky on me!" he confided. "She comes on to me in a red leather outfit and slowly undoes the zipper . . ."

I could picture the whole scene. Elizabeth loved sex and games.

Several years later, I was wearing my own red leather jumpsuit when Richard arrived from Switzerland with his new wife, Suzy Hunt. Suzy was a model from South Africa, five nine and blond—quite the opposite of Elizabeth. Richard had met her on the ski slopes. She had shared a ski lift with Brook Williams, his stand-in, and she had begged to meet Richard. Unable to stand being alone, Richard succumbed to her charms, and a quick romance led to a quick divorce from her race car–driver husband, James, and a quick marriage to Richard.

When Suzy saw me in my jumpsuit, she took me aside. "Love, what are you wearing?" she asked. "I have to have one. Rich will love it, since red is his favorite color and it stands for Wales."

Oh, my God. I had a truly designer moment. Should I let wife #4 wear the same red leather jumpsuit as wife #2 and #3? (Richard and Elizabeth had married each other twice!) I gave in. "Of course. I'll make you one next week," I promised, and hoped that Elizabeth would forgive me.

And so I made it, and Suzy loved it and wore it everywhere. Suzy was photographed with Richard more in my jumpsuit than in any other outfit.

Elizabeth never said a word.

Richard's marriage to Suzy Hunt lasted six years. She met a guy in Puerto Vallarta, a friend of all of ours, and left all the movie crazies to settle down with him in Mexico and help manage a hotel.

Sally Hay was next. She had been a production secretary for Richard during the filming of *Wagner* and had also previously dated Brook Williams. Sally was a medium-size normal-looking girl. She looked like Richard's secretary and was very eager to change that by having me design some French high fashion for her, including . . . one red leather jumpsuit.

Everything He Wants

Los Angeles, 1964–1985

Jane Fonda is the opposite of Goldie Hawn. Goldie is herself and never changes; Jane seems to become the woman she thinks her lover wants. The first time I saw Jane, we were sitting side by side at Alexandre de Paris hair salon. It was July 1964. Jane had just finished filming *La Ronde* with Roger Vadim.

Alexandre was trying to talk her into a sexy hairdo, and she would have none of it. She wore tweed sheaths and a *Glamour* magazine flip with a barrette on one side.

The next time I saw Jane was at Victorine Studios in Nice. She was shooting *Barbarella*, also directed by Roger Vadim, Brigitte Bardot's ex-husband and Jane's new one. He was helping her climb into a harness lift. She had Bardot's silver-blond hair in comic book curls, a G-string bottom, and a silver breastplate with her nipples sculpted in relief.

The *next* time I saw Jane, she was with Donald Sutherland after filming *Klute*. They were in Paris with her hairdresser, Paul McGregor, who did the *Klute* haircut for me as well (the hairdo I wore at my wedding). Donald's ex-wife, Shirley Douglas, was the daughter of a well-known Canadian politician, and so Donald knew politics. Jane was his new love and soon she loved politics as well. The sex doll transformed into "Hanoi Jane."

The *next* time I saw Jane, she and Donald were raising money for what they were describing as a worthy cause but without offering too many specifics. She was in L.A. and it was Oscar time. Jane convinced Elizabeth and Richard to donate $20,000 to her worthy cause. It turned out that the money was for the Black Panthers. Not that there's anything wrong with that, but it might have been nice to let the movie stars know where their money was going.

Five years later, in my house in Normandy at Christmas, Nathalie Delon got a phone call and handed the receiver to me. "Vicky," she said, "talk to my friend Eldridge Cleaver. He's in Paris and wants to become a jeans manufacturer."

The Black Panthers had moved on, and so had Jane.

The *next* time I saw Jane, she was raising money from rich Hollywood housewives for her husband Tom Hayden's campaign for the U.S. Senate. She was wearing Chanel and auctioning off her Andy Warhol self-portrait so Tom Hayden could win.

Jane had just started filming an exercise video, with my friend Shirlee Fonda, her stepmother. Shirlee and I were guests at the fund-raiser.

Shirlee was planning to manufacture and design Jane's exercise outfits. An exercise devotee for more than twenty years, Shirlee convinced Jane that it was the new thing. Suddenly Jane appeared everywhere in Shirlee's gym clothes, with Shirlee's muscular slim figure.

Later Jane would marry Ted Turner and become an Atlanta billionaire's wife.

Later still, Jane would become a Christian spokesperson.

Recently I saw Jane on TCM in an interview after she had written her memoirs. She actually spoke about morphing into different personalities. She said that writing her memoirs was a process of self-discovery.

The morphed actress reminds me of why it is so hard to marry someone in movies or theater. The stars and the rest of the team are living in a world of acting, constantly aware of how they are perceived, always on camera, always saying what is expected in the script, always charming, far from reality.

It explained my problems with Ron. Except for a *few* down-to-earth actors such as Goldie Hawn, Meryl Streep, and Elizabeth Taylor, who are oblivious to what others think of them, movie people are emotional chameleons. Elizabeth never changed herself for anyone. She was always over-the-top.

The Beginning of the End

Paris, winter 1981

How can you tell when it's really over? Cher sings, "It's in his kiss." When the feeling is gone, it's gone, and it doesn't come back. As an ex-mistress myself, I should have known what it meant when the fireworks stopped igniting. After one too many duds, I thought marriage counseling for Ron and me might light some old sparks, but no such luck. In fact, the sex counselor—who looked like he didn't get much action— informed me I was oversexed.

"I should hope so!" I told him. After all, I made a living out of selling sex, helping women get men with my sensuous designs. "Sex is my job and I love sex and I love my job!" I yelled, and left the session. We did not return to the counselor.

The beginning of the end was when Ron came back to Paris from filming *Wagner* with Richard Burton. He told me to "find a new boyfriend." I had been angry with him for bringing home a houseguest, Brook Williams, who wound up staying at our apartment for a month. Our 1930s mirrored art deco bar in the living room had become their daily hangout. One day I walked in and said, "The bar is closed." I told Brook he had to go and I would "help him pack," a great line of Tennessee Williams's from the film *Boom!* The fight that came after Brook's immediate departure down the old French staircase with his tattered suitcase in hand was the worst one ever. Our young boys hid out in their bedroom.

The next night, with my husband's "permission to date," I went alone to Yanou Collart's cocktail party in honor of Mikhail "Misha" Baryshnikov and wore a gold lamé snakeskin print strapless dress with a "love-me" bow on one side. I fell for the handsome Russian dancer hook, line, and sinker, and caught the twinkle in his pastel blue eyes. As we sat next to each other on the couch, I ran my hand down his thigh, then gave his thigh a little squeeze, just above the knee. "May I feel your muscle?" I asked innocently. It worked! Misha and I were dancing and kissing when Ron suddenly appeared at the party and forced me to go home.

After another horrible fight, Ron moved into the guest bedroom that Brook had vacated the day before. We decided to do the French thing and live together for the kids but have separate lives.

The next week I went to Castel's nightclub alone for the first time in my life, at last really living like a Frenchwoman. I wore a skintight white and gold lamé mini-mummy dress and high gold snakeskin sandals. My legs were bare and tan. I walked up to the bar alone, ordered pink champagne, and stared out at the disco floor watching a beautiful blond man dance at the center, under the twinkling multicolored glass ball. When the dance was over, he walked back to the bar alone and spoke to me in bad French with a Russian accent. He was in town to dance, he told me; Vladimir mentioned he was in the Bolshoi Ballet as he ordered me another champagne. I gladly accepted.

Aha! I thought. I missed out on Misha but I will now take revenge with another Russian ballet dancer. It was a magical, meant-to-be moment.

We didn't get to dance together. Vladimir walked me home, but we never made it to my apartment. We stopped to kiss and he dragged me into a nearby seedy hotel. In a cheap room, we made love until dawn under a purple neon hotel sign that kept blinking off and on. I was officially freed from my marriage to Ron—and I learned some new positions.

The next day, exhausted but filled with confidence to start on my life as a bachelorette, I left for New York (the boys were left with our Irish nanny) and went to an ultrachic dinner party on Park Avenue wearing the perfect outfit for a seduction: a red leather strapless gown. Red is the best color for attracting a man. I created it specifically for seduction, never realizing I would be in need of the dress myself! I carefully surveyed the room and found a potential lover seated on a couch in front of the fireplace. I decided to try the "thigh squeeze" again. I sat down next to the handsome, well-built, silver-haired gentleman and tried my new technique. "Oh, what lovely slacks," I cooed, with just a gentle squeeze above the knee. "The fabric must be British!" Within minutes we were off to Doubles, a posh private club on the Upper East Side, and then to his home with a view of Central Park, and a bed in the window.

Ron should not have told me to "date"!

THE KNEE-SQUEEZE TECHNIQUE

Sit down next to a man and place your hand on his bended leg, five inches above the knee. Pull your hand down slowly to just above the knee. Squeeze hard.

The gesture should be accompanied by one of these phrases:

Warren Beatty
The Man Who Really Loved Women

Among the eight women at the fashionable table, very well placed in the dead center of the terrace, were a Parisian fashion designer (*moi*), an actress who had costarred with Warren, a producer's wife, a hotel owner's daughter, an agent, and three housewives, one of them married to Ron's tailor. The eight of us were sitting in Ma Maison having lunch. I had designed the menu cover, a painting of the restaurant, so I loved eating there when in Hollywood.

The subject of our conversation was Warren Beauty (Elizabeth Taylor's nickname for him.) We realized that every single one of us had slept with him. What are the odds of that happening at a table of eight? Not low at all, if you know Warren. He loves women! All women! He loves them completely, except maybe his sister, Shirley MacLaine. Every woman was a target. Warren had patience. He could wait years and years.

The lunch at Ma Maison was hilarious. We all told our Warren stories and they were all similar. I'd known Warren for years, but I was married to his friend Ron. That probably wouldn't have prevented Warren from sleeping with me, but I was in my loyal-wife mode, especially when it came to my husband's friends. However, earlier this particular year, I had met Warren in the lobby of the Ritz-Carlton in New York. We were checking in at the same time and we wanted the same suite. Being the gentleman, he let me have the room. I told him I had recently separated from Ron. Licensed to kill.

The phone rang the next morning. "What's new, pussycat?" came his famous refrain, copied from Woody's first movie.

"Oh, nothing, Warren," I said. "I'm having a fashion show tomorrow, a fur collection for Dennis Basso, a new company."

"Oh," said he. "What are you doing right now?"

"Nothing."

"Well then, what are you wearing right now?"

"Nothing."

"In that case, why don't you come up to my room?"

He had taken the same suite with the view of Central Park right above me. I grabbed a towel, wrapped it around my naked body, and raced barefoot up the stairway, excited to have the chance to see what all the fuss was about!

Very well-endowed, Warren seemed to be able to go on for-ever. Pleasing the woman seemed to be his focus. As I rode him bronco style with my head and hair whirling around, having a great time, he was often interrupted by various women call-ing—not for sex, but to discuss their current love lives. Excited by multitasking, Warren was having a great time as well, with his phone under his chin and his hands and body all over me. He was gentle and rough, distant and yet dear. Warren was the male ver-sion of Dr. Ruth. Extremely intelligent and kind, he could dish out advice without missing a stroke. We made love nonstop as he was talking with great concern to one of his exes, who seemed to be suicidal. He must have calmed her down, since he seemed pleased with himself. Lovemaking with Warren, over one hour erect, was well spent, for me at least, and I left the room in a daze.

It seemed that he never actually climaxed, as we happily passed the afternoon together. I had to leave at five, as he was expecting his latest girlfriend, a model. I suppose he had to save something for her. After leaving Warren nude in bed, me in my towel, I passed girlfriend du jour in the hall. Beautiful as she was, she was Warren's number two because he was officially dating Isabelle Adjani at the time.

I have to assume that Warren changed completely when he married and fathered so many children with his beautiful and brilliant wife, Annette Bening. I did notice that Warren was a hypochondriac—his floor was covered with books and pill bottles. Could the fear of AIDS have calmed him down, or was Warren one of the only rabbits who could change? The exception that proves the rule? He was a brilliant guy, capable of anything, including a total change. The thing that made Warren so very special while he was a bachelor was that he was there for every ex-girlfriend in every way. Nobody could stay mad at him.

Years later, when they were in their twenties, I explained to my two sons how to be good boyfriends or partners. "Warren Beatty is the example of what women love and need. A man who loves women, loves to please them, and loves to listen."

Farewell to Richard Burton

Céligny, Switzerland, 1984

As I rode to sleep the owls were bearing the farm away . . .
—DYLAN THOMAS, *"Fern Hill"*

They say people know when they're dying by the strange little things they say and do. Richard Burton called us in Paris a few days before his death. The phone call was weird, disjointed and nostalgic. He talked for over an hour to both of us, and he hated phones! He was saying good-bye.

Days later we got the call from Switzerland, from Sally Hay. She told us that he had died of a stroke in the library while reading a book. Ron said, "She killed him!" He meant Sally. "Rich died of boredom." Elizabeth Taylor was a very hard act to follow.

The funeral was a circus. The Burton-Taylor family members and the entourage were to fly to Céligny and stay in two tiny inns in the center of town. Elizabeth Taylor was banned. Sally flatly refused to allow her to come.

Richard had owned a small chalet on a lake outside Geneva since his early days with Sybil, his first wife. He had hung on to it the way he clung to his old green Olivetti typewriter. Elizabeth never wanted to live there; it was in a small, obscure village. She owned a glamorous chalet she had bought with Eddie Fisher high in the Alps in Gstaad behind the Palace Hotel, and that's where she wanted to go. When the Burtons were in residence, they were treated like the king and queen of the mountain. With a 360-degree view from the balcony, Elizabeth could survey her domain.

During his subsequent marriages to Suzy and Sally, Richard got his wish to return to his first simple home in the tiny village he adored.

His plan, however, was to be buried "at home" in Wales. Elizabeth Taylor was determined to be buried there beside him.

Sally chose to bury him in Switzerland.

Any funeral involving Welsh people is never sad. Richard's remaining sisters and brothers gathered in the local pub to have a brew, talk about the good old times, and sing! Elizabeth's children gathered at the pub with Richard's daughter, Kate. Elizabeth's daughter Liza took charge of calling Elizabeth and connecting her to the Welsh contingent; phone calls went back and forth all day between California and Switzerland. The plot thickened.

I spoke to Elizabeth later. "You must come," I said. "I'll speak to Sally."

Elizabeth was already packed.

But Sally would have none of it. "She is not coming. I'm his wife—over my dead body."

I had to call Elizabeth and tell her the answer was a very final *no*.

The morning of the funeral, Sally asked me to come up to her room and help her dress. She was in her fancy silk underwear, unwrapping boxes of clothes I had just sent from Paris. I had been designing her clothes, just as I had done for Suzy, out of love for Richard (and to "pay back" Elizabeth and Richard's loan to start me off). Sally took some three evening gowns from the tissue paper and proceeded to try them on. I was stunned. We were due to bury Richard in a few hours.

"Vicky, let's fit these now while you're here," Sally said.

Though stunned I had to follow along. So I grabbed my trusty tape measure from my purse.

"Now I'll finally be able to go out and wear these things," she said. After our fitting, she put on a smart Jean Muir deep purple floral suit and she matched the colors of the flowers exactly with new pink, purple, and gold Bulgari earrings and a necklace. Then she proceeded downstairs to play hostess.

The Welsh contingent, furious that Elizabeth couldn't come, decided on the spot to have a second funeral in Wales just for her, on the very plot where she'd planned to be buried next to Richard.

I couldn't wait to get to a phone and tell Elizabeth about fitting the dresses on Sally. I was unable to imagine that someone could be so cold over her beloved, but Elizabeth excused her, saying, "Oh, she must be in shock."

I hadn't thought of that. For years afterward, Sally dressed up as Mrs. Richard Burton, the widow, wearing my gowns. After that day in her bedroom, I never made her another dress. And I never saw her again.

The worst moment for me was being in the library after the funeral, where Richard sat and read and wrote in his diary before he died. I sat down in his chair just for the feeling of him and looked to his table and lamp where he rested his book. Inside the open book was a photo of Richard and Ron on their previous film, *Wagner*.

In that photo, Ron, my husband, was holding and kissing another woman under a tree.

Richard Burton's death was the death of a great love story. Elizabeth and Richard never in all their years apart stopped phoning each other, never stopped loving each other. Maybe she was hoping, like Scarlett O'Hara, that "Tomorrow is another day . . ." and she would get him back before it was all over.

Elizabeth's Passion

After Elizabeth's first *and* second breakup with Richard, she dated the used-car dealer Henry Wynberg, a Hollywood single man who later dated my girlfriend Maggie Eastwood, Clint's lovable ex.

Henry was a very clever entrepreneur who came unknown from Holland and made it big in the Hollywood business world. One day in London in Norma Heyman's "salon," Henry tried to persuade Elizabeth to do a fragrance.

Elizabeth was not convinced. "Dearest Henry, big movie stars don't put their name on products." I thought about it and decided to do a perfume of my own. I named it Vicky Tiel and begged Elizabeth to change her mind. She refused. It was beneath her.

Fortunately for Elizabeth, she and Henry broke up and he negotiated a "separation deal." She finally agreed to produce her first fragrance and share a small royalty as a reward for all he sacrificed in Hollywood to be with her for two Burton breakups. At the ends of their careers, wild spending had consumed a lot of their fortune. "The Burtons" didn't have the film careers of their youth, but Elizabeth had White Diamonds. Like Coco and her Chanel No. 5, White Diamonds brings in hundreds of millions today. Luckily my perfumes are still selling, too, after twenty-one years, and Elizabeth and I both have Coco to thank—and Richard, too, for insisting we meet her. Elizabeth was the first big movie star to become a fragrance icon and make it okay.

Peaches and Steve Say Goodbye

1982

Steve DeNaut loved the life he grew up with in California and he stayed. We remained close for more than twenty years. I lived in Paris and he lived near Laguna Beach, only a phone call away. We had each other for advice, consolation, a happy voice on a rainy day. We had each other's backs, something Ron never seemed to achieve; Ron was interested only in my front. I realized our relationship was all front; we never really knew each other, he wouldn't reveal himself completely.

Steve had never remarried after Brenda married Mike Arquette and my departure from New York. He yearned for a relationship with his daughter Lisa DeNaut, now Rosanna Arquette. She refused to let him into her life and wouldn't even acknowledge him as her real daddy. This broke Steve's heart and his only solution was to move on and have more kids. But with whom?

Our geographical distance was insurmountable. In California he had his folks, his brother and sister, and the South Coast Repertory in Costa Mesa, where he was a company actor and acting teacher. Steve never became the movie star he should have been. The limelight of his youth was a moment he lost, much like Gene Kelly's character, Noel Airman, in *Marjorie Morningstar*. Steve peaked too young.

On the phone one summer in the mid-1980s, he confided

in me about a romance he'd been having with the manager of the theater company, a sharp businesswoman and "a beautiful person." He felt that marriage and fatherhood with her was the solution. I could only agree. He then surprised me with a sweet demand: Would I spend a glorious last weekend with him for "closure," and then we would say good-bye forever. He wanted to be true to his future wife; no more contact *ever* (something Richard and Elizabeth could never achieve).

My marriage to Ron ended at Richard Burton's funeral when I found the photo of Ron with some girl. How poetic, to spend a weekend of passion with my first true love, and we could both release ourselves from the bonds of Peaches and Steve and be happy with new partners.

I flew to L.A. We stayed at a hotel hanging on the cliffs overlooking Laguna Beach with the deep blue ocean roaring outside our window. We walked the sandy cove below at sunrise and sunset. Otherwise, we never left the room and ate only room service. It was funny: In all our years together, we never ate a meal—even in the movies we always tried to have sex, never eat.

We reminisced over our twenty years apart: what we'd missed, what we'd accomplished. In the big bed we said good-bye with intense, last-time lovemaking and the deepest, softest kisses. I realized that with Steve I was myself: unashamed, unrehearsed, without makeup, without beautiful clothes. He knew me and loved me . . . Peaches, dressed and undressed.

On Monday night I took the red-eye to Paris. When we kissed and hugged good-bye at the gate at LAX, I knew I could move on. I would find a love like Steve again! I would find someone unlike Ron, someone whom I could trust to be true, someone deep, someone real.

Steve's marriage to Lisa Palmieri took place within a week.

His mom called me the next year to say they had a beautiful daughter, Jessi DeNaut.

Many years later I got a disjointed phone call from Steve, much like the call I had gotten from Burton. His voice was somber. I mentioned the book I was writing about us. He told me softly, "Baby, you were the one."

Steve died of cancer a few months later.

The End of It All

The death of Richard Burton was the end of it all. The end of my marriage to Ron and the end of Elizabeth's dreams that one day she and Richard would reunite, remarry, and begin a new stage of their lives as the beautiful older couple of the theater, reading scripts together in their chalet in Gstaad, appearing on Broadway occasionally, as they had done in Noël Coward's *Private Lives* and in other brilliantly directed theatrical classics—always to great acclaim. It was not to be.

Looking back, Richard was the glue in our lives. He was the glue in the intricately woven puzzle of so many different personalities, between Hollywood and Europe, between obscure theater actors and celebrity photo-op starlets, royalty and world-renowned authors, zillionaires and rugby players, great chefs and Hollywood producers, bodyguards and politicians, *Vogue* photographers and paparazzi who surrounded him his every waking moment for the last thirty years of his life.

When he died, these players who starred in his life went back to their four corners of the world, never to reunite in the literary salon that he and Elizabeth had created in majestic hotel rooms and location trailers. Elizabeth could have never pulled off these salons on her own, nor would she have wanted to live in such a formal way, almost like a royal court.

Burton's life was a constant banter of words, dialogues, and arguments fueled by drink and endless trays of food. After the funeral, Ron and I went back to Paris, upset that Elizabeth never got to join us to grieve with the family who loved her Richard.

We were facing another terrible reality. Ron had worked almost exclusively for the Burtons for over twenty years, and now Elizabeth had moved back to Bel Air to more or less retire.

Ron had to find another movie star (and he did soon after—Kevin Costner and Dennis Quaid, both manly American versions of Richard).

At his age and with his reputation, Ron could not be just another makeup man on the set. He was the *stars'* makeup man: Elvis, Marilyn, Debbie, Elizabeth, and Richard.

And I sensed that the "Hollywood Ron" I had fallen in love with was gone, too. Perhaps the insecurity of starting over at fifty-three in a town that is an altar to youth caused Ron's breakdown, but something was definitely gone beyond his best friend. His swagger had disappeared. In his place was a lost, sad, often drunk, and distant man trying to turn our home in Paris into a cocktail party, not an intellectual salon.

I could have excused his behavior as grieving for his best friend, yet the distance was almost welcome at this point in our marriage. The Ron I had known for more than twenty years was more than slipping away from me. I didn't desire him anymore. I just didn't care. I didn't care what he did during the day or what he said or what he meant. I wanted to sleep alone with Chi Chi. Inside me was a deep anger that wouldn't subside. I'd had *enough*.

I thought of Miles and Woody and Marlon and Misha and the other one-name-and-you-know-who-he-is men I had turned down who would have been great notches on my bedpost even if they weren't marriage material. At ninety I would have died with a great smile on my face. What a waste! As I thought of these missed opportunities I got angry, and then I got angrier. Eventually, I just let go and detached.

I had known deep down when I met Ron that he was a cheater. He had cheated on his wife with me and had cheated on me recently with my close girlfriend Odile Attinelli, Nathalie Delon's best friend and our favorite fashion photographer. I had never known, or perhaps I had never *wanted* to know, the extent of my husband's cheating, but suddenly I did want to know. A reliable source confirmed the recent dalliance with Odile, and something snapped in me. I gave up caring about *us* anymore. No more attempts to recharge our romance with vacations to Venice and Saint-Tropez each year to rekindle our love in a sexy location.

Before, when Ron had told me to "date" and later, when we tried to stay together for the kids' sake, something changed. I just couldn't imagine another kiss from him. Something was permanently broken. Richard was our glue, and he was gone. I asked Ron to move out.

I wanted a new "us" in my life. I dreamed of someone who would love only me. I had to move on and go look for him. I would put some notches on my bedpost until I found him.

What would I wear?

PASTA HEART ATTACK

After our separation, I continued to eat Ron's pasta and think kindly of him. We had our beautiful boys. We had our memories. Ron had two more wives after we were divorced, and a possible third—the kids aren't sure. At seventy-five he had a heart attack but survived. He outlived Richard Burton, who died at fifty-eight. The drinking did not do Ron in; it was his famous fettucine Alfredo, a recipe he had learned in Rome when we did the Burton movies and lived with them on the beach above Centro Corsetti, a restaurant in Torvaianica. Mama Corsetti taught Ron to make this pasta from scratch.

MAMA CORSETTI'S FETTUCINE ALFREDO

1 pound fettucine

1½ sticks butter

1 cup heavy cream or crème fraîche

½ cup grated fresh Parmesan, plus a few tablespoons more to sprinkle on top

½ cup chopped lardoons sautéed in olive oil

fresh-ground pepper

1. Cook the pasta al dente in a tall pot.

2. In a double boiler, cook the butter, cream, and cheese over medium heat, whisking frequently.

3. When the sauce is smooth, pour it over the pasta, along with the lardoons (pour off any leftover olive oil). Top with some more Parmesan and black pepper.

Mama Corsetti gave me a large brown square antique pepper mill from the 1930s, and we took it everywhere. When we separated, Ron got the mill house, but I got the pepper mill. I use it every day and think of Mama Corsetti and the beach near Rome.

Pastel Paradise

1983

My newfound boyfriend from the knee squeeze (not Baryshnikov) became my full-time lover. We would meet all over America and England. He was the president of the U.S. Croquet Association and though he lived mostly in Palm Beach, his croquet matches took place all over the world. A former advertising executive, he had been the boyfriend of a Palm Beach socialite.

The croquet matches took me to Florida, a new destination for me. After all, the Burtons had never filmed there. As soon as I laid eyes on Florida, it was love at first sight, the same way I felt the first time I arrived in Paris. The palm trees and the turquoise water were a perfect antidote to my Parisian smoky gray palette. Any excuse, and I was off to Florida.

I discovered a crowd of glamorous women in Miami and Palm Beach and began to "do" the society balls where the object of each female guest was to get her photo in the "shiny sheets," local versions of gossip magazines. My evening gowns were the perfect complement to their diamonds, emeralds, and rubies. Elizabeth had taught me well: white jersey with emeralds, lavender with rubies and sapphires, diamonds with anything, especially jeans, and always keep a few slinky black dresses in your weekend suitcase in case someone invites you to a ball.

Dressing women in Florida added a new dimension to my European color palette: hot pink, turquoise, lime green. Plus: bold prints, ball gowns, and ruffles. Florida was, after all, in the South.

A sleek, elegant client of mine was divorcing her husband, Elton Cary. A soon-to-be-divorced and wealthy man was not going to last long on the market in Miami. Elton was tall, silver haired, and always tan. He reminded me of John Forsythe in *Dynasty*. It was the '80s and *Dynasty* was big. I was not convinced that I could fit into Elton's world of charity balls and dressing up for dinner. He took me on a carriage ride around Central Park and professed his desire to become my lover. No knee squeeze necessary, only a sort of business proposal. Would I consider it? But Elton just wasn't my type. I went back to my girlfriend's apartment and went to sleep—alone.

I woke up at six A.M. with an epiphany: Why not give another physical type a chance? Elton didn't have my must-have baby blue eyes. His eyes were lime green.

Bad boys, musicians, athletes, film folk, motorcycle dudes—enough. Try a suit-and-tie guy for once. Try green eyes—*very* Richard Burton. I hopped in a cab at dawn and called Elton on the house phone at the Pierre Hotel.

When he answered, I said, "I'm downstairs. Can we make love now?"

He replied, so unlike the men of my past: "Give me a second, honey, so I can brush my teeth."

Afterward, as I confided to my girlfriends, I was in shock. Much like Warren, he could keep it going for an hour. Suit-and-tie guys could be good in bed. Little did I realize that some bad boys hide in the suit and tie. They are wolves in sheeps' clothing. The croquet player was out. The businessman was in. I discovered a new maxim: Give a man who is crazy about you a chance.

Overnight I had a lover with a chauffeur, a boat, and a big bank account. I was leaving the film world for *Miami Vice!*

Elton and I began a two-year romance. I would fly to see him every few weeks for long weekends. I was also deeper and deeper in love with Florida. I loved the colors, the pale green water, the baby blue sky with multicolored rainbows, and the pink and yellow art deco buildings. It was a pastel paradise. Every evening Elton would come home early from the bank where he was president and we would go down to his sixteen-foot Cary fishing boat (that he had built himself), whip out into Miami Bay, and fish for snapper under the bridge until it got dark. We gave the fish to the chef of the Palm Bay Club for our lunch the next day. Then we would shower and I would get all dressed up in an evening gown or a cocktail dress, and we would go to dinner at the most expensive restaurants in Miami. When we waltzed in, we got the best tables and nonstop service.

Elton's closet was the size of a bedroom, and his suits were all color coordinated with light gray starting near the door, going into smoky gray, then into black, and pale greens and pale pinks going into wine. Yes, he had pink suits. *Eek!*

The fashionable crowd in Miami was much like the Burtons' in Europe: the kings and queens of glitz. Diamonds and rubies were worn with tennis clothes. I increased the number of gown designs in my collection for these new clients who could go to a ball every night of the week. This new lifestyle seriously helped my couture business grow, and at last I had places to wear the most beautiful gowns I designed.

Sometimes I would go out with Elton in a curly "Marilyn" wig and black sunglasses in a white sequined "Happy Birthday, Mr. President" sheath. I would pretend to be a hooker. I would wiggle and play dumb in front of people he knew and say, "How much you gonna give me if I do you right here in the ladies' room?"

Elton and I had a lot of fun. A snake rabbit, he told me he was finally divorcing his wife and he was also giving up his mistress from the last years of his marriage. I saw her once and named her "Dippity-do." She looked like Daisy Mae in pale pink shorts and the big blond curls of my Marilyn wig. I would later realize he had a trashy favorite type: the dumb blonde. Was I another dumb brunette?

Elton worked in banks and companies he owned with his wife. In the beginning, all the money had come from her family. The boat business he owned with his best friend, Don Aronow, the race boat champion, was independent from his wife. He and Don were on various bank boards together.

Don had built his empire with the success of the Cigarette boat. Later, he created the Donzi. The drug dealers and the Coast Guard were both his clients. Don and Elton also both owned helicopters, but Elton eventually sold his. Don would fly around and visit his buddies and land on their lawns. Before Elton and I became lovers, Don Aronow was a friend who flew by copter to the Rogerses' parties in Westport. Helicopters replaced Rolls-Royces as '80s status symbols.

In 1987 I asked Ron to finalize our divorce and he agreed. He had pulled himself together, bought a Porsche, and begun dating a Crazy Horse saloon stripper young enough to be his daughter. I felt he wouldn't mind if I married Elton.

To celebrate the divorce, I took Rex and Richard to Egypt. They were eleven and nine. They wanted to escape Paris life and ride camels in the desert like Indiana Jones.

It's said that a visit to Egypt always alters your life. The pyramids are the ancient spiritual center of the universe. We hired a private camel driver and rode into the desert. He took us deep into the center of Queen Seti's tomb. I closed my eyes and listened to the ancients speak.

My Driver is a Hit Man

Cairo, 1987

If you want to know happiness for a lifetime, help others.
—CHINESE PROVERB

The sun rose coral pink over the pyramids, turning the earth a dusty rose as I rode along the desert with my two sons on camelback. I was looking for shops that sold ancient perfume bottles. I was preparing designs for the Vicky Tiel fragrance I was about to launch at Saks, and Rex and Richard came along to help me find the perfect blue-green bottle. Ancient Egyptians first used perfume around 1500 B.C., and blue-green bottles from 400 B.C. were still obtainable. You just had to search.

Before we left Paris, I informed my two young sons that divorce from their dad was inevitable. I thought that we would continue our lives without him, since I was certain that he would leave me in Paris and return to Hollywood to work.

The trip to Egypt was a way to begin our life as a threesome. What better place to start afresh than Egypt? Let's turn a bad thing into a good holiday. Let's celebrate the divorce with a party in the desert. The boys were glad to be on the trip with me. We booked rooms at Club Med. It was one of our happiest times together.

At night, back at the hotel, I called Elton, only to be told by his secretary that he had gone to the Carolinas to play golf. But wait a minute—he didn't play golf. I called my travel agent, a Vicky Tiel dress client, and asked to have Elton's footsteps traced and to find out if he had betrayed me. I sensed something wrong. My travel agent, who had access to some great inside sources and information, found out that "Mr. and Mrs. Elton Cary" were in Hilton Head. Not again!

After packing the most beautiful pale turquoise bottles and sensual fragrances I had found, I flew back to Paris with the boys, left them with the nanny, and then flew straight on to Miami. I went to Elton's apartment and waited for him. He returned— luckily, alone—at three in the morning and was quite shocked to find me there. He confessed that he had been with another woman. Probably another trashy blonde with a real Marilyn "wig."

How could I have fallen for a snake rabbit? Looks could deceive. Moreover, his apartment was loaded with my clothes, furniture, oil paintings, and books. I decided not to fight with him. I was exhausted from the Cairo–Paris–Miami trip, so I slept for a few hours and then locked myself in his enormous walk-in closet with the fifty suits. There was a phone in the closet.

I called a close friend and client in Miami. She had been a showgirl married to one of the men who made Las Vegas a success. In the 1950s he was the one who had put the horse's head in the gangster's bed. I knew she would have good advice.

She told me, "Don't worry, Vicky. Stay in the closet. I'll send my driver over. He's very professional under pressure. He was a hit man. Just go downstairs, get in the limo, and he will take you to our plane and the pilot will fly you back to New York. Get out now before Elton charms you back into his bed!"

I followed her advice and by noon I was back in New York via Teterboro Airport and fast asleep an hour later.

The shock of losing my husband and my "fiancé" one right after the other was a bit much. For the first time in my life, I was in no mood to go back to work. A real break from designing and from parenting was necessary. Where to go?

Where else but the Big Easy? For years I had been visiting New Orleans and dressing the glamorous beauties Pam Halter and Dathel Coleman there. Marie O'Neill, another Southern beauty and a close friend, let me stay with her in her pink town house in the Garden District. I could recover from my double whammy. When I arrived, I cried for two solid days and stopped only to watch the Yankees play on a big TV with her husband, oilman Jim, and discuss my situation with his daughter Terry O'Neill, the current president of NOW, who was taking action for women's equality. What action could I take other than to change my choice of men?

A few weeks after breaking up with Elton, all Miami woke up one morning to read in *The Miami Herald* that Don Aronow, the Cigarette boat owner and Elton's best friend, had been gunned down in Thunderboat Row by a hit man (hopefully not my friend's driver). The rumor was that the murderer was none other than Don's latest mistress's husband.

My heart told me it wasn't true. The police later confirmed that she was both Don's and Elton's mistress. They had shared her. Was she the woman in Hilton Head posing as Mrs. Cary? I never found out. I never saw Elton again.

Through Elton, I had become part of a circle of friends that included Don's wife, his ex-wife, his children, and all their colleagues, some of whose various "business" dealings were questionable, to say the least. Eventually the police determined that the murder was related to another boat builder and involved the sale of boats used to run drugs. Don had at the same time made boats for the Coast Guard to catch the drug boats. It was rumored that Don was working for the CIA. The more I learned, the more I decided I had made a very lucky escape from Miami.

But now, after a week eating the world's best fried oysters in Galatoire's and Commander's Palace, I still wasn't ready to leave fantasy world and return to reality, but I was getting stronger about never going back to Elton. Where else could I go?

It was the first time since the age of eleven that I had no one to love and no one to love me. A mini-depression had enveloped me like a fog. I had no desire to work, to draw, to meet clients, and most of all to be social. I wanted to hide, preferably with a glass of wine—French wine, *bien sûr*.

In the past, whenever I'd had sad thoughts, I'd go to nature. I'd find the largest tree and lie on the ground and stare up through the branches, seeing only the sky, or I'd find a flower with a beautiful color and put my face next to the petals and bring the color into my body, feeling it as a balm over my wounds. Now, an inner voice told me to be practical and get some serious help.

I looked through my client book. Aha, Key West! Nancy Friday lived there and at that time was considered America's foremost sex expert, with her bestselling book *My Mother/My Self*. She should be able to get me through the double breakup with some excellent advice. She would understand.

Thank God for girlfriends.

Meeting Mr. Right

Key West, 1987

Nancy Friday and her husband, the novelist Bill Manville, had been my friends since the sixties when Bill ran the *Playboy* office in London and Nancy was pals with Norma Heyman.

Nancy and Bill had discovered Old Town Key West and its laid-back, hedonistic atmosphere. They joined a community of successful writers and artists who purchased charming old conch houses and turned them into breezy hideouts with the year-round promise of sex, sun, and sand. Jimmy Buffett, who had rented my first apartment in Paris on rue du Dragon from me a few years earlier, called Key West "a sunny place for shady people"!

From New Orleans, I flew to Miami, then hopped on a commuter plane to Key West, then a pink taxi to Southard Street. I arrived on Nancy's doorstep on a Sunday morning at ten o'clock. During our phone conversation the night before, she had assured me that the change of scenery would do me good and generously offered the use of her guest cottage. She told me she had been working on a new book but would be glad to offer comfort and advice.

While I was waiting for her to answer the doorbell, Bill emerged, looking disheveled, unshaved, and upset. "Oh, Vicky," he wailed, "Nancy just left me!" Her cab had just pulled away.

Even though my hostess had flown the coop, I had no other place to go, so I moved my suitcases into the guesthouse. That night, Bill and I sat in his whitewashed kitchen, outfitted with a bar overlooking the sparkling pool. Sipping wine, he told me that Nancy had fallen in love with Norman Pearlstine, editor of *The Wall Street Journal*, and had ended their marriage just in time for my arrival. I was so disappointed. Not only for Bill, but for myself. Where was the advice and help she had promised?

But it all worked out. Bill and I had each other's shoulders to cry on. I told Bill about Elton and said, "I'm over the glamour boys. . . . I want a real man who is secure, who can fix things and screw me." I also wanted someone I could be alone with and be at peace with. Bill explained that he and Nancy, ironically, had worked together on a book called *Jealousy* and had discovered that the main cause for failed relationships is that most primitive of all emotions. Too bad their insights could not save their own relationship.

"It's all about the clash of egos," he said. "You've got to find someone who is not competing with you. Find someone in a different field, a totally different category!"

Hmm. My mother told me this, about a Jewish doctor.

He went on. "Ron was an artist like you, only you're more successful. And the boyfriend is a businessman, but it's his wife's money that financed his deals. You, on the other hand, are a self-made woman!" I was already starting to feel stronger as he spoke. "Vicky, you should find a guy in a noncompetitive field like a teacher or a mechanic or a fisherman! You liked to fish with your fancy boyfriend in Miami, why not go looking for a fisherman in Key West?"

Not a bad idea. I love being around water and boats and fishing. Hmmm . . . A man from a different category.

The next day I dressed in a white T-shirt and skintight white stretch jeans, and rented a pink bike. I made a point of taking off my signature star diamond necklace. I cycled down to the docks where the houseboats and yachts were anchored. I rode past the fishing pier and saw all the charter fishing boats lined up. I checked them out, looking from one boat to the other.

Suddenly a guy yelled, "Hey, lady, you want to rent my boat?" And there, in all his glory, was husband number two!

He had the most exquisite crystal blue eyes with the longest curly eyelashes I had ever seen on a man. He was tall and muscular and very tan, with a head of curly brown hair, and wore very short cutoff gray sweatpants, obviously without the encumbrance of underwear. Later I found out that this deliriously perfect male specimen had instantly confided to his friend, Captain Craig Snell, "You see that lady in the white pants? I'm marrying her!" Ah, the power of tight white pants!

They called him "Big Mike" or "Hammerhead," and he had been in Key West first as a marine and then stayed for the Mariel boatlift. He decided to stay there permanently and do the Hemingway thing. Part of Mike's charm was how much he hated clothes. He barely owned any, and "barely" was a look he had perfected. No shoes, no underwear. Just skin and shorts.

Looking into Mike's beautiful blue eyes, all the painful memories vanished—and the happy ones, too—in a puff of smoke. It was as if I'd been hypnotized. All memories of every man I'd known faded the instant we met.

On our first date, he spent all the money he earned from selling fish that day to take me to an early dinner at an expensive restaurant on Duval Street. I was surprised when he ordered a Coke. He asked me what I did for a living. Afraid to tell the truth and scare him off, I said, "I fly between Paris and Miami" (not quite a lie). "Oh, a stew," he said, assuming I was a stewardess. I nodded.

After dinner, we went diving in the coral reef off Key West. Mike bought some bait fish and chopped it up in little pieces. Then he taught me how to feed the pastel blue angelfish by hand. Their mouths felt like little kisses. We made love underwater as best we could, and by the time we came up for breath, we both knew we would never be apart.

Later that night we checked into the Hampton Inn across the street from the Garrison Bight Dock. After an amazing night of lovemaking, our room was a total mess. Both beds were disasters. The next day the motel ran an ad for new maids.

On our second date, I asked Mike if I could buy him some shoes as a gift, and he accepted a pair of leather flip-flops. Then I brought him back to Bill's conch house. Bill approved.

"Finally someone listened to my advice," he said happily. "You went out and got yourself a fisherman."

Having sanctioned our union, Bill offered to rent us his guest cottage month to month. We lived there for a year. My life changed just a little; I commuted from Key West to Paris, not Miami to Paris.

My boys agreed to return to boarding school in the fall so I could invest time in Key West and my new life, but they came often to "fun fish" at night for sharks and fish the Bimini world tournament.

The first phone call to my new Key West home came from a charming fashion guy from Columbus, Ohio, whom I had gone out with in New York a few times. Somehow, he had found my number in Key West and was calling to invite me to a party on a yacht in Palm Beach, where he had just purchased a new home.

Mike grabbed the phone. "Hey, man," he said. "She's taken," and slammed down the receiver. Between the long-haired fisherman with no shoes and the Palm Beach billionaire, there was no contest.

Looking for a Man in a Different Category

Life in a conch cottage in Key West was very different from Paris. I awoke every morning to the fragrant smells of jasmine and the sweet songs of thousands of colored birds. The salty ocean breeze floated in the air. WELCOME TO PARADISE was written across the wall of the one-room airport terminal. When tiny prop planes pulled up to The Conch Flyer restaurant instead of a proper terminal, it was the first sign Key West was a different kind of place.

There were the palmetto bugs. Giant three-inch black bugs that crawled out anytime you moved a piece of furniture. It made no sense for a female to scream, as men paid no attention. These bugs are an everyday part of the funky population of tropical paradise and, besides, the large bugs all eat mosquitoes. Killing any large bug is a bigger mistake.

I asked Mike, "What do I do about a maid?"

He walked to the closet and handed me a broom.

Fortunately, the cottage was small, but eventually I found Larry, Bill Manville's friend and part-time hairdresser, to help me around the house and cut and curl my hair right in my own home.

The kids had come for a visit and loved the beach, sunset cruises, and shark hunting at night with Big Mike. He was called Big Mike not only for his size but also his large personality. He was the whole show.

My diet changed from rich French foods to fruit and fish. I was tan and trim from swimming in the pool we shared with Bill.

Bill owned three small cottages that formed a circle around a central patio deck with a blue-and-white tiled pool and hidden tropical gardens filled with frangipani and hibiscus trees. No one could see in from the street. That was the tradition in Key West. Unlike Paris, where everything happened on the streets.

The entire lifestyle was different and I loved it. No dress-up parties. No makeup, no glamorous hairdos. Instead, lazy days with tall yellow or lime green drinks with umbrellas and sunburned people dressed only in shorts and the barest tops, riding everywhere on pink bicycles. Even the famous and powerful rode bicycles.

I was lying on the couch eating mangoes from my own trees, watching the traffic cruise down Southard Street, when the phone rang. It was Elizabeth! She was in L.A. after a big birthday party in Tangiers. Malcolm Forbes had been escorting her for the last few months and threw a fabulous "native" party in her honor at his home.

"Everything happens in tents in the desert," she told me.

I was getting all the details when I said plainly, "I hope you're not sleeping with him."

Miss Naïve Movie Star had nothing to say.

"When I stayed with my boyfriend Elton Cary, I saw him, Elizabeth, in the elevator of the Mayfair Regent Hotel at two A.M., going upstairs with a young black stud muffin in leather pants, biker jacket, and heavy metal."

There was a giant pause. "Well, he's such a dear. What a shame."

Elizabeth didn't take that well. I think she had glimpsed a future of flying around the world in eighty days on Forbes's planes to his vacation houses in Morocco, Tahiti, and France.

"Elizabeth, have you ever considered choosing a man from another category?" I asked.

"Oh, no, I don't know. Not really. Where would I meet him?"

"Listen, I have found a nice regular guy, an ordinary American guy from the real world, someone who completes me and does what I can't do. Why don't you give it a try?"

Enter Elizabeth Taylor's husband number eight . . . Larry Fortensky!

Vicky Teel for the Night

O ur days in Key West had a predictable rhythm. Mike kept busy at the pier with his fishing expeditions. Known as a shark expert, he and his buddy "Big" Gene Lemire would take customers out at night on a boat, hoping to find sharks. Often they would tag and release them, but occasionally they would capture one and hang the trophy on the dock. They could sell the meat or fins to Japan. Each day I admired my new companion more and adjusted to his life-at-home style. I really didn't miss the fancy dinners and parties, as long as I could be with Mike.

After three months I told him, "I'm a dress designer with a shop in New York and in Paris."

Tears came into his eyes. "I'm just a fling, you're gonna leave me."

I grabbed his hands and put them around my waist and kissed him. I said, "I'll never leave you."

We have been together twenty-three years.

Eventually, though, my career had to continue. I had to keep designing clothes, and I needed to travel to my shop in New York and back home to the kids in Paris. I wanted my man to come along and he agreed to learn about my "other life." He bought some jeans and white shirts, we locked up our sweet little cottage, and we flew off to New York. We visited my apartment on the forty-fifth floor of CitySpire in Midtown near Bergdorf. Mike was afraid to go to the windows and look down—he was scared of heights since a bad parachute fall as a marine and a fall off a building in Cuba during the Mariel boatlift.

Next we flew to Paris, and after a few weeks of strolling around the City of Lights, walking along the Seine, and exploring the charming little side streets and shops, I finally asked Mike what he thought of Paris. We were walking hand in hand in front of Notre Dame, and he looked at me and said, "It's just so . . . it's so . . . *old*!" He admitted to being a fish out of water and missed the sunny beaches of home.

On his first week in Paris, Mike bought a tux. We went to the Best Dressed awards together. I was selected as one of the 10 Best Dressed Women in the world. It was our first night out together to introduce Mike to my "fashion world." I had to go.

The Best awards are organized by Massimo Gargia of *The Best* magazine in Paris. Some of the other best-dressed women of the year included Princess Soraya of Iran and Lauren Hutton (her again!).

The night began quite well. Mike was seated next to LaToya Jackson and her husband, Jack Gordon. During a dance, Massimo cut in and pulled me to the side. "Princess Soraya wants to know 'how much you want' for Mike," he said.

She apparently wanted to buy him. I burst out laughing and couldn't help but run and tell Mike. Big mistake! He didn't laugh; he grabbed my arm and made me leave. At least I had my Best award.

He raced down the staircase of the Grand Palais. I lost a diamond-and-emerald earring trying to keep up with him, which made Mike even angrier. When I told him how much the earring cost and that I couldn't leave it behind, he found it for me and then raced into a taxi and left Paris the next day for the Keys.

I had been afraid that my success as a designer would scare Mike off, but once he saw my boutique in Paris, and my dresses hanging in Bergdorf's in New York, he confided his own worry to me. In a rare moment of self-revelation, he told me that now that he saw what a big deal I was, he was sure that I would eventually leave him. It was hard for him to understand, as it was for many of my skeptical friends, that I would want to stay with him forever.

After a few months of commuting between Paris and Key West, Mike and I went into business together. We found the most beautiful charter fishing boat, named her *Vicky Tiel*, and docked her at the Pier House at the end of Duval Street in the heart of Key West. The fashion editor of *The Miami Herald* wrote an article titled "Fashion and Fish" with a photo of me on the boat.

My glamorous friends in Miami and Palm Beach thought I'd lost my mind until they received Christmas cards in 1988 with a photo of twenty-nine-year-old Mike and forty-three-year-old me, arms entwined, with my boys on the boat and a backdrop of a glorious Key West sunset. I never heard another word.

With the charter business taking off, Mike decided to promote my new perfume, Vicky Tiel, on the boat, while also promoting nighttime shark fishing. He ordered one thousand T-shirts with VICKY TIEL FOR THE NIGHT printed on them.

When we didn't have clients, we would take the boat fun fishing alone and dive for fresh lobster. Vivien Best Demonge said, "Everyone wants to do what you did, Vicky, only nobody does!"

The final surprise was when Mike went on the Internet to trace his family history. I would never have guessed that the beautiful young man without clothes on the Key West dock came from a royal Scottish family. The Hamiltons, descended from the House of Stuart, had settled the South via Nansemond, Virginia. Mike Hamilton could have been allowed to join the exclusive Chevy Chase Country Club (a membership out of reach to most presidents) as a son of the American Revolution.

Mike was my perfect man. He was also my perfect opposite. Everything I couldn't do, he could do. He was kind and intelligent, he loved nature, and best of all he was not a rabbit. I could leave for work, fly, and return. After a few years together he understood that I was in for the long haul.

LOBSTER AT SEA

1. Take a boat out to sea in the Florida Keys and pull up a lobster from your trap or catch one under rocks by diving down or snorkeling.

2. Cook the lobster in its shell in the microwave for 1 minute. Don't overcook, or it will be rubbery.

3. Melt a stick of butter with paprika, salt, and pepper.

4. Crack the lobster, pull out pieces of lobster meat, and pour the melted butter over it.

5. Pull a mattress onto the deck of your boat, make love, and fall asleep under the stars.

If you are unfortunate enough to have to do this at home, get a lobster from the fish store, put on your bikini, and follow steps 2–4. Then make love anywhere you like.

" Up A Tree "

Key West

I had been reluctant to drive since hitting that police officer in
Paris after the long lunch with Dorian Leigh. Unfortunately,
in our new home in the Keys, I *had* to drive. I could ride a
bicycle in Key West, take cabs in Paris and New York, but when we
moved to our home on the beach in Summerland Key, the local
supermarket was several miles up Route 1 in Big Pine Key.

"Babe," Mike said one day, "you gotta get real! We have hur-
ricanes here and I could be on my boat in the Dry Tortugas and
not come home. I could nip around Cuba and escape the storm,
but you're going to need a car to evacuate."

Well. I sat up and listened. Shopping for groceries in su-
permarkets, something I'd never done before, was already on
Mike's to-do list in order to "get real." Yikes. I had always had a
chauffeur, Monsieur Puippe or Augusto. And now I had to drive.

I passed the driver's test in Key West with flying colors. Little
did they know I had crashed four cars. My first crash was at sixteen when Daddy bought me a white Studebaker Lark convertible. I skidded in the rain and spun around and into a pregnant
woman pushing a baby carriage. No one was hurt except for the
picket fence I knocked down. The woman had fallen out of fear
and was badly shaken but fine, thank goodness.

The second crash was in Malibu, when trying to spy on Ron

and his wife (remember, the one he was leaving?) playing tennis. I crashed my brand-new yellow Morgan convertible into the tennis court.

The Morgan was fully restored when I crashed it again, this time on Sunset Boulevard driving by a new shop called Holly's Harp. I saw a *copy* of my famous Liza gown, a caftan in bias chiffon, named for Elizabeth Taylor's daughter, who had found a skirt with bias points in her travels. The dress had been a bestseller at Henri Bendel in New York, and now my creation was being copied by a new designer whom I'd even met in New York. I drove my car into the rear end of the car in front of me while staring at my Liza in the window.

That totaled my Morgan. Of course, my last crash was the cop in Paris. Most people literally refused to get into a car with me.

Hoping that I would turn over a new leaf, I bought a red convertible sports car and everything went well for a few months, until Christmas.

Mike had been partying too hard in Bahama Town and forgot to come home for Christmas dinner. My houseguest, the model Nicolle Meyer (the favorite of photographer Guy Bourdin in Paris), had gone to bed. Having had one too many Blender Blisses, I was ready to search for Mike and bring him home.

I got in the car, put it in reverse, and sped backward down my long driveway. I ended up in the gumbo-limbo tree in the center of our circular driveway.

My car was caught about six feet up in the low branches and I was dangling out of it somewhere. The cops came. Fortunately my neighbor was a lawyer. He determined that you cannot arrest someone for drunk driving on her own property, and the cops left.

I called a cab and took off to Bahama Town, looking for Mike, whom I found asleep at a party.

The next day I drove Nicolle home to her place across the tip of Florida on Captiva Island. She mentioned that I drove a lot better when I didn't drink.

BLENDER BLISS

Pick the fruit of the trees in your garden—or your grocery store. The proportions are equal parts fruit and rum.

2 bananas
2 mangoes
a few teaspoons of coconut juice
Bacardi light rum
ice cubes

Mix everything in the blender until the liquid is smooth. Pour it into tall 1950s painted glasses—do not drink out of the blender! Do not drive.

I think this is most blissfully drunk sitting on the porch looking at the water. But it is good anytime, anywhere.

WHAT'S AN ADDICT?

Was I an addict, or just another '60s girl who had too much fun? A friend of mine, whom I'll call Henri, a recovering heroin addict, gave me his best description of who is an addict and who is not.

Growing up in the Bronx, he and his best friend drank, smoked pot, did speed, you name it, as teenagers.

His best friend went to L.A. and became a movie producer in the '70s. Henri went to Paris and became an antiques dealer. Both discovered heroin and both sniffed, then shot heroin until the '80s. His friend stayed in L.A., married, had kids, got to produce big-budget films, and finally said to himself, "Heroin is interfering with my life. I'll quit." He did, and he never started again. He had an occasional drink but never did drugs. He was *not* an addict.

Henri, on the other hand, quit about the same time, had only one drink a day, and in two months was back on hard drugs. He was incapable of quitting. He *was* an addict. He could not stop on his own and he used every excuse: It was too hot, it was too cold, his wife was a bitch, his friend died, he had too much money, he lost a job. . . .

Which one was I? Unable to decide and afraid to end up in another tree not my own, I decided to quit for good. *Everything*: pot, cigarettes, champagne, and, sadly, French wine.

Mink and Manure

The final house we owned on Key West was actually twenty-five miles east on a small residential island called Summerland Key. A crazy coincidence was that Fred Neil, my friend the Village folksinger, lived there, too, only the Key was so private that I never knew he was there until I read his obituary in the paper.

Our house was on stilts, directly on the beach, on a rare half acre with a gate and a long driveway. One restaurant, Monte's Seafood, was nearby. Every day fishing boats pulled up and sold fresh fish.

I planted a huge tropical garden so the house was hidden from the street. On the beach we had a hammock in the gumbo-limbo tree along with tree sculptures I made out of hanging lobster trap balls. Mike painted our bedroom sunshine yellow and the sand came right up under the house. A commercial for my new perfume, Sirene, was shot on the dock next to my beach. The boys came from Paris for all their vacations. It was a dream home until two things happened.

Mike began to notice fewer fish on his outings. He asked his clients to tag and release, a no-kill policy. We also noticed our beach and water landscape changing. One day I found that my pet parrot fish had left the ocean in front of the house. They had lived there a year. The coral was now a cloudy spot of white powder. After five years of diving and knowing each nook of our island, we realized we were experiencing climate change.

Then in 1998 Hurricane Georges knocked our socks off (and part of the roof, too). Worst of all was the damage to my tropical garden—orchids, palms, passion flowers, and jasmine were a soup mix, all over the yard. But the killer was my oleander, swept away when the tide rode across our garden to the road. I could not bear to watch the cleanup. I ran away to Paris, my other home.

Mike called me in Paris. He told me to come back and drive from Tallahassee on I-10 to Alabama. "When you see something you like, get off the road and buy some land. If you're lucky, you can find a house on a river. There're some old plantations tucked away—you can do your Scarlett O'Hara thing."

He was right. I met my girlfriend, Sam Moses, who had a dress shop in Tallahassee. We got into her BMW with her large chow, Max, and went house hunting.

After two days of searching with the help of a Realtor, we drove up a long driveway and saw the Blackwater River and a primitive untouched forest surrounding a small house. I ran down to the river, peeled off my clothes, and jumped in.

Sam turned to Stephanie, the Realtor, and said, "She'll take it."

The property, known as the old "Baptism Hole," was in the middle of a state forest, in the middle of nowhere, an hour from any town. It was *perfect*.

I called Mike and said, "I've found our 'Green Acres.' You can build us a plantation."

He said, "Yeah, mink and manure!"

I replied, "I'm finished with wearing animals, unless maybe a vintage piece. I'm going to raise them instead. It will be more like draped chiffon and manure."

THERE'S ALWAYS A BETTER RIVER

In 1985, Ron got to keep our mill house on the river Eure in our divorce settlement, and I got to keep my shop in Paris. Soon after the papers were signed, Ron moved into the mill house with his latest girlfriend, a jazz singer. I was barely able to get anything out and had to leave behind the English oak furniture I had handpicked in the Cotswolds. Even worse, I never got to retrieve the two English landscapes Elizabeth had given me as a reward for smuggling Daisy to London. The man Ron eventually sold the home to "furnished" refused to let me have my art and furniture.

It was heartbreaking. I had lost my beautiful sixteenth-century home. How on earth would I ever find another home on a river where I could swim? If only I had known then not to suffer so.

Today we own land on both sides of the pristine Blackwater River and I have a "sugar sand" beach all to myself, where I can swim year-round, au naturel.

Whenever you think you have a life-shattering problem, remember: THERE IS ALWAYS A BETTER RIVER.

Life in the Deep South

Today my life has peace and balance. I live on my farm in the Deep South and also fly to Paris every few months and New York every three weeks. I get a bit of everything. The high-low life.

The farm Mike and I live on has ponds filled with catfish and bream. We have five dogs and two cats, all rescued, on forty acres. Our next-door neighbors have a horse ranch and a stud farm. Their family and ours have the only farms on the Blackwater River, with its white sand bottom, flowing from Alabama to the Gulf. The rest of the land is protected national forest.

We also have a swimming hole at the foot of the front yard. It used to be the baptism spot for the Red Oak Church. Carolyn Williams, another neighbor, comes over once a week and we wash our hair while we float in the river.

People ask, "Aren't there snakes in there?" Yes, there are plenty. We have rattlers sunning themselves on the riverbanks. They won't bother you if you don't bother them.

Last week I saw a black snake near the swimming hole. Carolyn said she'd seen him before. "He's been comin' around," she said. "He generally hides when people come. He won't hurt you," she reassured me.

I had gotten used to giant insects the size of a child's hand in Key West. Here it's snakes. I'm not worried. It's worth it to find peace and quiet.

Carolyn told me that to keep a man from straying in the Deep South, you need three things: (1) perfect iced tea in the fridge at all times, with fresh mint; (2) a good recipe for chicken and dumplings; and (3) you know what the third thing is.

We have nine-foot-wide porches all decorated like living rooms surrounding the house, a front porch with a lime green rocking chair for sunrise, and a swing on the back porch for sunset. On the front porch I can sit drinking Carolyn Williams's iced tea while facing in any direction and watch birds, squirrels, and foxes. Mike raises English bantam chickens, which live in our front yard and sleep in our tall oak tree, and their little babies, called "biddies," are protected by our dog, Baba the Beloved, a golden Lab-huskie mix. We have fresh eggs, our own well water, and two planted acres. There are more than a hundred roses, along with pear, peach, and lemon trees, which are all great for making jams and Lisa Fonssagrives's dartois. Not to mention blackberries and figs and green grapes on twenty-foot-long vines.

A family of swallows lives in the chimney. They come out every night at sunset and fly overhead, dipping down to sing "hello" to me as I swim in the pool. My fashions are short caftans I design in Tunisia, where my son Richard has a home, and I'm always barefoot like Mike.

There's a goddess statue who pours water into the pool from an antique urn. Wind chimes jangle on the porch next to hammocks and swings covered in Martha Stewart retro flower prints.

The décor inside is *Father Knows Best* meets shabby chic, with original 1950s fabrics in all the rooms. The couches and curtains and all the bedrooms have multicolored chenille blankets and '50s print fabric.

When I show Lynne Rogers, who is now a chic Beverly Hills

decorator, the photos, she says, "Oh, no! It's everything I ran away from when I left home in Pensacola in the fifties."

Mike, born in 1958, likes to say, "Vicky collects everything from the fifties, including me!"

CAROLYN WILLIAMS'S PERFECT ICED TEA

Put 5 tea bags and 2 cups of water in a large bowl. Microwave on high for 5 minutes.

Pour the tea into a 2-quart pitcher and stir in ⅓ cup of sugar until it dissolves. Add water to fill the pitcher. Refrigerate.

Serve with a sprig of fresh mint.

MISS SUSIE RUTH DOWDY'S CHICKEN AND DUMPLINGS

1 stewing chicken
2 cups self-rising flour
1 can condensed cream of chicken soup
salt and fresh-ground pepper

1. Put the chicken in a large pot and cover it with salted water. Bring it to a boil, then lower the heat and simmer for 4 hours. Remove the chicken and set aside.

2. Put ½ cup of the broth and the flour in a mixing bowl and knead on a floured surface. It will be a thick paste.

3. Roll out the dough and cut into ¼-inch thick strips 1½" by 1".

4. Reheat the broth until it comes to a rolling boil. Add the cream of chicken soup and mix thoroughly. Drop in the dumpling strips; they will sink to the bottom. When they rise to the top, turn down the heat and let them sit.

5. Reheat the chicken in the remaining broth, if necessary. Cut the chicken into pieces, skin and debone it, and shred. Put back in with the dumplings.

6. Serve the chicken in large bowls, with the dumplings and broth.

Aunt Dora's Greatest Romance

1992

When my clients lament that they're sixty and alone, either divorced or widowed, and that there's no hope left for romance, I tell them about my aunt Dora to cheer them up.

My aunt was married several times in New York to various husbands, each one wealthier than the last. Finally she married a heart surgeon, Hershel Meyer, and he bought her a penthouse in the Beresford on Central Park West, with a wraparound terrace. Dora was an avid Communist and wrote radical left-wing books and poetry in the '50s, and eventually (thanks to Joseph McCarthy) she left the States.

Dora settled in a ritzy suburb east of Paris, in a three-story house hear the Bois de Vincennes. She entertained Russian dignitaries there in the late '50s and was invited to meet Chairman Mao when her Communist poetry became all the rage. Aunt Dora believed in equality for the masses but Dior couture suits for herself.

My father was proud of my success and felt himself responsible because of his don't-have-sex-for-shoes lecture. But his sister was not. I visited her quite often, and she never failed to reprimand me for my bourgeois career choice: making ridiculous frou-frou gowns for oversexed, overprivileged women. I didn't see her as often after she bought a beach apartment in Tel Aviv. In Jerusalem, her plays were produced in the Yiddish theater.

In the late '80s, Uncle Hershel died, leaving her alone, with a lot of property. Worried about Dora, my father asked me to visit her. I obeyed and found out the surprising news that she was in love with her Israeli publisher and he'd moved into her large apartment overlooking the sea!

"He always loved me," she said, "but I was married."

Abraham was sixty-five and Dora was eighty.

Later, just before she died, Dora whispered to me, "Make sure Abraham gets to keep the apartment in Tel Aviv. Vicky, I finally had the best sex ever!"

Aunt Dora's death in 1992 caused a lot of grief in the otherwise happy life of my father. He had never remarried, and he retired at the age of forty-five to North Miami, where he played tennis, chess, the mandolin in an orchestra, and dated all the available women in his four-tower condo on the beach.

Daddy called me to Miami. He missed his beloved sister, whom he had visited in Paris yearly. He told me, "I've been falling a lot on the tennis courts." He was seventy-nine. The doctors told him he had Lou Gehrig's disease.

Three months later, from the hospital in Miami, he called me to drive up from Key West. "Please get Mike to come and kill me; he must have friends with good pills." Daddy didn't want to be paralyzed. Mike agreed.

I told Daddy please not to get Mike in trouble. Tibetan Buddhists kill themselves with their mind only; so do American Indians—remember Dustin Hoffman in *Little Big Man* (Daddy loved movies): "You close your eyes, find your third eye, and focus on it. Follow the colors until you pass over to the other side."

I bought a Walkman with earphones and loaded it with Mozart's Requiem, one of Daddy's favorite pieces. I said, "Daddy, first practice. Close your eyes and do what I say—and promise later to let me know if you reincarnate!"

It was my birthday, October 21. I kissed him good-bye. "I'm going to leave now and come back tomorrow," I told him. Mike was taking me to dinner on Big Pine Key and I didn't want to miss it.

By the time I got to Key West, Daddy was dead. The doctors didn't know the cause, so they wrote down pneumonia. My son Richard and Mike helped me bury Daddy in his tennis clothes with his favorite racquet and fresh balls.

A year later, I had a personal appearance at Neiman Marcus Bal Harbor and I took the limousine to Daddy's cemetery. I wore my best black sheath and Chanel heels. At Daddy's grave, I went down on my knees and kissed his name on the headstone.

At that exact moment a dime dropped from the heavens (there were no trees nearby) and landed on his name. I had no money on me, so it was a message from Daddy—the nonbeliever—that there was life after, *something* after, and he had a dime to spare—or had his beliefs turned on a dime?

Five years later, on another visit to the grave, there was only one tree growing in the vast cemetery—right next to Daddy's grave, and it was leaning left (Aunt Dora's influence)!

WORKING WOMEN VS. WOMEN WHO WORK

As the couture business in Bergdorf expanded, my company's manager, Carmelita de Jesus, hired a talented assistant, a Jamaican fashion diva, twentysomething Akilia Shedira. When asked about her ambitions, she replied, "There are two types of women: working women and women who work. I am a working woman."

How well put. I had come across these strong differences in my clients.

Working women have to work for their own personal power. They love accomplishing goals.

Women who work have to work until a man, an inheritance, or a windfall falls into their lap. Women who work also dabble at work part-time or on charities to fill up their days and provide conversation at lunch. They always hope someone else will worry about income. If they are French, the state often pays.

Motherhood and being a wife are jobs, and these women work hard as homemakers, but their *power* comes from independence, and independence comes foremost from a paycheck.

When you don't know how to earn your own money—or buy your own shoes—you feel fear and lose your power.

The Delta Queen

1993

I was almost sixty and nothing had changed. I was flying to Palm Beach from Paris via Atlanta, and the French *hôtesse de l'air* would not let me into the first-class cabin.

The *hôtesse*, in her well-cut navy blue Air France uniform, did not approve of my ripped jeans and ripped jean jacket. I had cut out the piece on my shoulder above the pocket on both sides, so I was wearing a peekaboo bare-shoulder look.

She wanted me to sit in seat 32G coach, even though I was holding a boarding pass for 1B first class in my hand. The head hostess appeared and told me that if I did not sit down immediately in seat 32G, I would be thrown off the plane.

"I'm a fashion designer in Paris," I yelled. "You should see how John Galliano at Dior dresses! I'm conservative compared to him."

Badly dressed and badly behaved, I finally sat down. How could this happen to a platinum 100,000-miles-a-year passenger? I had to accept the bad seat, bad food, and bad attitude if I wanted to get to Mar-a-Lago, Donald Trump's place on the ocean, where Neiman Marcus was throwing a pool party for fall and my clothes were the highlight. I was expected for dinner at the Palm Beach home of Maria and Raymond Floyd, the golfer. Too many people would be upset if I didn't show. I sat down in 32G, closed my eyes, and fell asleep.

Didn't the hostess realize the antitravel look is for those who *really* travel? The well-dressed couple in first class is actually the pretty secretary sleeping with her older boss, hoping to move up to trophy wife. Hasn't the hostess ever flown with Julia Roberts or Meg Ryan? They can look like bag ladies. Renée Zellweger is always in workout clothes.

I had on my standard travel look. Nylon hose are the first thing to burn up. If the plane goes down, anything synthetic will melt (that includes your bra). Only real cotton will do: cotton jeans, cotton socks, heavy-soled leather Steve Madden oxfords—*not* high heels—and, most of all, any T-shirt with a hood to keep your hair from burning. Leave it to a designer to think of the perfect outfit. It comes with the territory.

Upon arrival in Atlanta, I stormed over to a red-coated manager to file a complaint.

"I have a better idea than that," came a voice behind me. "I'm Leticia Moise from CNN Atlanta. May I do a story on this? I'd love to hear what the folks of Atlanta think of your outfit and if they would let you stay in first class."

A few days after the filming, I was shown on CNN News as "the Fashion Designer Thrown Out of First Class." Ms. Moise spoke as I modeled my ripped-jeans look down the red carpet in the center aisle of the airport.

She decided to get some public opinion.

"Would you let her into first class?" she asked an overweight man in a sweat suit.

He looked me over, then responded into her microphone, "Hell, no!"

VICKY'S TRAVEL TIPS

- Wear layers, such as a T-shirt and a hoodie, in case of air-conditioning or heating problems. Keep socks in a tote along with a large wool or cotton scarf.

- Wear makeup and jewelry to be fabulous in case the man of your dreams sits next to you. Remember the knee-squeeze technique. Wear a low-cut top underneath if you want to show him your assets. Do not wear tight skirts or pants. No undies, either, as bacteria can grow in "space."

- Carry your business cards—flying is a perfect occasion for networking.

- Always keep a day's worth of food in case the plane stops on the runway for hours. Nuts, fruits, chocolates, and peanut butter sandwiches are good. (Water is free.) Nothing creamy in jars will pass security.

- Turn flying into a holiday in your head with great snacks and music, your favorite book to read, gossip magazines, and *fun*.

- School reunions, gyms, sports, and travel are great places for finding someone to love!

Elizabeth Taylor's New Year's Eve at Home

2000

Elizabeth always called her favorite caviar "gray babies." Gray babies are the Iranian belugas sold in light blue six-inch containers. They are giant gray beads like pearls. The dark smoky ones and small black ones are real gourmet no-nos. The bigger the better.

Ron told me of a night thirty-five years earlier at Debbie Reynolds's house after Elizabeth stole Eddie Fisher. Ron was doing Debbie's makeup for the powerful role of Unsinkable Molly Brown, who made a fortune mining in Colorado, but personally Debbie was crying in Beverly Hills this night. Ron would soon leave America with Elizabeth to work on *The Sandpiper* in Paris.

Debbie had bought a very large tin of black caviar—not gray babies—and had set it on the coffee table in front of Ron. Friends of Debbie's were around the room having cocktails. Debbie was pouring her heart out to Ron and then got angry at him for eating too much caviar.

Ron told me, "Debbie had no chance of keeping Eddie when Elizabeth decided she wanted him. Elizabeth was much too generous a person to not get any man she laid her eyes on. Elizabeth would have given me *my own* caviar tin."

I introduced my new husband, Mike, to Elizabeth Taylor's

New Year's Eve Dinner for the Millennium New Year 2000 while we were in Paris. First we watched fireworks over the Eiffel Tower explode from the window of our apartment on quai Henri IV. Then we retired to the bedroom, where we placed three trays of caviar "sandwiches," champagne (for Mike), pastries from Café Mille Feuilles on the rue de Buci, and delicious macaroons from Ladurée and watched all the New Year's celebrations around the world on French television.

This is the sexiest candlelight supper, with the one you love.

ELIZABETH'S CAVIAR "SANDWICHES"

Use large Idaho potatoes. Prick the skin, then rub the outsides with cooking oil (not olive oil) and bake at 350° for 1 hour.

Cut the potatoes in half lengthwise. Scoop out the insides, leaving only a little white potato clinging to the skins. (Save the insides for mashed potatoes tomorrow.) Fill one potato half with sour cream or crème fraîche. Top with about 2 tablespoons of beluga caviar or "gray babies." Sprinkle on minced fresh onions. Put the top on the sandwich and eat with your hands.

The Perfect Body, 21st Century

It's no longer the clothes you bring to the body.
It's the body you bring to the clothes!
—JOAN KANER, *fashion director, Neiman Marcus*

I know of one New York socialite who had liposuction on her hips and the fat returned a few months later—on her knees. They doubled in size. There's no place to go but down.

One day in the early eighties I was in Miami showing my collection in Claudette Candib's mirrored ballroom on Sunset Island. There were ten of Miami's great beauties there, all undressed, and so was I. We were trying on my latest Mummy dress—the horizontal bias-cut, all draped jersey dress that I had created for Goldie Hawn.

Suddenly Fran Harris looked at her perfect body and touched-up face in the mirror and screamed, "Oh, my God! What is this?" There were three wrinkles on top of her knees. I examined them closely and then looked down at my knees. I had them, too.

Later that day Fran told me she had called her doctor. There was no operation possible. Knees had to bend. And we had to live with the wrinkles from that day on.

Ten years later, Fran and I sat in the Neiman Marcus dining room at the Bal Harbor mall and laughed about the day we met our wrinkled knees.

"I've learned to live with wrinkled knees, and elbows, too," she told me. "I've accepted myself the way I am. I decided to be the best I can be at fifty and not compete with another age group. I've had my glory days and now it's time for me to find other things to concentrate on."

The perfect body is a myth. Perfect is different in the eye of each beholder.

The typical Vicky Tiel customer has a feminine body and loves it. She has a husband who married her for her curves. My clothing accentuates those curves: Most of my dresses have an inner construction with twenty-four bones to maximize the feminine shape. My Scarlett O'Hara corset silhouette is a horror to designers who prefer a straight-as-a-stick little-boy body on women.

I once spoke with my teacher James Galanos about this. We both appeared at the I. Magnin trunk show the same day. The store had made a mistake and booked our shows simultaneously. We didn't have a problem. I told the management that our clients were on opposite poles of the spectrum. Mr. Galanos refused to dress or fit "large" women (he meant busty). He did not sell size fourteen or above. He designed for his dream woman, petite Nancy Reagan, and would not compromise. I told him bisexual French men often liked the little-boy-looking girl, since it was close to being gay but still straight.

The point of my fashion, I told him, was less clean chic, more sexual chic. My dream client is any woman with curves. Moreover, I wanted to help a woman find a man and keep him. It wasn't for any intellectual concept, or for another woman's approval. It was just all about sex and feminine power. The right dress has magical power.

The good thing about my fashions is that they never change. A dress with power can be worn forever. It's not about a trend; it's about the body being its beautiful best.

IT TAKES A LOT OF WORK—AND BUCKS—
TO LOOK FABULOUS

CHECKLIST

- 2 bust implants, size 34D

- Liposuction on stomach, butt, hips, and back

- Botox injections in laugh lines, forehead, eye wrinkles, upper-lip lines

- Eyelid surgery to take off the fatty, sagging top lids

- Laser tooth whitening

- Silicone injections inside lips for a puffy bee-stung mouth (don't overdo!)

- Upper-lip implant for especially thin lips

DRAWBACKS

- Every woman ends up looking the same, like the Stepford wives.

- You can't move your face.

- It is hard to laugh.

- It all drops eventually and you have to do it again. And again.

- This stuff hurts.

- It takes a while before you are willing to go out in public.

- If you did all of the above, it would cost around $25,000, and none of it is covered by insurance.

The Fairy Tale Life of Aimee de Heeren

Summer 2003

Among the grandest grande dames of the twentieth century, Aimee de Heeren was also my longest-term, most faithful customer. I began dressing her in 1968 and continued to design her party clothes until her death in 2006. Her exact age was a matter of dispute, but with Aimee, the years didn't count. Born stunningly beautiful in Brazil at the turn of the century, and quickly becoming noticed in Europe in the '30s, Aimee spoke six languages and collected art, jewels, museum-quality furniture, and friends of all ages along the way. In 1941 Aimee was selected by *Time* magazine as one of the ten best-dressed women of the world along with Wallis Simpson and Babe Paley.

Aimee (translation: "to love") was the only client I fit in her home, whenever and wherever she happened to be. She lived in Paris on the Left Bank in a house with a full-acre garden in the back. In New York she owned a double-wide brownstone on East Ninetieth Street, which sold for $33 million (after her death). In

Palm Beach she had a magnificent villa on the sea near the Kennedy compound. Best of all, she had a castle in Biarritz, on the Spanish border, with a five-acre garden overlooking the sea.

Aimee had the finest taste in men, furniture, friends, food, and wines, although she didn't drink. She taught me about a carefully planned life of extravagance, exercise, and excellence. She certainly excelled at everything she ever tried.

She was also an incredibly nice person. She befriended not just royalty like the Duke and Duchess of Windsor, but people from all walks of life. She kept the same measurements for the forty years I knew her. Her secret, she told me, was moderation and small portions. She did yoga and meditation, and she took Chinese herbs fifty years before they were fashionable. She introduced me to Chinese herbs, which I got in New York from the famous Dr. George Wong. Aimee showed me a note from Dr. Wong: "It is important for women to experience sexual happiness on a regular basis, as this will invigorate the flow of female energy to enrich and rejuvenate the mind and the body."

Aimee's other great passions were entertaining in royal style and appearing ageless in amazing gowns of the latest fashion, which only women in their thirties and forties would dare to wear. She set a high standard in Palm Beach and Europe.

Her great love was her husband, Rodman de Heeren, heir to the Wanamaker department store chain in Philadelphia. He died in 1983 at age seventy-four, leaving her his fortune and an incredible collection of art and homes. They had one child, daughter Cristina, who was born in Spain and also raised in Palm Beach. Cristina is the founder of an organization devoted to preserving flamenco dance and culture.

One day in 2003 I received a phone call in New York requesting me to create a unique gown for Aimee's birthday. The party was to be held in her château in Biarritz. Aimee was inviting all her international friends for a last party to say good-bye. She was losing the ability to dance and didn't want to "go out" without a last hurrah. Parties were given in her honor later in her life, but this event was her last as the reigning hostess.

I was chosen to design her greatest gown ever, and I wanted it to be a showstopper. It had to be deep purple to properly show off her diamonds, amethysts, and rubies.

I flew to Biarritz and was put in an incredible suite with a bathroom unchanged from the 1930s, except for the perfect plumbing. The towels and linens all bore Aimee's monogram. I found her in her art deco–mirrored dressing room and helped her into the gown.

She spoke to me in a still melodic voice. "Vicky, I must not wear just this necklace. It's my last party. I'm going to the vault and take out *everything*. I want to wear the lot."

When she was finally dressed, I told her how Elizabeth Taylor went to the Rothschilds' Ferriéres château in France with a one-inch rock on every finger.

Aimee smiled and said, "Why not? *Moi aussi!*" And she did.

I took her photo to show Elizabeth one day and let her know that she was not alone in her devotion to "wretched excess."

Aimee's party, in her ballroom overlooking the enormous terrace bathed in the July moonlight, was stupendous. We danced and laughed and celebrated Aimee.

She told us she was ninety, but we knew she cheated on the years and assumed she was ninety-five. Aimee was escorted that night by an infamous rich and gay playboy.

Well past midnight, the party finally ended and the magical night was over.

I flew back to New York the next day with my photos and

memories. Aimee never ordered another gown. In her remaining years, she walked with help around the gardens of her various homes. She died peacefully in 2006. Some of the obituaries say she was 99, but the official one says 103. So at her party in 2003, where she wore my purple corset gown and danced for hours, Aimee would have been 100 years old!

AIMEE DE HEEREN'S GINGER TEA

Aimee often invited me to tea on her Louis XIV banquette after a dress fitting. She always served ginger tea, telling me it was her secret for longevity, in addition to specially prescribed Chinese herbs.

1. Slice large pieces of ginger very thin.

2. In a porcelain cup, pour hot water over 4–5 slices.

3. Let steep for 3 minutes.

Aimee's other secret was walking every afternoon. A nurse would help Aimee walk around the streets of Paris or New York, holding Aimee's arm while Aimee held a silver-handled cane with the other hand.

A Typical Day with a Bunch of Ladies

January 17, 2001

I naugural fever from the post-Bush election parties was over. The women who hand-sew my designs in Paris were exhausted, complaining that they could not possibly make another dress. I was in New York, in my salon at Bergdorf's, anticipating a typical day with ladies who lunch.

My first client of the day was an elegant chinchilla-clad woman, fortyish, whose husband had just appeared on the cover of *Fortune* magazine. She wanted me to create an important ball gown in two weeks for her very first post–*Fortune* cover event. We chose a pale celadon green with silver beads to go with her new emerald-and-diamond necklace, her tan, and her green eyes. The gown would provide the magic touch she required in her new position in New York society. As the wife of an important CEO, the event would be her "inauguration" as a newly crowned princess of corporate America. I promised to bead a bag to match the dress. My only problem: Who would sew the dress? It had to be made in two weeks.

While I pondered this challenge, I looked in on a fitting session in the next dressing room, where three women were gathered. One was a dimpled blonde, about thirty, very housewifey.

In the next chair sat a short-haired brunette with schoolteacher looks, and finally a pretty mom-next-door type in her midthirties. She was standing on a pedestal, wearing the gown chosen for her son's upcoming bar mitzvah, an $8,000 lilac-and-silver tulle dress, covered with beads. The friends were there for moral support.

The dress needed to be shortened, and the fitter and I began to fuss with the seven layers of Lurex crinoline. We were under the dress. Suddenly the woman's cell phone went off and she screamed into it, "Well, break down the door and shoot the motherfucker if you have to!"

The fitter and I stayed silently at our task, under the tent of fabric, marking the flimsy layers of crinoline. It turned out that the client, who seemed to be just another housewife, was, in fact, the district attorney of a major nearby city. With her busy schedule, she had clearly mastered the art of multitasking.

While we worked, she barked orders to a squad of police who had encircled a drug dealer's home. The dealer was apparently holding a female hostage, handcuffed to the shower stall. Once the police broke in, they found that the hostage had $1,300 cash on her. My client then yelled into her phone, "She's not a hostage, you assholes, she's a dealer, too! Lock her up."

Emerging at last from the crinoline, I smiled up at her and said, "I agree. Lock her up!"

Entitlement

I was lying on my son Richard's futon in our loft on the Left Bank. Lying next to me was George Segal, a friend from *Who's Afraid of Virginia Woolf?*, and his wife, Sonia. George reconnected with Sonia at their forty-fifth high school reunion, and he married his childhood sweetheart. (Note: High school reunions are wonderful places to find husbands late in life, and maybe even somebody who already loved you once upon a time.) Sonia and I were lying on each side of George. If it had been the sixties, when all three of us had lived in Greenwich Village, we'd all be smoking pot. But now it's the twenty-first century and we were all drinking *thé des mûres sauvage* (wild blackberry tea) and watching game three of the NBA playoffs, the L.A. Lakers against the Philadelphia 76ers.

Sonia and George fell in love as students in school in Bucks County, Pennsylvania, and were Sixers fans. I was a converted Sixers fan after seeing Allen Iverson's brilliant game when he slashed through Shaq and Kobe's defense. David vs. the Goliaths. Elizabeth taught me always to root for the underdog.

Earlier that day, George had walked into my shop. He was showing Sonia his hangouts in Paris. He looked around, very disoriented.

"George," I said, "you're looking for my conversation pit. I filled it up with cement in the seventies."

In those days, Americans in Paris would come over to sit on my Indian pillows, get high, and listen to sitar music or Miles Davis or *Tubular Bells*. Now the shop was quiet. The walls were white, with white chiffon Greek drapes, and the look was more Dorothy Draper, with the simplicity of the forties.

"We've cleaned up our bodies and our spaces," I explained to George.

Paris goes on as the backdrop of classical beauty, but we change. I no longer drink, do drugs, or party, but I always have fun! Life itself is the party. "Life itself is the sweetheart," wrote Willa Cather, and it's my favorite quote ever.

"Vicky, that's the difference between you and Barbra Strei-sand," said George. (I was surprised to be mentioned in the same sentence with the Great One.) "You both amaze me. You're almost the same in your power. You both have such . . . entitlement. You're both so creative and into everything before any-one else. The only difference is, you have  more fun. She's like your friend Woody. They both worry."

"George," I responded, "everything that counts happens to you by the time you're three. My mom used to tell me over and over how beautiful and talented I was, and I believed her. My dad treated me like an adult. Maybe their parents are to blame? Maybe they were negative?"

George was listening intently but with one eye on the game.

"Then the next problem is puberty," I went on, "how you are perceived at thirteen or fourteen when the opposite sex decides if you're popular or not. That's a killer. I was a cheerleader. I had true power in a high school of two thousand students. This weekend we're having our high school reunion in Chevy Chase. I'm getting a photo of all the ex-cheerleaders together. I'm sure they're all amazing women today."

And finally, between slam dunks on the TV screen, I said, "So, George, tell your kids to tell their kids:

"You are beautiful.

"You are wonderful.

"You are talented.

"You are walking miracles.

"It worked for me."

The Art of Survival

Thousands of people have talent. I might as well congratulate you for having eyes in your head. The one and only thing that counts is, do you have staying power?

—NOËL COWARD

When I was in my thirties, I thought about the enormous role luck had played in my life. I knew I was one lucky woman. In the beginning, I was lucky to go to Paris with Mia Fonssagrives, with her family's connections to the world of high fashion. And when I was only twenty, what luck to have met Elizabeth Taylor, who turned out to be a great mentor. And thanks to the Burtons, I was lucky to be introduced to

Coco Chanel, my idol, and imagine that she was passing the torch to me. I was also lucky to have met Edith Head, who advised me to choose between costumes and retail.

In my forties, I was wise enough to realize that luck had definitely played a role, but so did my own chutzpah. Luck can land you in the right place at the right time. But having landed there, *then* what? Not everyone has the nerve to take the next step. It's how you use the luck you are dealt that makes the difference.

I had to be strong to have survived some serious disappointments in my personal and professional life. Yet I continued to go to work every day, no matter the circumstances or emotions. Work was always there, a part of my life I could control and count on.

One day, in my late fifties, I woke up and realized I was about to have a forty-year career without a break! Collection after collection, season after season, and finally, at that point in my life, no fear of failure on the horizon.

My moment of self-congratulation didn't last long. A few days later, a young new buyer arrived at Bergdorf's and sauntered into my salon. He told me he didn't like my work. He said my designs were old-fashioned. He wanted to revolutionize the stock and my look was out. He advised me to "see the writing on the wall."

Having waited forty years to fail, I told him with a smile that I was grateful for his warning. I asked him to let me know a few months in advance when my time had come, so I could take care of my employees and take that long-overdue vacation!

The following week I saw the chairman of the Neiman Marcus Group, Burt Tansky, and told him I was thankful for the twenty-five years of partnership and not to worry. I was happy to retire and move to my Florida farm. In my case "out to pasture" would be "out to swamp."

He looked at me quizzically and then burst out laughing.

Without a word, he walked away, shaking his head and roaring with laughter.

Eventually the young buyer moved on and out, and I'm still doing collection after collection for Bergdorf's. By now I know that it's not about luck, or chutzpah, or even hard work or ethics or relationships. Survival is simply a gift from the universe. And I'm making the most of it!

One of the inevitable results of surviving is that you are surrounded most of the time by people quite a bit younger than you are. Don't complain about it, or even mention it. Being around young people is an advantage. Keep an open mind and heart, and you'll find that youth is contagious.

Learn to think of yourself as ageless, and *shazzam*—you will be.

VICKY'S TWELVE TIPS FOR SURVIVAL

- Find work that flows easily. Time stands still when creative juices flow. You'll know it when it happens.

- Don't expect overnight success. If you do peak early, immediately start planning your "comeback."

- Don't count on making money quickly. Louis Féraud told me that it takes seven years to make it in fashion, and if you last fifteen years, you are classic. Money should not be the goal. Lasting is the goal.

- Find a niche. Eliminate competition. If there is competition, don't be jealous. Ignore it.

- Try to go into business without a backer, even if the backer is your spouse. The backer may want to dictate to you or fire you or even divorce you.

- Learn patience. Not everyone is going to love your work. Ignore them and wait for someone who does.

- Be your own best promoter. Believe in yourself.

- Work harder than everyone else.

- Stay young and healthy. Listen to and even learn to enjoy current music, books, plays, and movies.

- Live in the present, not the past. *These* are the good-ole days.

- Stay forever young at heart.

THE RED SHOES

Lucie Belle was born in March 2007 to my son Rex and his beautiful wife, Ani. Lucie Belle loves fashion, jewels, boys, and drama. Her very first sentence, at one year old, was, "Oh, my God."

For Lucie Belle's birth photo I made her a pearl gray lace corset ball gown with a full tulle skirt and a lace stole with a gray organza rose on a bandeau across her head.

Lucie Belle had the good fortune to welcome a baby brother, Roman, and become a big sister, afterward declaring she would be marrying her brother and would need a red dress to go with her red shoes.

Fashion starts young. At three, Lucie chose her own clothes. Red patent leather Mary Janes are her favorite shoes, and when the handsome salesman presented her brown oxfords, she politely answered, "I don't think so."

I called Mike from Paris (covered in pink paint) to remind him of the day we met twenty-three years ago. "It's been swell," I told him.

Mike answered, "I'd rather be on a roller coaster than a merry-go-round."

Today, the drama continues . . .

Life Runs Full Circle

In 2004 I drove north of New York City to look for a mountain home. I was in search of fresh air and more closets. I wanted a sweet home to live in and to write and read and paint in. Accompanied by my son Rex and his then-fiancée, Ani, who wanted a family weekend getaway spot, we found an isolated log cabin with a view of the Catskills and all three of us fell in love.

We moved in and weekended there for five years. Little did we know the cabin was built by our neighbor Dave Cummings (who owned a lot of property on the mountain) for his daughter and son-in-law, a Key West fisherman and a friend of my husband's.

Yet the greatest surprise of all, proving that everything in life happens for a reason, was that living a few miles away was Liza Todd Burton, Elizabeth Taylor's beautiful daughter. Now a sculptor of horses, she lived on her horse farm one village away. Liza of the Chiffon Caftan was now Liza of the Saddle.

Both of us had been "brought up" by Elizabeth, living large, living our childhoods out in the Dorchester in London, the Plaza Athénée in Paris, and the Excelsior in Rome. Now we were both living off the same road in the middle of beautiful nowhere, living fabulous, living real, and now together again.

BOOKS ON THE SHELF AROUND MY BED

I have biographies, travel, art, self-help, and current affairs and even an atlas nearby:

The Language of Letting Go—Melody Beattie

Tamara de Lempicka: A Life of Deco and Decadence—Laura Claridge

The House at Sugar Beach—Helene Cooper

Collapse—Jared Diamond

Infinite in All Directions—Freeman J. Dyson

The Soulmate Path—Monte Farber, Amy Zerner, and Arielle Ford (gift from Amy Zerner)

Arrogance: Rescuing America from the Media Elite—Bernard Goldberg

Bias: A CBS Insider Exposes How the Media Distort the News—Bernard Goldberg

Haunted Britain and Ireland—Richard Jones with the Fortean Library

The Undiscovered Self—Carl G. Jung

The Liars' Club: A Memoir—Mary Karr

Furious Love: Elizabeth Taylor, Richard Burton, and the Marriage of the Century—Sam Kashner and Nancy Schoenberger

The Culture of Narcissism—Christopher Lasch

Megatrends Asia—John Naisbitt

The Roses: The Complete Plates—Pierre Joseph Redouté

Jane Trahey: On Women and Power—Jane Trahey

The Way of Life: Tao Te Ching: The Classic Translation—Lao Tzu (R. B. Blakney, translator)

Blood Is Dirt—Robert Wilson

World Atlas (Oxford University Press)—always on the shelf!

And some novels and short stories:

London Fields—Martin Amis

Disgrace—J. M. Coetzee

Prey—Michael Crichton

Smoke and Mirrors—Neil Gaiman

July's People—Nadine Gordimer

The Partner—John Grisham

The Wind-Up Bird Chronicle—Haruki Murakami

Lush Life—Richard Price

INDEX